MA   ...S POLICY REFORM

MANAGING POLICY REFORM

*Concepts and Tools for Decision-Makers
in Developing and Transitioning Countries*

**Derick W. Brinkerhoff
and
Benjamin L. Crosby**

Kumarian
Press, Inc.

Managing Policy Reform: Concepts and Tools for Decision-Makers in Developing and Transitioning Countries

Published 2002 in the United States of America by Kumarian Press, Inc.
1294 Blue Hills Avenue, Bloomfield, CT 06002 USA

Copyedit, design, and production by Joan Weber Laflamme, jml ediset, Vienna, Va.
Proofread by Kathleen Achor.
The text of this book is set in 10/12 Adobe Caslon 224 Book.

Printed in Canada on acid-free paper by Transcontinental Printing and Graphics, Inc. Text printed with vegetable oil-based ink.

∞ The paper used in this publication meets the minimum requirements of the American National Standard for Information Sciences–Permanence of Paper for Printed Library Materials, ANSI 239.48–1984.

Library of Congress Cataloging-in-Publication Data

Brinkerhoff, Derick W.
    Managing policy reform : concepts and tools for decision-makers in developing and transitioning countries / Derick W. Brinkerhoff and Benjamin L. Crosby.
        p.   cm.
    Includes bibliographical references.
    ISBN 1–56549–142–4 (pbk. : alk. paper)
    1. Political planning. 2. Political participation. 3. Democratization. 4. Developing countries—Politics and government. I. Crosby, Benjamin, 1941– II. Title.
    JF1525.P6 B75 2002
    352.3'4'091724—dc21

                                                                                    2001038797

11 10 09 08 07 06 05 04 03 02   10 9 8 7 6 5 4 3 2 1   First Printing 2002

We dedicate this book to all the people with whom we worked and from whom we learned about policy change, and to Jeanne Foote North, who helped to make our work possible.

Contents

I

POLICY CHANGE:
IMPLEMENTATION PERSPECTIVES AND CHALLENGES

II

A TOOL KIT FOR POLICY REFORMERS
AND STRATEGIC MANAGERS

Illustrations

TABLES

FIGURES

BOXES

Preface

As countries make the difficult transition to democracy and economic liberalization, numerous policy changes are necessary. Decision-makers and reformers have tended to focus their attention primarily on the technical content of these reforms. These are important concerns, yet a singular focus on the technical aspects of reform ignores a major element of achieving results. Success in pursuing reforms requires recognizing that reform is about process and people (who wins and who loses from reforms), as well as about content. This is a particularly important facet of managing governmental affairs in a democracy.

Democratic governance requires an efficient, effective, and accountable public sector that is open to citizen participation and that strengthens rather than weakens a democratic political system. Because citizens lose confidence in a government that is unable to implement policies or deliver basic services, the degree to which a government is able to carry out these functions can be a key determinant of a country's ability to sustain democratic reform.

From 1990 to 2001 the U.S. Agency for International Development (USAID) funded the Implementing Policy Change Project (IPC) to develop tools and approaches to improve the process of policy implementation in ways that encourage and enhance sustainable democratic governance. During that period IPC worked in more than forty countries on reform efforts across a wide variety of development sectors, from regional to national to local levels, with government officials, private sector entrepreneurs, and civil society groups. For example, at the national level in Zambia IPC consultants worked with the president's cabinet to improve communications between line ministries and senior government officials to make the translation of policy into practice more effective and to improve accountability. At the local level in Bulgaria an IPC team assisted municipal governments, business associations, and civil society groups to increase citizen participation in policy and program decisions, develop transparent and accountable budget and finance systems, and improve local service delivery. In West Africa an IPC team supported the creation of national business associations and helped these groups lobby their governments for policy reforms. In Zambia, Bulgaria, and all the countries where IPC provided assistance, we found committed people from whom we learned as much if not more than they learned from us. IPC was not a one-way transfer of tools and knowledge but a collaborative learning endeavor with many contributors.

In this book we assemble in a single volume the conceptual frameworks, techniques, tools, and lessons from IPC's accumulated ten years of experience. Harder to capture, though, are the excitement and satisfaction that we encountered in collaborating with people around the world in government, the private sector, and civil society on policy reform and implementation. Any tool kit simplifies reality, and through our shared collaborations we were constantly reminded of the complexities of policy change and of the importance of situating tools within specific sociopolitical and organizational contexts. So it is with a combination of gratitude toward those we worked with and humility in recognition of the intricacies of making reforms successful that we have written this book. It is aimed at helping to navigate the "how" of policy change. Based on a task framework for managing the policy-implementation process and on field-tested analytic techniques, the book provides:

- Ideas for policy designers, decision-makers, and managers to improve the quality of policy decisions taken and the effectiveness of the organizational, human, and financial resources applied to implementing them.
- Strategies to improve the implementation feasibility of ongoing and future policy reforms, and to foster stronger links between democratic governance and policy management across a range of development sectors.
- Tools for designing, managing, and influencing policy reforms that can be used by reformers in government, donor agencies, nongovernmental organizations (NGOs), civil society groups, and the private sector.

The book brings a strategic perspective to bear on governance and policy implementation, recognizing its complexities and the need to highlight the technical, political, and institutional dimensions of policy change. The approach focuses directly on applicability to reform issues in the context of democratization and improved governance and delineates management strategies for dealing with these challenges. The positive responses we received from developing and transitioning country policy managers, USAID and other donor agency staff, and academics and students indicate a need to continue to disseminate these tools and approaches. We hope that members of the international community and developing/transitioning country individuals and groups that design, guide, manage, and/or influence the policy process will find *Managing Policy Reform* a useful resource.

Acknowledgments

This book would not be possible without the enthusiastic collaboration, commitment, energy, and insights of all the people in the countries where IPC worked. So, first and foremost, we want to recognize and thank them for their contribution. We do so collectively, because the list of individuals is too long to include everyone who has helped us along the way, although we in no way intend to diminish the contribution of each. Next, we acknowledge the U. S. Agency for International Development's Center for Democracy and Governance, which provided the financial resources through the Implementing Policy Change Project (Contract No. AEP–5470–I–00–5034–00) that made the book possible. Patricia Isman Fn'Piere, the project officer for IPC, gave us constant support as well as helpful suggestions and comments on the chapters as they evolved. We gratefully acknowledge her commitment to learning and dissemination of best practices in the area of policy implementation. Over the years the members of the Development Management Network, an informal association of practitioners, academics, and students, have given us peer review and feedback on earlier versions of much of the material included here. A special note of thanks goes to Jeanne Foote North (USAID retired), project officer for the first phase of IPC, whose dedication to development management, the primacy of the perspectives and needs of policy stakeholders in developing and transitioning countries, and the need to document and synthesize lessons learned was instrumental in making this book a reality. We thank Coralie Bryant, Professor, School of International and Public Affairs, Columbia University, and two anonymous reviewers for their helpful comments on an earlier version of the book. We would also like to recognize the support of Stephanie Y. Wilson, International Group Vice-President, Abt Associates Inc., and Lawrence Cooley, President, Management Systems International. Finally, the views expressed in this book in no way represent the official position of USAID, and any failings and shortcomings are the responsibility of the authors.

I

POLICY CHANGE

Implementation Perspectives and Challenges

I

Introduction:
Implementing Policy Reforms

This book is about how to implement policy reforms in developing and transitioning economies. Development policy has long been the domain of economists and sectoral specialists located in both international donor agencies and developing countries. These experts know a lot about the technical content of good policies, which is the "what" of policy reform. They frequently feel stymied, however, when it comes to translating those good policies into concrete results. Many a frustrated minister has asked his or her staff, "Our policies are sound, why are they not implemented?" This question is often echoed by the parliamentarian who wonders why the laws the parliament passes do not produce outcomes or lead to improvements in citizens' lives.

The minister's and the parliamentarian's questions concern the "how" of policy reform, which is the topic of this book. The following chapters examine the process side of policy change, participation and stakeholders, and issues that arise in organizing the "how" of reform (multi-organizational structures and coordination).

FROM POLICY CONTENT TO PROCESS

Answers to the "how" question have evolved through several generations of international development theory and practice, as well as of policy analysis and evaluation. What we present in this book draws upon this broad base. A rapid and, of necessity, oversimplified look back sets the scene.[1]

Economic precepts have remained the backbone of policy advice given to governments on how to achieve the "take off" to growth and development since the 1950s. This first generation of policy prescriptions informed the economic stabilization and structural adjustment programs

3

of the International Monetary Fund (IMF) and the World Bank, begun in the late 1970s and 1980s, and remains at the core of these policy reform packages today (see Thomas et al. 1991). Stabilization reforms focused on staunching fiscal deficits, reducing balance of payments, and bringing down inflation rates. Structural adjustment followed by realigning exchange rates, modifying trade regimes, reducing subsidies, changing tax policies, shrinking the public sector wage bill, and strengthening markets. Within the framework of the broader macroeconomic packages, sectoral adjustment packages sought to extend structural reforms to deal with specific sectoral issues.

First-generation policy analysis relied heavily on economic models that seek "first-best" solutions that maximize socioeconomic welfare for the greatest number of citizens under free-market conditions.[2] The "how" question did not arise, since these economic models assumed that the best policies would be implemented because (a) governments are interested in maximizing welfare for all citizens (the "benevolent" state), and (b) governments have sufficient administrative capacity to implement policy choices effectively. However, experience revealed that the best (technically "correct") policies often were not adopted or implemented. The gap between prescription and real-world application led to a critical reexamination of the assumptions underlying economic models of policy reform (see, for example, Bates and Krueger 1993, Frischtak and Atiyas 1996, Haggard and Kaufman 1992, Haggard and Webb 1994, Waterbury 1989).

Scholars and practitioners initially focused on the role and capacity of the state as the missing elements, which opened the door for the inclusion of politics and institutions as categories of inquiry in policy analysis and design, which led to the next generation of analytic approaches and development models. This second generation encompasses institutional economics and political economy, and focuses upon the interplay among state, market, and civil society.[3] Key concepts are transaction costs, incentives, and interest groups, all of which are related.

Transaction costs emerge as a function of the institutions through which economic exchanges are mediated, with markets and hierarchies (states) forming the two ends of an institutional continuum. By ordering differing patterns of transaction costs, these institutions (which encompass rules, norms, and behaviors serving collective ends) influence various actors' incentives to enter into, or not, economic transactions (see, for example, Nabli and Nugent 1989). Policy models based on institutional economics favor reducing the role of government in the direct provision of goods and services and increasing the role of the private sector and civil society (see, for example, Picciotto 1995).

Political economy places the impacts of political variables at the center of explanations of policy outcomes. It emphasizes how incentive patterns are a function of underlying political objectives and interest group interactions (see, for example, Meier 1991, Bates and Krueger 1993). The state, political economists hold, risks capture by interlocking circles of economic and political elites. From the perspective of small farmers or local businesses, for example, the average developing-country government, far from being benevolent, represents a "predator," a resource-extractive state whose policies add significantly to the costs of doing business. Thus successful policy reforms must offset the influence of entrenched interest groups, reduce opportunities for rent-seeking, and strengthen the countervailing power of civil society.

The "how" question from this second generation of policy approaches focuses upon recognizing that institutions and politics matter (see Burki and Perry 1998) and that building capacity is necessary (Grindle 1996, 1997). Critical to rearranging the relationships among state, market, and civil society is their capacity to fulfill new functions. The emphasis on capacity reflects the realization that while economic liberalization may call for a smaller, less interventionist state, the tasks of effectively fulfilling governmental functions in a market economy with an active civil society require a stronger state than most developing countries have (see Callaghy 1990), and one that operates effectively at multiple levels in "polycentric institutional arrangements" (Ostrom et al. 1993).

The third generation of policy analysis approaches responds to the lessons learned from the policy dialogue and reform experience of the 1990s and into 2000, in which the importance of the "how" question became paramount. The technical aspect of the question concentrates upon issues of reform sequencing and the interactions among the various components of macroeconomic, sectoral, and governance reforms (see, for example, DeJanvry et al. 1993, Haggard and Webb 1994). In addition, third-generation techniques see policy reform as a process. This shift means that policies are dynamic combinations of purposes, rules, actions, resources, incentives, and behaviors leading to outcomes that can only imperfectly be predicted or controlled.[4]

Third-generation policy analysis recognizes the complex interactions among policy statutes, stakeholders, implementors, and sociopolitical environments. The process perspective calls for an additional set of tools that incorporates social and institutional factors more centrally into technical policy alternatives. It advocates that policy tools are more useful to policymakers in helping to guide policy development and implementation as it unfolds, rather than in choosing among competing policies a priori (for example, Weiss 1989). Further, it suggests that policy emerges from the bottom up, not just from the top down (see, for example, Winter 1990, Coston 1999, McGee and Norton 2000).

MANAGING THE PROCESS DIMENSION
OF POLICY IMPLEMENTATION

A major implication of the third generation of policy analytic approaches is that if policy is a process, then successful policy outcomes depend not simply upon designing good policies but upon managing their implementation. Instead of identifying ideal solutions up front and top down, policy implementors need to iteratively develop "second- or third-best" answers that collaborating agencies and stakeholders can agree upon. The best technical solution cannot be achieved unless there is cooperation, which means making modifications to accommodate the views and needs of the various parties involved. This encompasses what Schon and Rein (1995) call "reframing" policy issues. When problems are encountered, addressing them calls for shared analysis and joint action, both inside and outside of government, and for building strategic planning and management capacity along with technical skills (see Nelson 1994a, Stone 1996, White 1990).

The policy implementation process is at least as political as technical, and is complex and highly interactive. Besides technical and institutional analysis, it calls for consensus-building, participation of key stakeholders, conflict resolution, compromise, contingency planning, and adaptation. New policies often reconfigure roles, structures, and incentives, thus changing the array of costs and benefits to implementors, direct beneficiaries, and other stakeholders. Experience has shown that an inwardly focused, "business as usual" approach will fall short of achieving intended results. For example, across Africa, forestry and wildlife departments' efforts to implement new community-based natural resources management policies met with limited success at the outset because the departments failed to make structural and procedural changes to accommodate the new policies (Brinkerhoff 1999b). At first, they left their policing and enforcement role unchanged while trying to foster collaborative and participatory relations with local communities.

Further, political will and indigenous leadership are essential for sustainable policy reform and implementation. No amount of external donor pressure or resources, by themselves, can produce sustained reform. It takes ownership, both of the policy change to be implemented and of any capacity building efforts intended to enhance implementation. Unless someone or some group in the country where policy reform is being pursued feels that the changes are something that it wants to see happen, externally initiated change efforts, whether at the local or national level, are likely to fail. Such individuals or groups serve as "policy champions" or "policy entrepreneurs" (Kingdon 1995). Without policy champions who are willing and able to be effective leaders for change, sustainable reform is not possible.

POLICY IMPLEMENTATION AND DEMOCRATIC GOVERNANCE

Since the late 1980s and early 1990s policy reform in developing and transitioning countries has taken place within the context of democratization. There has been a worldwide increase in the number of countries shifting to democratic forms of governance in response to both national and international forces (see Diamond and Plattner 1996). Economic liberalization and democratization are closely interconnected, though debate is ongoing on the nature of those connections and their sequencing.[5]

Definitions of democracy vary from a narrow focus on electoral procedures for the selection of political leadership to expansive characterizations of broad popular participation in both politics and the mechanics of governing.[6] For our purposes, we consider a political regime to be democratic if it has the following: procedures that assure meaningful competition among individuals and groups for political power; broad participation in the choice of leaders and policies, and in the allocation of societal resources; and a high degree of civil, political, and economic liberties. Under democratic regimes governments face strong pressures to be efficient, effective, accountable, transparent, and responsive.

One reaction to these pressures has been a rethinking of the role of the state. Both economic and democratic reforms have focused on decentralizing, privatizing, and downsizing government to create capacity to provide basic services and critical public goods effectively and equitably, and to manage the marketplace transparently.[7] In developing countries the demands of globalization and economic liberalization are moving governments forcefully in this direction, though the pace and extent of this shift varies around the world (World Bank 1997, Rondinelli 1999).

Besides a revised role for the state, democratization transforms the way government relates to citizens. As developing and transitioning countries proceed down the path to democracy, changes take place in how all sectors of society interact "to coordinate the aggregation of diverging interests and thus promote policy that can credibly be taken to represent the public interest" (Frischtak 1994, vii). This interaction is the essence of governance, which is more than simply government. Governance reforms seek, on the one hand, to engage citizens more fully and effectively in politics and policymaking, often by strengthening civil society (see, for example, Burbidge 1997). On the other hand, reforms aim to modify how public agencies operate so as to infuse them with democratic principles. Democratic governance can be characterized in terms of the following operational features.

- It exhibits high levels of transparency and accountability; that is, information is made available and widely shared, decision-making processes are open, and public officials are held to account for the use of resources and the achievement of outcomes.

- It provides for increased citizen participation, particularly of marginalized groups, and for decision-making by local bodies that is accessible to citizens.
- Its structures and procedures permit the incorporation of the views of a range of societal groups in the formulation of policies (policy pluralism) and the equitable delivery of public services; they also redefine the role for the state (less direct service provision, creation and maintenance of a "level playing field" for economic activity, and empowerment of non-state actors).
- It operates within an institutional and legal framework that recognizes and respects human rights and the rule of law.

Democratic governance concentrates attention upon significant process questions. How do citizens exercise influence upon, and oversight of, the state? How do public leaders and agencies operate responsibly and responsively to carry out their mandates? How are social relations managed among different classes of society to assure inclusion, fairness, and equity? The answers that a particular country's governance system provides will go a long way in configuring the context for policy implementation. Conversely, how policy implementation is managed can contribute to shaping how a country operationalizes democratic governance. For example, sectoral policy implementation that fosters the participation of civil society groups can contribute to the creation of social capital (see Evans 1996). This can build citizen skills and confidence with democratic procedures (see Brinkerhoff 2000, Das Gupta et al. 2000). Subsequent chapters elaborate upon these issues.

CONTENTS OF THE BOOK

Building on the third-generation perspectives on policy process and on analysis and experience related to democratic governance, the book's chapters offer approaches and tools that can help policymakers to deal successfully with process, showing how the process side of reforms can be systematically assessed and managed. The book is organized into two major sections. The first part, "Policy Change: Implementation Perspectives and Challenges," consists of five chapters. The first chapter introduces the topic of the book and presents an overview of the key concerns relating to policy reform implementation, process approaches, and democratic governance. Chapter 2 presents IPC's policy implementation task framework and the strategic management model. It considers how the reform process looks from the perspective of developing/transitioning country decision-makers and managers, and identifies the key challenges that they face. The task framework helps host country managers divide the policy process into discrete tasks, which can then be addressed systematically. The strategic management model assists them to identify long-range targets, scan their operating environments, match their organizations' structures and resources to the challenges they face, identify key constituencies, build alliances, set priorities for and plan actions, and make adjustments and adaptations to reach performance objectives over time. The chapter previews how the tools contained in Part II can be used for strategically managing the policy implementation process.

Chapter 3 deals with citizen participation in the policy process. Identifying stakeholders that can be mobilized into constituencies for pursuing reform, and developing strategies for dealing with winners and losers are central problems for policymakers and managers. Many reforms are derailed or undermined by failure to take sufficient account of the need for supportive constituencies. Democratic governance puts a premium on participatory mobilization of stakeholder support. Unmanaged participation, however, can impede reforms. This chapter discusses both the benefits and the limits of participation, and addresses how to channel participation effectively to build constituencies and to promote democratic governance.

Chapter 4 examines the multi-organizational nature of policy implementation arrangements. In policy implementation the arena for action expands beyond the authority of a single manager or agency, and often extends far beyond the public sector. Policy reforms often compel actors that have never worked together to synchronize operations and harmonize procedures. Countries around the world are experimenting with cross-sectoral partnerships that bring government agencies together with non-governmental actors in a number of development sectors. This chapter examines partnerships as a mechanism for implementing reforms that can effectively combine the efforts of NGOs, civil society, and the private sector with those of government to achieve results.

Chapter 5 extends the exploration of the multi-organizational dimension of policy implementation undertaken in the previous chapter and examines the challenge of coordination. The chapter looks at what coordination is and the issues involved in designing and managing coordination structures and procedures. The chapter offers some guidance on different coordination options and some solutions for coordination problems, and then turns to a discussion of coordination venues that can help different policy stakeholders to work together.

Part II, "A Tool Kit for Policy Reformers and Strategic Managers," presents a set of analytic and process tools and techniques. Its seven chapters constitute a basic tool kit for planning and managing the policy reform process strategically. Each chapter describes the particular tool, relates it to the strategic management model and the policy implementation task framework, and illustrates how to use it. The chapters cover stakeholder analysis, policy characteristics analysis, political and institutional mapping, workshops for managing policy reform, advocacy techniques for reform, conflict resolution, and policy monitoring.

ANALYTIC METHODOLOGY AND DATA BASE

IPC was both a technical assistance project designed to provide technical advice and analytic support to countries faced with particular policy implementation tasks and problems, and an applied research effort to advance knowledge about policy implementation in developing and transitioning countries. For the first phase of the project (1990–95) IPC's working hypothesis was that strategic management approaches and process tools could facilitate policy implementation in developing and transitioning countries.[8] The second phase (1995–2001) expanded this hypothesis: Strategic management approaches and process tools could help governments and civil society groups to achieve policy reform outcomes in ways that enhance democracy and democratic governance. IPC's methodology consisted of successive iterations of (a) identifying policy process concepts, tools, and best practices; (b) applying them to various field situations; (c) reviewing the field application experience to modify and refine the concepts and tools; and (d) disseminating emerging lessons for subsequent application and critical review.[9] The project's field activities took place in response to requests from government officials or civil society groups who approached USAID or from USAID staff themselves. Thus, contrary to standard research designs, we did not select country cases or policy situations for analysis. Rather, they selected us. IPC's demand-driven mode of operations posed significant problems for systematic investigation and hypothesis testing.

We sought to overcome these problems through the iterative process noted above. More specifically, this led to numerous forays into the literature on development policy, political economy, participation, civil society, democratization, public administration, and strategic management. Second, in the course of testing and revising our knowledge in practical applications and real-world situations, we engaged our in-country collaborators in discussions of the concepts, tools, and approaches that IPC teams employed to bring their unique perspectives to bear on testing the utility and applicability of strategic management and policy process tools and approaches. Third, we wrote up our reflections and experiences and shared them with a variety of audiences, both in the practitioner and academic communities, to obtain critical feedback. This iterative process helped us to refine our analytic tools and approaches over the life of the project, to develop a framework for policy implementation (Chapter 2), and to track some commonly occurring themes, such as participation (Chapter 3), multi-organizational implementation structures (Chapter 4), and coordination (Chapter 5). The implementation task framework presented in Chapter 2 and these common themes served as our informal analytic protocol, and over the life of the project we used them to look for lessons from our field activities.

Operating within IPC's mandate to provide technical assistance in a variety of countries around the world, we aimed to produce and apply broad insights into policy implementation and the factors affecting success, as opposed to in-depth knowledge of particular countries, regions, or policy sectors. The geographic range of IPC fieldwork extended throughout the developing and transitioning world, with the majority of activities in Africa (35), followed by Latin America and the Caribbean (10), the Middle East (3), Eastern European and former Soviet Union countries (7), and one country in Asia. Sectorally, the experience base was also broad, as Table 1.1 illustrates. The appendix at the end of the

Table 1.1 Sectoral Distribution of IPC Field Activities

Application	Examples
Sectoral	Economic: export, trade and investment; privatization; fiscal/tax; regional economic; export regulation (diamonds)
	Private sector: small and medium enterprise; private sector development
	Agriculture/livestock
	Natural resource management/environment
	Social: education; social safety nets
	Health: HIV/AIDS
	Telecommunications
	Urban development
Governance	Anti-corruption
	Decentralization/local government
	Judicial reform
	Administrative reform
	Cabinet offices
	Citizen consultation
Organization capacity building	Communications
	Policy coordination
	Policy analysis
	Strategic management training
	Agency restructuring
	Budgeting

book provides a summary description of IPC's field activities during the period 1990–2001.[10]

INTENDED AUDIENCE

The primary audience for this book consists of policymakers and implementors in developing and transitioning countries. Our target is on the practitioners confronting the challenges of formulating, implementing, and/or monitoring policies within democratizing settings. There are, however, others who will find the book of direct relevance to their ongoing activities. The full list of our intended audience includes:

- *Government policymakers and reformers* who wish to enhance the implementation feasibility of the policies they promote and the effectiveness of the resources they assign to carry them out, to increase the responsiveness and accountability of government to citizens; and who seek guidance and ideas on how to structure implementation processes, how to manage multiple organizations in the policy arena, and how to deal with difficult implementation problems.
- *Private sector, NGO, or civil society organization members* who wish to increase their voice and clout in the policy reform process and to become more strategic and effective policy advocates and influencers within the context of democratic systems.
- *Donor agency staff* who wish to improve the chances for successful implementation of the sectoral policy reforms and programs they design and oversee, and/or who wish to enhance the prospects for democracy and good governance in the context of the country programs they are responsible for.
- *Policy analysts, technical/sectoral specialists, and management professionals* who work with governments, NGOs, civil society groups, private enterprise, or donors in multi-organizational settings to design, implement, or monitor policy reforms and to strengthen democratic governance.
- *Trainers in management schools and policy institutes* who wish to provide their students with cutting edge approaches and tools for understanding and managing policy reforms and their implementation.

NOTES

1. This section draws extensively on Brinkerhoff (1997b).

2. Analytic methods, such as the general equilibrium modeling techniques that emerged in the 1970s and 1980s, have fine-tuned these models to their present-day level of sophistication (see, for example, Taylor 1990). Sectoral applications employ sector-specific input-output matrices to assess policy options; for example, pricing and marketing of agricultural commodities (Monke and Pearson 1989). At the program and project level, first-generation techniques introduced cost-benefit and rate-of-return methodologies to arrive at a decision-making calculus to rank order national investment priorities and/or select among alternative investments (see, for example, Adler 1987, Gittinger 1982, Little and Mirlees 1991).

3. Among the streams of investigation that form the theoretical basis for the second generation are the "new institutional economics" (North 1990, Harriss et al. 1995), the "new political economy" (Meier 1991), and the "new institutionalism" (Ferris and Tang 1993). In the words of Oliver Williamson, "The new institutional economics is preoccupied with the origins, incidence, and ramifications of transaction costs" (1979, 233). The new element in the new political economy is the recognition that developing country governments are neither wholly predatory nor totally devoted to self-aggrandizement at the expense of pursuing policies that yield some set of wider benefits to citizens. This modified analytic framework recognizes the "perspective of public choice theorists (all predatory, no productive activities) and the conventional welfare economics perspective (all productive, no predatory activities) as two special cases" (Rausser 1990, 824). Reality lies somewhere in between, which leaves the door open for sincere interest in pursuing beneficial policy goals and altruistic behavior (Grindle 1991). As Lewis states, there are "instances of government decision and action that appear to have been driven neither by class nor by self-seeking but by the actors' notions of the public interest" (1989, 80). This modification means that decision-makers might be interested in using the results of policy analysis to achieve espoused policy goals. It places a premium on understanding the institutions involved in a particular policy situation and the incentives they create (see, for example, Cammack 1992, Klitgaard 1991, Rowe 1989). The new institutionalism emerges from the confluence of the new institutional economics, the new political economy, and other social science disciplines. This broad stream combines a variety of perspectives: organizational studies (Powell and DiMaggio 1991), public administration (Ferris and Tang 1993), anthropology (Ensminger 1992), political science (Ostrom 1990, Ostrom et al. 1993), and the progressively expanding scope of economics within the new institutional economics paradigm (Clague 1994, Clague 1997, Picciotto 1995, Picciotto and Weisner 1998). Among their contributions is an increased understanding of the factors that are critical to matching institutional arrangements with policy choices and service delivery modes in various sectors to deal effectively with the institutional problems those policy regimes pose (for example, free-riding, corruption, information asymmetries, uncertainty of outcomes, and so on).

4. There is an extensive literature on policy design and implementation as process, both in the U.S. domestic context and in the writings on international development. On the policy process in the United States, see Lindblom (1968), Kingdon (1995), Stone (1996), Schneider and Ingram (1997), and Sabatier (1999). On policy implementation in the United States, see the classic Pressman and Wildavsky (1973), Palumbo and Calista (1990), and the recent overview of the literature in O'Toole (2000). On the policy process and implementation in developing/transitioning countries, see, for example, Brinkerhoff (1996b), Chhibber (1998), Grindle (1980), Horowitz (1989), Grindle and Thomas (1991), Meier (1991), Lindenberg and Crosby (1981), and White (1990).

5. An important analytic stream of investigation has focused on the interactions between, and the sequencing of, economic and political liberalization. Analysis, theory-building, and operational conclusions have for the most part been based upon case studies (see, for example, Bates and Krueger 1993, Haggard and Webb 1994). An influential debate on these topics can be found in the October 1994 issue of the *Journal of Democracy* entitled *Special Issue: Economic Reform and Democracy*. From that issue, see, for example, Armijo et al. (1994), Geddes (1994), and Nelson (1994a). See also Diamond and Plattner (1995) and Nelson (1994b). A frequently cited quantitative study of these interactions is Knack and Keefer (1995).

6. The literature on democracy and democratization is huge, and our treatment of it here is necessarily partial and oversimplified. Besides the references cited in the previous note, see the regional studies on Africa and the former socialist economies in Bratton and van de Walle (1997) and Clague (1997), respectively.

7. These reforms consist of a loosely bundled set of concepts drawn from the pioneering administrative change efforts in Australia, New Zealand, and the United Kingdom (the New Public Management), and later from the United States (the Reinventing Government movement). For an analytic overview of the New Public Management, see Ferlie et al. (1996). On Reinventing Government, see Osborne and Gaebler (1992) and NPR (1996). Regarding the application of the New Public Management in developing countries, see Polidano (1999), Laking (1999), and Wallis and Dollery (2001).

8. This working hypothesis was elaborated into a set of propositions (Brinkerhoff 1992, 2):
- *Proposition 1*: The strategic management approach to policy implementation can be effectively transferred to developing/transitioning country organizations and managers.
- *Sub-proposition 1a*: The strategic management approach to policy implementation can be operationalized in a set of concepts, techniques, and processes.
- *Sub-proposition 1b*: These concepts, techniques, and processes can be learned and applied by developing/transitioning country managers through technical cooperation, networking, institutional strengthening, and dissemination activities.
- *Proposition 2*: Adoption and application of the strategic management approach by developing/transitioning country organizations and managers will improve the effectiveness of policy implementation.

- *Sub-proposition 2a*: The conditions under which the strategic management approach contributes effectively to improved policy implementation can be identified and analyzed.
- *Sub-proposition 2b*: The collaborative process and learning dimensions of the strategic management approach are generic to implementation of policies across a broad range of sectors.

9. The dissemination function of IPC included presentations at workshops, seminars, and conferences; the preparation of documents and reports, many of which are available at the IPC website <http://ipc.msi-inc.com/ipc.html>; and formal publications. Among the latter, see, for example, the 1996 special issue of *World Development*; Brinkerhoff (1996b) contains the overview piece for this issue.

10. Other sources of experience that inform the book come from USAID-funded projects that have applied some of the management strategies and tools that IPC has developed and refined. These include, for example, Partnerships for Health Reform, a worldwide health policy reform project; and the Green Project, an environmental policy and institution-building project in El Salvador.

2

Managing Policy Implementation

Through our judicial reform program, we want to see an independent judiciary in our country, where the legal framework fits our development needs and supports private investment, where judges are respected, and we have the resources we need to function effectively.
   —Minister of Justice and the President of the Supreme Court, Guinea-Bissau

The Southern Africa Development Community (SADC) intends to establish a harmonized set of policy agreements in the telecommunications and transportation sectors that will facilitate regional trade and economic growth, and that will increase cooperation among member states.
   —SADC representative of the regional telecommunications and transportation committee

Our education reform program will enhance equity and cultural and linguistic pluralism, redress the educational deficits of our indigenous communities, and contribute to democracy and economic development in Guatemala.
   —Parity Commission for Education Reform, Guatemala

As these three examples of policy goals from countries where IPC worked illustrate, new policies are full of hope: If policy prescriptions are followed, then social and economic problems will be solved. However, without attention to what is needed to bring about results—that is, without focusing on implementation—those hopes may not be achieved.[1] Chapter 1 argued that managing policy implementation is as much a "how to do it" problem as it is a question of determining "what to do." In Guinea-Bissau implementing judicial reform involved modifying the constitution, drafting a variety of new legislation, creating a separate budget category for funding the judiciary, building capacity for judges and other court officials, conducting a communications campaign regarding the role and functions of the judiciary, and repairing physical infrastructure. In Southern

Africa an important element in implementing the regional telecommunications and transportation policy protocols consisted of negotiating and building agreement among government officials, representatives of the private sector, and citizens' groups on the specifics of the new provisions and how they should be applied. In Guatemala, in the aftermath of protracted civil strife, making progress with education reform encompassed decentralization and reorganization of the educational system, broad-based community participation, resource redistribution, and conflict resolution, all of which were complicated by a change in political leadership at the outset of the policy reform.

In each of these cases, and in the other countries where IPC provided assistance, implementing new policies presented myriad challenges that placed the "how" of reform at the forefront: changes in roles, institutional and resource constraints, new patterns of interactions with other agencies and with citizens, demands from new constituents, and pressure to show results in short periods of time. This chapter offers a way of understanding and managing these implementation challenges. We first examine the nature of policy implementation and some of the factors that contribute to the difficulty of implementation. We then present the policy implementation task framework and the strategic management model that informed the activities of IPC over the life of the project. Both consider the reform process from the developing country policy manager's perspective and identify the key challenges to be faced. The task framework helps managers charged with reform divide the policy process into discrete tasks, which can then be addressed systematically. The strategic management model assists managers in identifying long-range targets, scanning operating environments, fitting organizational structures and resources to the challenges faced, identifying key stakeholders and constituents, building alliances, setting priorities among and selecting strategic options, and making adjustments and modifications to reach performance objectives. But first, let us turn to the question of why policy change is so difficult.

CHARACTERISTICS OF POLICY CHANGE IN DEVELOPING AND TRANSITIONING COUNTRIES

Looking across a wide range of policies, we can identify several characteristics of policy change that appear to be generally applicable. Each of these holds major implications for implementation. First, *the stimulus for policy change often comes from sources outside of government*. These outsiders can be new political leaders assuming power following a democratic transition or regular election, powerful interest groups with a change agenda, or international donor agencies.[2] In the late 1970s and throughout the 1980s, when many developing countries were undergoing economic crisis, structural adjustment programs introduced substantial changes in macroeconomic policy frameworks as part of the conditionalities for loans and assistance packages (see, for example, Krueger 1993, Rodrik 1993). Frequently, negotiation of reforms took place among a narrow set of actors with conditionalities agreed to only reluctantly.

In the late 1990s and into the new millennium the stimulus for change is increasingly from groups within the country, for example, from political movements and civil society. This transformation is partially due to the worldwide shift toward democratic governance, which opens up the policy process to a broader range of citizens, and (to differing degrees) challenges governments to be more responsive and accountable (see, for example, Grindle 1996). It is also due to the increasing strength (again to differing degrees) of civil society (for example, Burbidge 1997, Coston 1998c, Edwards and Hulme 1992, Harbeson et al. 1994).

Second, and a corollary to the first characteristic, *policy change decisions are highly political*. Policy reform is political.[3] It addresses fundamental questions of what is to be done, how it is to be done, and how benefits are distributed (see Lasswell 1958, Lindblom 1968). Policy change is thus, in many instances, controversial. When change occurs, relationships at various levels and among stakeholders are shifted. A new array of policy winners and losers emerges, and often the losers are deeply entrenched and can exercise strong and effective opposition (Frischtak and Atiyas 1996, Haggard and Webb 1994, Lindenberg and Crosby 1981, Grindle 1999). The existence of powerful opposition helps explain why it is often so difficult to get policy change processes moving, or in some cases why it stalls before it can begin.

For example, this was the case with railway privatization in Mozambique, which was proposed during the period immediately following the end of the civil war, when large numbers of soldiers were being demobilized. USAID, in cooperation with the World Bank, provided assistance to develop possible policy alternatives for generating employment. However, the idea of laying off railway employees at the same time that the job market was already flooded ultimately could not generate sufficient support to overcome political opposition (see White 1997).

Third, while politicians and external interest groups may have a lead role in the initiation of policy change, *those most actively involved in the formulation of the policy changes tend to be technocrats*. Technocrats generally operate under a different decisional calculus than that of either the political or the administrative leadership. While politicians take care to manage their constituencies, technocrats are concerned with technical solutions, maximizing output, and rationalizing scarce resources. Political trade-offs are generally not factors in technocrats' policy formulation equations (see Grindle and Thomas 1991). Getting technocrats to think about losers, opposition, and other political factors is not a simple matter.

The evolution of natural resources and environment policy exemplifies this characteristic. Early generations of environment policy reforms were designed by scientists and conservationists based on scientific and technical criteria, which resulted in policies with a heavy emphasis on resource protection, essentially aimed at fencing off resources from users. The next iteration of these reforms incorporated social and anthropological variables, particularly in community-based natural resources management policies, and the policy mix shifted to combine conservation with sustainable use (see Western and Wright 1994). Currently, the centrality of political and institutional factors to these policies has become well recognized (for example, Ribot 1995, Brinkerhoff 1999b).

Fourth, *reformers are frequently new to government and unfamiliar with the environment for policy implementation.* In democracies and transitioning countries, many governments come to power based on the promise of reform and sweeping change. Because they are neither wedded to established routines nor mortgaged to entrenched interests, reformers may be quite effective at the outset of the new government (Waterbury 1989). However, they are also very likely to be unfamiliar with the state's administrative structures, unaware of the time and energy required to overcome bureaucratic inertia and resistance, and unschooled in using the levers of power to accomplish change.[4] Veteran bureaucrats know that reformers can be worn down; if that is not possible, they can be outlasted, since reformers will likely be around for only a very few years.

For example, this characteristic was evident in Zambia when the Chiluba government first took office. At the time that IPC worked with the new cabinet to improve the effectiveness of policy management, the neophyte ministers were unfamiliar with their ministries and with the machinery of government. It took some time before they learned how to exercise their decision-making authority and to translate that into action (Garnett et al. 1997).

Fifth, in most cases the *resources needed to carry out policy change either do not exist or are in the wrong place.* Budgets are prepared on an annual cycle and may not include the resources needed for new efforts. The allocation of resources represented by a budget is the product of understandings and arrangements arrived at over considerable negotiation and commitment of interested and often powerful actors, and cannot necessarily be shifted easily (see Caiden and Wildavsky 1974).[5] Resources can be reallocated, but only with the consent of these actors; the political consequences of proceeding without their consent can be drastic. The difficulty of reallocation points up the critical role of external resources for initiating the policy change process, both as a catalyst and to buy time to negotiate the reallocation of the budget.

For example, in Namibia, once HIV/AIDS became part of the national policy agenda, programmatic action was initially delayed until budget cycles freed up resources within the health sector to be reallocated. Later, as HIV/AIDS was recognized as a policy problem with broader ramifications than just health, the health ministry resisted relinquishing control because it meant that others would receive a share of the funds it managed for HIV/AIDS policy implementation.

Finally, *policy change requires that government organizations adapt and modify to new tasks.* Changes in government organizations can be made, but often with only great reluctance and difficulty. New policies may demand that extensive modifications be made or new organizations created. It should not be assumed that existing organizations are not performing important tasks or that they have considerable idle capacity. What the organizations do or what they produce is the product of understandings among interested parties about what and whose needs should be satisfied. Procedures, routines, and organizational culture are built and become institutionalized around such understandings. While changes can be instituted, the process is neither simple nor quick.

For example, health policy reform as pursued around the world involves significant changes in the role of ministries of health, shifting their emphasis from direct provision of health services to funders of services provided by the private and nonprofit sectors and to monitoring quality and consumer satisfaction (WHO 2000). Health reform also creates new organizations, for example, health-insurance fund agencies in the public sector or family practice firms to provide basic services in the private sector. In many developing and transitioning countries ministries of health are struggling to understand their new roles and to build the new capacities and attitudes required to implement reform successfully. Similarly, new private sector entities also wrestle with how to provide new service packages, interact with funders, meet quality assurance standards, and respond to customers.

IMPLEMENTING DIFFERENT TYPES OF POLICIES

So far we have discussed the characteristics of policy change as if all policies exhibited the same degree of implementation difficulty and complexity. Clearly this is not the case. In the international development arena one key distinction is between policies that are "stroke-of-the-pen" or "self-implementing" measures and those that are long-haul and incremental (see Haggard and Kaufman 1994, Nelson 1989). The former are also referred to as first-generation policy reforms, because they are associated with the first wave of economic stabilization and structural adjustment and consisted of single-event policy changes, such as exchange rate devaluation, tariff reductions, and interest rate shifts. The latter are called second-generation reforms, due to their association with the next in the sequence of International Monetary Fund and World Bank adjustment programs, which consisted of longer-term institutional and social policy changes, such as civil service reform, privatization of state-owned enterprises, new forms of service delivery, social safety net programs, and so on.

In terms of implementation a general consensus exists that there is a quantum leap in difficulty and complexity between the first and second generations of policy reform. Stroke-of-the-pen policies, which were devised by a small team of technical specialists and were done quickly without advance notice, were much easier to put in place than long-term incremental reforms that extend over many years. One of the mistakes of second-generation reform implementors, at least initially, was to assume that the strategies and tactics used for first-generation policy change would work equally well for long-haul reforms. IPC's experience focused on long-term, incremental sectoral policies, along with associated organizational and governance reforms (see Table 1.1). Thus, our discussion of managing policy change is limited to the second and subsequent generations of reforms.

Within that broad category of policies we borrow from Lowi (1972) and Grindle and Thomas (1991) in making some additional distinctions among implementing different types of policies. A critical differentiation is to look at policies in terms of their costs and benefits. Who gains the benefits, and are those benefits broadly or narrowly distributed? Who bears the costs and where are those costs concentrated? This topic is discussed in more detail in Chapter 7; however, we preview a couple of salient points here. Lowi classifies policies into four types, each of which has different patterns of costs and benefits: distributive (subsidies, infrastructure siting), regulatory (for example, industry regulations, pollution controls), redistributive (for example, tax and social welfare policies), and constitutive (procedural). His argument is that the type of policy determines the kind of politics and interest-group dynamics that take place during policy formulation and implementation. Grindle and Thomas elaborate a variant on this perspective, and besides examining features of policy costs and benefits, they look at the impetus for a policy and at how and where the politics surrounding the policy play out.

We see these distinctions as useful to (a) differentiate the level of implementation difficulty and complexity among policies; (b) help policy managers to decide where to look in terms of which actors they will need to interact with, and where those interactions are likely to take place; and (c) anticipate the likely array of winners and losers. Based on our experience with IPC, though, we consider the task framework presented below to offer a sufficiently generic management approach as to apply to a very wide range of types of policies. While the degree to which one or another of the policy implementation tasks applies to a particular policy can vary, we argue that all the tasks need to be addressed to assure successful policy management.

THE NATURE OF POLICY IMPLEMENTATION

Before presenting the task framework, however, it is worthwhile to discuss briefly what makes policy implementation different from implementing projects and programs. Some view policy implementation as similar to project or program implementation, but on a broader scale. However, assuming that policy implementation is simply project/program management writ large will lead reformers astray. Perhaps the most significant differences are the following:

- *Policy implementation is rarely a linear, coherent process.* Programs and projects have a beginning and an end; there are specific time-lines; targets and objectives are clearly specified for each phase; and plans and actions are defined to reach those targets. But with policy implementation, change is rarely straightforward. While policy statutes set goals and objectives, the extent to which those are clearly stated in terms of a sequence of cause and effect can vary, and they are frequently vague or leave operationalization until some later stage of the process.[6] As a result, policy implementation can often be multidirectional, fragmented, frequently interrupted, unpredictable, and very long term. How to sequence actions, what priorities to pay attention to, and who to include can be hard to determine and can vary over the long life of the policy change process.
- *No single agency can manage the policy-implementation effort.* Projects and programs have project managers or program heads. Whether part of a larger agency or independent, it is generally clear who is in charge. But in almost every case, policy implementation requires the concerted actions of multiple agencies and groups, both within government and outside, from civil society and the private sector. Even if one of them is nominally the lead agency, in reality no individual entity is "in charge."[7] Authority and responsibility are dispersed among the actors involved, which means that traditional command-and-control management is rarely applicable.
- *Policy implementation creates winners and losers.* Projects and programs provide benefits to those they affect. When policies change, new groups will benefit, but those groups who profited under the previous policy will not only cease to benefit but may actually be placed at a serious disadvantage. What complicates policy implementation is that the losers are usually in a much more powerful position to defend their interests, oppose, and resist change than those who

stand to gain. Particularly for regulatory policies there are often cozy relationships among legislators, executing agencies, and interest groups that favor a particular policy equilibrium and that are difficult to displace.[8]

- *New policies generally do not come with budgets.* Programs and projects have budgets. Were it otherwise they would not exist. Policies, however, particularly at the start of the reform process, rarely have more than the promise of resources. Making progress means lobbying for new funds, identifying existing sources of implementation support, and negotiating for resource reallocation. All of these efforts are subject to the vagaries of the budget process and shifting political winds.

If the (oversimplified) metaphor for project management is bridge construction, then policy implementation can be likened to urban renewal. The image comprises an assembly process at multiple sites; dependent upon the coordinated actions of government, community members, and businesses; often starved for resources, and as a result subject to stop-start dynamics; often controversial and conflictual; incremental and long-term; and requiring continual reshaping of its various components to produce the results called for.[9] With this vision in mind, let us now turn to the task model.

POLICY IMPLEMENTATION AS A SET OF TASKS

International development management can be thought of as a blend of strategy, tactics, and operating routines (see, for example, Brinkerhoff and Ingle 1989, Brinkerhoff 1991, Kiggundu 1989, Paul 1983). The particular mix that makes up the appropriate blend depends upon what kind of objectives are being pursued and what the manager's role in the organization is. Brinkerhoff (1991: 12–13) develops a continuum to describe project and program tasks, distinguishing between program management tasks as relatively more strategic and project management tasks as more relatively operational in nature. In applying this perspective on management to policy implementation, we modify Brinkerhoff's framework and conceive of policy implementation as an extension of the strategic end of the continuum. It includes the following tasks: policy legitimization, constituency building, resource accumulation, organizational design and modification, mobilizing resources and actions, and monitoring progress and impact. This is illustrated in Table 2.1.

As the table shows, the major emphasis in policy implementation is on the strategic end of the continuum. However, it also reveals that the tasks of project and program management are germane for the operational tasks

of policies, once their components are specified into programmatic outputs. Let us examine more closely each of the tasks involved in policy
implementation.

Table 2.1 A Continuum of Implementation Task Functions

Policy implementation	Program implementation	Project implementation
(emphasis on strategic tasks) ⟵————————⟶		(emphasis on operating tasks)
• Legitimization • Constituency building • Resource accumulation • Organizational design and modification • Mobilizing resources and actions • Monitoring progress	• Program design • Capacity building for implementors • Collaboration with multiple groups and organizations • Expanding resources and support • Active leadership	• Clear objectives • Defined roles and responsibilities • Plans/schedules • Rewards and sanctions • Feedback/adaptation mechanisms

Policy Legitimization

To make progress with implementation, key decision-makers must view
the proposed policy as legitimate. To acquire legitimacy, some individual,
group, or organization must assert that the proposed policy reform is
necessary and vital, even though it will present serious costs. This step
involves the emergence or designation of a policy champion, some individual or group with credibility, political resources, and the willingness
to risk that political capital in support of the policy.

Sources for policy change can emerge, as mentioned earlier, from a
variety of sources, both within a particular country, from government or
civil society actors, or from external actors such as international donor
agencies. Whatever the source, it is important that the policy be recognized as legitimate and worth pursuing early in the implementation process. This will open the door to developing ownership for the change.
Because the policy will likely require a significant shift both in attitudes
and actions, it is important that the "legitimizer" or policy champion
state that the new policy actually represents the preferred behavior, that
the policy is considered valid and desirable.

The more contentious the policy issue, or the more the new policy
departs from past practice, the more important will be the legitimization
function. The history of gender policies in international development is a
good example (see Snyder et al. 1996). In this case the task of convincing
key decision-makers in countries around the world of the importance

and legitimacy of gender has proven to be a long-term endeavor, and in many countries it has been hampered by women's low status and lack of political clout. Increasingly, policymakers and policy implementors recognize the gender dimensions of a wide range of sectoral policies (for example, women's important role in agriculture) and accord legitimacy to gender-sensitive policies and programs.

Constituency Building

Since support is frequently absent, an adequate constituency for the reform must be developed; the reform must be marketed and promoted. Constituents are those who will benefit by the change in some manner. They may be consumers of the service provided, providers of inputs, or officials within the implementing agency who find their position or status enhanced by the change. Constituents may also be groups with some influence in the direction of the change, or those that can bring some sort of resource to bear in support of the change. Constituents are the winners in the policy change process. They are positive stakeholders who will lend their support and commitment to the policy champion. Constituency building complements and amplifies the legitimization process. It aims not only at gaining acceptance but also at institutionalizing the change by creating a new set of beneficiaries with an interest in seeing the reform effected. Constituency building creates and mobilizes positive stakeholders in favor of the new policy (see Sabatier and Jenkins-Smith 1993).

Once the constituency members have a stake in the change, they will be more likely to mobilize to defend their interests. Policy managers or reformers should not assume that because a policy is sound or correct, support will automatically be forthcoming or that stakeholders will clearly and immediately see that it is in their interest to support the change. Bates and Krueger (1993) argue that potential constituents/beneficiaries of economic reform often have difficulty in seeing how their own interests are benefited and thus not only play a marginal role in initiating reform but may be difficult to mobilize as well. Such groups, without some way to calculate how they will be benefited, are unlikely to participate.

Development of strong constituencies requires that policy managers market the reform in language that makes the change both understandable and appealing to potential supporters. They also need to assist potential support groups to recognize and articulate their interests in such a way that supports and strengthens the reform initiative. In certain cases, even if a group has a good idea of how its interests can be positively affected by the policy change, it may have no outlet to express its demands or opinions. Frequently, policy winners may not know how to play the "policy game," but potential losers most certainly do (see Bardach 1977). Building support also means showing those with positive interest in the policy change how to play the game, how to be useful, informed, and determined support.

Putting together a constituency at the outset of the policy change process can be a difficult task. Since the benefits of policy change are mostly felt only in the long run, a certain amount of faith on the part of the new constituents will be necessary. In the meantime the losers will seek to maintain the status quo. Support for the new policy must be of sufficient importance to overcome or at least neutralize the forces opposing implementation (see Gillespie et al. 1996).

Resource Accumulation

To implement a new policy, human, technical, material, and financial resources must be allocated to the effort (Grindle and Thomas 1991, Mazmanian and Sabatier 1989). While external resources may cover a portion of what will be needed, gathering sufficient resources generally means cutting those directed to old policies. With the all too common problem of dwindling resources for all activities of government, competition for scarce resources increases. Debt burdens and financial crises add to the difficulties in resource accumulation. The inability of governments to redistribute resources to new priorities is frequently the cause of program or project shutdowns once donor resources have been exhausted. The task of resource accumulation means both securing initial funding and assuring the policy a place in the government's budget allocation process (Ames 1987). Making sure that budget allocations translate into steady resource flows is another aspect of resource accumulation. For example, agricultural research policy in Africa has been plagued with stop-start funding that has severely curtailed policy impacts (see Idachaba 1998).

Low or unstable levels of financial resources are not the only problem. Many developing countries also suffer from a scarcity of skilled human resources. Not only do many countries simply lack the skills for certain kinds of new policies, but in some cases the pool of talent that might easily acquire those skills has been depleted through war, repression, disease, and emigration.

The problem of lack of sufficient resources for implementing policy change is difficult to overstate. Frequently, the agencies charged with implementing a new policy have limited resources and capacity. In many cases a simple injection of funds is not enough. For example, when a country decides to devolve service delivery functions to local government, for which contracting out is required, much more is involved than an

intergovernmental resource transfer. Do local governments have accounting systems in place? Do they understand the rules for competitive bidding for services? Can they manage budgets and undertake quality reviews? Managing the resource implications of new policies requires time
and attention to the development of new skills and capacities.

Organizational Design and Modification

The introduction of new tasks and objectives accompanying policy
reform will likely cause modifications in the implementing organization(s).
However, organizational design and/or modification pose several problems. First, because of the existence of entrenched procedures and routines, and alliances with existing constituents and interests, there is frequently resistance to making changes in either the mandate or the
structure of the established organization. Staff may not be committed to
the new policy or may be opposed to it. For example, many "old-school"
foresters are opposed to new natural resource management policies that
transfer substantial control of forests to local communities. Second, the
tasks called for by reforms may be substantially different from current
ones, and the organization lacks the capacity to handle them. This is
frequently the case when reforms transform agencies that formerly provided services directly into contract managers and overseers of services
provided by the private sector.

With significant policy change an agency can be affected in terms of its
internal arrangements and of its relations with its operating environment.
Internally, what the agency does and how it goes about those tasks may
change. New tasks will call for new structures and procedures. Continuing the natural resource management example, forestry departments have
been restructured away from the military and police models of the past
toward community development models, which de-emphasize hierarchy
and control and stress cooperation and citizen participation. Externally,
since policy reform cuts across individual organizational boundaries,
implementing organizations will need to pay more attention to the external environment and to interacting, communicating, and cooperating with
the organization's external stakeholders. Under the new community-based
natural resource management policy regimes, forestry departments, which
previously operated relatively independently, must interact with other
ministries (for example, rural development, agriculture, health), local
governments, NGOs, and local community groups. Since successful actions by one entity may depend on the implementation of complemen-
tary actions by other agencies, there will be greater need for sharing information and resources, and more concerted coordination (see Chapter
5). New interorganizational structures, such as partnerships, may emerge
(see Chapter 4).

As decades of experience with institutional strengthening have demonstrated, retooling organizations is difficult. New ideas, structures, or methods may be ignored or modified to adapt to systems already in place. Simply ignoring the new directive for change is a classic response. Since the turnover rate of cabinet ministers is high in most developing and transitioning countries, agency staff knows that if they stall long enough, the minister and the new policy directive may simply go away.[10]

Because of the difficulty in establishing new routines or tasks in organizations, it may be easier and politically more feasible to create new structures rather than overhaul older ones. However, there are trade-offs. Staff in existing organizations understand the budgeting, procurement, financial, and personnel systems of government and are likely have their own political networks. These can be helpful to reformers if they can be enlisted on the side of change, but they are an impediment if through inertia or intent they oppose change. Creating a new organization has the benefit of beginning with a (more or less) "clean slate" and supportive actors, but often it takes time for the new entity to begin to be effective. Often the old organization remains in place and can cause problems through subtle sabotage or outright opposition. For example, many countries that have established new environmental agencies have seen them suffer through such growing pains and turf battles with existing, well-established ministries.

Mobilizing Resources and Actions

If policy change is to achieve results, then resources and actions must be mobilized in the appropriate directions. Before resources are mobilized and actions initiated, policy change tends to be largely a paper exercise, but the mobilization task shifts the policy from paper to action, causing some to win and others to lose. It is around this task that policy reform is likely to encounter stiff resistance and generate conflict.

Mobilization of resources entails both planning and doing. It includes the preparation of concrete action plans, clarification of performance targets and standards, and then the conduct of those activities. Frequently this task involves breaking the reform package down into a sequence of action steps. Many reforms begin with pilot sites for demonstration and learning. For example, health policy reform in Egypt began with pilot tests in primary health care clinics in several locations in the city of Alexandria, where new basic service packages and provider payment schemes were tested before roll-out to other parts of the country. Similarly, in Zimbabwe new wildlife management policy that increased community control over natural resources in buffer zones around national parks began with pilots under the CAMPFIRE program before expanding to other places. Moving through the sequence from pilot, to roll-out, to full coverage requires policy managers to achieve some early successes that will build confidence, communicate those to stakeholders, learn from the pilots to fine-tune expansion, and keep progress moving.

Important to continued forward progress is attention to incentives for policy actors to adopt new modes and practices required by the policy change. If adequate incentives are not provided, resource mobilization will be impaired. If those in control of the resources within the implementing organization do not perceive adequate benefits for modifying their behavior, then the policy will not move forward. Likewise, if consumers or clients of the policy change do not perceive benefits, they will not modify their behavior and thus will undermine the policy's aims. It is also likely that the incentive needs of external and internal stakeholders will be different. Unless compelling reasons and positive incentives are given, actors are likely to resist the mandated changes. Thus, managing this implementation task calls for a collegial and collaborative management style (rather than autocratic or hierarchical), and negotiation and conflict resolution.

Monitoring the Progress and Impact of Policy Change

If policy changes are successful, then their impact will be evidenced in some manner or another such as transformed behaviors, greater or improved benefits to consumers or clients, and more effective or efficient production and use of resources. However, not all policy change strategies produce positive benefits or results despite good intentions. Some may produce unintended and unforeseen results and/or negative impacts. For instance, economic stabilization and adjustment reforms can exacerbate socioeconomic inequities if they are not quickly followed by strategies aimed at addressing the needs of the poor and marginalized.[11] It is therefore important to attempt to ascertain what effects policy changes produce, and to correct or adjust implementation should unsatisfactory results appear.

Because many policy reforms are long term and the benefits and impacts do not show up immediately, monitoring of progress in the form of process indicators is important. Some of these process indicators relate to monitoring the set of the implementation tasks described here, and others to the action sequence of pilot, roll-out, and expansion mentioned above. Tracking these indicators will facilitate learning and error correction, which can help avoid negative policy impacts. Monitoring is also vital for purposes of accountability, to assure that policy managers and implementing agencies are fulfilling their prescribed obligations. Monitoring may be carried out by a variety of actors, not simply implementors themselves. Possibilities include policy beneficiaries at the community level, civil society organizations (for example, so-called watchdog NGOs), think tanks or universities, international bodies (for example, Transparency International for anti-corruption efforts, or the International Union for the Conservation of Nature for environmental policies), or government entities (for example, legislative oversight committees, or ombudsman offices).[12]

Monitoring policy change requires mechanisms both for periodic review and evaluation and for tracking policies across multiple agencies over several years. The interaction of policy change among agencies is not always obvious. Impact in one agency's behaviors and outputs may come relatively rapidly and clearly, while in another it may be much slower and more ephemeral. Though these differences may be caused by the nature of the policy or perhaps by a lack of resources at critical stages, they will have the overall effect of complicating the construction of manageable monitoring indicators.

Because policy implementation involves multiple agencies, the question of who monitors and reports on a comprehensive picture of overall policy impacts can sometimes be problematic. On the technical side it is important to track the cumulative and interactive effects of all implementing actors on the production of policy outputs and changes. However, this can entail a heavy investment in monitoring and evaluation and risks creating a burdensome system that distracts from actual implementation. On the bureaucratic side, because monitoring and evaluation reports and results can be used for reward, punishment, and accountability, tensions and conflicts can arise when monitoring responsibilities are allocated. Of course, to a certain extent external monitoring and evaluation are central to the checks and balances that characterize democratic governance. In that context independent monitoring by public oversight agencies and civil society groups plays a key role in assuring accountability and responsiveness of policies to constituency needs and desires.

SEQUENCING, TIME, AND THE IMPLEMENTATION TASKS

As our preceding discussion implies, the implementation task model is roughly sequential (see Figure 2.1). Completion of the early tasks is requisite to the success of the latter. If those tasks to be completed at the start of the process are not adequately attended to, there will most certainly be problems in the completion of those tasks that follow, with growing consequences for the policy's successful implementation. That said, however, it is possible, and often in practice necessary, to focus on a later task before the completion of earlier ones. At certain points several tasks may be tackled simultaneously. For instance, once a decision has been made to implement a certain policy, some degree of legitimization has taken place, though it will need to be expanded to those with a role in implementation. Then the process of building support that will permit other actions to take place must begin. However, once the constituency building process is under way but not yet completed, it is advisable to begin developing strategies for accumulating resources, such as cultivating key members of the legislature's budget committee. Managers might also begin to think about and develop strategies for organizational modifications to permit the new policy to go forward. This might involve sending certain key personnel off for training in the skills that will be required for the new policy. If policy managers have taken on the responsibility for implementation of a new policy midway through the process (started by other managers), then they should make sure that the initial tasks have been sufficiently completed to provide the necessary base for completing later tasks.

Figure 2.1 Sequencing and the Policy Implementation Tasks

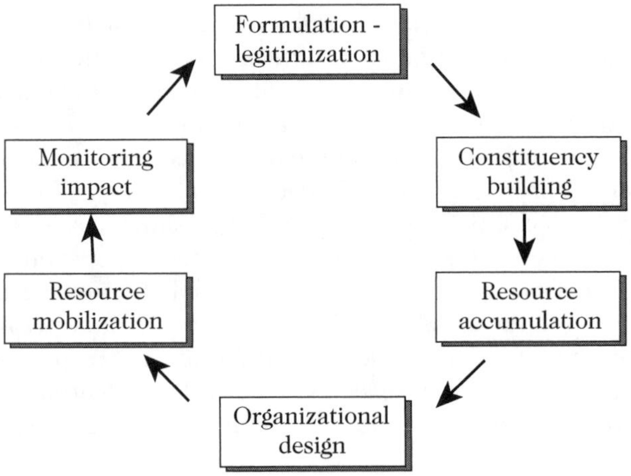

Since major policy initiatives tend to have many components, certain aspects of the new policy may be implemented at a much more rapid pace than others. For instance, when justice reform was undertaken in El Salvador during the mid-1990s, rapid and significant progress was made on several fronts, such as strengthening the role of the attorney general, separation of the police from the military, and professionalization of the judiciary. For each component, strong constituencies developed, budget reallocations were made to assure financing of the reforms, organizations were reformed, personnel retrained, and resources were fully mobilized toward the new policy's objectives. In other areas of justice reform, however, such as overhaul of criminal codes and procedures and reform of the legal profession (law school curriculum reform and codes of conduct), the issues evoked little interest. Revision in criminal codes and procedures engendered outright opposition. Thus the sequence of implementation for various components of the justice reform showed a pattern of uneven progress.

One of the most serious problems faced by policy implementation is the length of time that it takes to accomplish the process. As pointed out earlier, second-generation, long-haul reforms take several years or even decades to fully accomplish their objectives. This is particularly the case with complex and multi-component social reforms in health, education, and environmental policies. If a country takes twenty years to fully implement a reform, the government will inevitably change several times during the process. During that period large numbers of decision-makers (in the legislature, the cabinet, and the executing organizations) and interest groups will weigh in on the process and attempt to influence the direction of change and implementation.

For policy managers, the fact that policy implementation extends beyond a single political cycle in a country is a primary issue to be dealt with. To keep policy implementation tasks on track and moving forward, given the length of time required and the changing nature of sociopolitical conditions in most countries, what is clearly required is a strategic outlook on implementation. This is discussed later in this chapter.

Secondarily, the length of time required for implementing policy changes that are supported by donor agencies falls outside their three- to five-year programming cycles. Their short-term, results-based program design and management procedures do not easily accommodate most policy implementation time frames, which points up the indispensability of generating ownership and enduring constituencies. It is crucial that constituencies be developed that are capable of assuring that policy issues remain in play and that implementation remain on track through multiple governments and a changing cast of actors.

USING THE TASK FRAMEWORK

The implementation task framework is useful for a number of purposes. First, it can help to assess where the policy implementation process stands at a given point and provide a more accurate view as to what steps to take next and how long the process might take to accomplish. For instance, has the task of building an adequate support constituency been sufficiently completed so that policy managers can begin to think about how to use that support for obtaining needed resources? If not, then how much longer will the process take?

Second, the task framework may be used as a diagnostic instrument for pinpointing potential or existing trouble spots, problems, and roadblocks facing the policy reform effort. If policy implementers are encountering difficulties in obtaining resources for implementation, it may signal that insufficient attention was paid to developing a committed support base among key stakeholders such as political party officials, financial committees in the congress, or budget authorities.

Third, the task framework can be of considerable assistance in mapping out implementation strategies. As the earlier discussion emphasizes, any one of the tasks may involve substantial leadership, effort, and resources to accomplish, and may take many years to complete. The task framework can help policy managers to revisit the status of those tasks periodically and assure that reform progress will not evaporate or be derailed with a change of government. For example, when new political actors come to power, it is likely that the tasks of legitimization and constituency building will need to be undertaken again for these new stakeholders. Adjustments may be called for in policy monitoring, to make sure that the information and reporting on policy results are communicated to the latest set of decision-makers and that the policy message appeals to their concerns. A new administration may mean new organizations are created, some of which may need to be brought on board as members of the reform's implementation team. Certainly the resource mobilization task will require periodic ongoing attention to make sure that resource commitments remain in place and/or are renegotiated when governments change.

Fourth, the framework's recognition of the sequential nature of policy implementation tasks makes it simpler to identify what needs to be done and when. Among the most common problems in policy implementation are the tendency to set overly ambitious targets and, relatedly, to assume that the implementation process will move quickly and smoothly. However, if managers have a solid grasp of the task framework, they will be less likely to set unrealistic goals. Managers will have a much better sense of what can be done and will recognize that much of what needs to happen lies outside of their direct control. This can encourage managers to think and act strategically (see the next section) and to develop action plans collaboratively.

Another frequent error in policy implementation is placing the cart before the horse; in essence, skipping steps in the task cycle. Too often implementation strategies are adopted that assume levels of capability not yet possessed by the implementing agency. New tasks require new skills and modified organizations, but these requirements may take several years to be met. Obviously, for political reasons policy decisions often promise more and faster results than can realistically be achieved. Sometimes over-promising is the best way to take advantage of an opportunity for policy change. However, the task framework can be used to review what will be needed to generate some quick and visible results and to help make them happen even if all the requisite steps for long-term results are not yet taken. The framework is also useful as a guide for policy managers in communicating what will be necessary for ultimate success to both political actors and the public, which can help to adjust expectations.

Attention to the task framework and its sequencing can lead managers to ask the right questions and not make unwarranted assumptions about available human resource capacities or the suitability of a particular organization to carrying out a new policy. For instance, among the policy reforms undertaken by South Africa's post-apartheid government is health care financing reform. The ANC government moved quickly on eliminating some fees related to public health services and on modifying the budget allocation process for health, but much of the reform package depended upon significant changes in intergovernmental relations as part of implementing decentralization of service delivery and upon reprioritization of health sector spending to address equity and coverage for vulnerable groups. Analysis of the reform effort highlighted the problems of making assumptions about the health sector's readiness and capacity to move quickly in putting changes in place and noted the difficulties in reaching consensus on financing measures among key political stakeholders. Despite these difficulties some early and visible changes were accomplished that showed the public that health reform was under way, even though financing arrangements were not fully worked out. For example, immunization campaigns were conducted (polio, hepatitis B, measles), a clinic-building program was launched (400 new clinics and 152 expansions of existing ones between 1995 and 1998), and a school feeding program was carried out nationwide (Gilson et al. 1999).

Fifth, the implementation task framework can be a valuable aid to policy managers in the development of more realistic and accurate indicators for monitoring the progress toward impacts. As noted above, it should not be expected that a new policy can be implemented within a relatively short time period. With a better understanding of what might be expected within a given period of time, more realistic indicators can be developed.

Table 2.2 illustrates strategies and mechanisms that might be employed in implementing each of the six tasks. While the table is not meant to be exhaustive, it shows not only a range of different alternative strategies that might be used to carry out particular tasks, but also what sorts of mechanisms and tools can be used to carry out those strategies. Descriptions and applications of many of these suggested tools can be found in the chapters in Part II of this book. In keeping with the process focus of the implementation task framework, all of these tools and mechanisms concentrate on the "how" rather than the "what" of the policy's technical content.

Table 2.2 Implementation Tasks, Strategies, Mechanisms

Implementation task	Task implementation strategies	Task implementation mechanisms and tools
Creating legitimacy	• Raising awareness, questioning the status quo • Identifying policy reform champions • Creating new forums for policy discussion • Creation of bridging mechanisms • Developing convening authority	• Policy dialogue workshops • Public-private forums • Stakeholder workshops • Task forces • Blue-ribbon committees
Building constituencies	• Supporting policy champions • Identifying and mobilizing key stakeholders • Marketing, bargaining, and building coalitions • Dealing with realities of opposition • Mobilization of under-organized stakeholders or beneficiaries	• Stakeholder analysis • Political mapping • Policy network analysis and mapping • Lobbying and advocacy • Negotiated rule making • Association development
Accumulating resources	• Identifying and obtaining seed and bridge financing from internal/external sources • Negotiating with finance and budget authorities for a larger share of resources • Development of partnerships/exchange with other public agencies, NGOs, community groups • Creation and installation of new capacities • Upgrading human resources	• Lobbying with external donors • Public finance reviews • Transparent, accessible budget processes • Lobbying/bargaining • Identifying new skills and developing training programs for new skills
Modifying organizational structures	• Fitting new missions to old organizations or creating new organizations • Building implementation capacity	• Organizational diagnostics (SWOT [strengths, weaknesses, opportunities, threats] analysis)

		• Organizational retooling, reengineering • Creation of ad hoc task forces and cross-ministerial commissions • Policy coordination, management units • Public-private partnerships
	• Developing boundary-spanning links • Fostering networks and partnerships • Enhancing cooperation and coordination among implementing agencies	
Mobilizing resources and actions	• Developing concrete plans, performance expectations, and accountability; creating and carrying out doable activities • Identifying, creating, and/or altering incentives • Dealing with resistance and conflict • Governing the coalition and achieving compliance • Recognizing the importance of and mobilizing actions for early success • Communicating success stories	• Creation and implementation of participatory planning processes • Joint problem-solving workshops • Utilization of multi-party action plans • Innovative dispute resolution mechanisms • Creation of rewards system for performance and sanctions for under-performance
Monitoring impact	• Positioning monitoring in the policy and political arenas • Creating and positioning analytic capacity • Linking learning and operations • Establishing realistic performance standards and milestones • Establishing managerial mechanisms for application of lessons learned	• Cross-agency monitoring units • Citizen oversight panels, public hearings • Regularized performance review for implementing agencies • International monitoring groups • Policy impact evaluations • Civil society watchdogs, service delivery satisfaction surveys

As noted above, any single implementation task may well take several years to accomplish and transcend more than one government. Similarly, the more complicated the policy and the greater the resistance to change, the more likely that multiple strategies will be required. In the case of economic reform policy in Honduras, for example, just to create an adequate level of legitimacy (Task 1) regarding the merits of a market-led economic framework took several years. The policy analysis and implementation unit staff that IPC worked with used nearly all the proposed strategies and implementation mechanisms suggested for the task of creating legitimacy in Table 2.2. Policy reform champions had to be identified and persuaded of the need for policy change, new public-private forums that bypassed regular venues for discussion of economic policy (such as the congress, universities, and business associations) had to be developed, and bridging mechanisms for coordination created (in the form of specialized policy promotion agencies). During that period legitimacy for the new policy grew more rapidly among certain groups than in others. This, however, allowed the process of constituency building to begin among those sensing that new economic policies were needed. Stakeholder analysis and political mapping tools were then used to determine which areas required more support and among which sectors support could be capitalized upon.

POLICY IMPLEMENTATION AND STRATEGIC MANAGEMENT

Policy implementation requires the active intervention of policy managers and their organizations. Wherever they are located (for example, public agencies, NGOs, community groups, or business associations), policy managers need capabilities and skills different from those generally associated with routine administration. As Table 2.1 shows, policy implementation lies at the strategic end of the management spectrum. Traditional management skills tend to focus on the technical, internally focused needs of the policy and its administrative arrangements, whereas most of the barriers to policy implementation are process and/or externally derived. Though implementing organizations need to upgrade their capacities to be able to deliver on the substance of the new policies, those capacities must be balanced with others that will assist the organizations in securing and maintaining the support necessary for the longer haul. They will need skills that will allow them to compete with other organizations in the quest for resources to carry out new policies.

What sort of management skills can be realistically exercised to implement policy reforms? One answer can be found in the approaches and tools associated with strategic management (see, for example, Bryson 1988, Kiggundu 1996, Koteen 1989). Strategic management is outwardly focused. It is designed to assist in managing in times of turbulence, when inputs are unpredictable and change nonlinear, when resources are unavailable, when the change process is long term, and when a broader vision of organizational mandates and actions is needed.

Specifically, strategic management helps policy managers and their organizations by directing them to (1) look out to capture signals of change and transformation, (2) look in to examine how well and with what resources implementing organizations can respond to the changes mandated by the new policies, and (3) look ahead to ask what comes next and to put into place the resources/measures needed to get there. Getting the right balance among the outward-, inward-, and forward-looking functions is the essence of managing the policy process strategically. Box 2.1 summarizes the three-way orientation of strategic management. The outward- and forward-looking elements of strategic management are particularly essential for coping with the "nobody in charge" characteristic of policy implementation.

Box 2.1 Strategic Management's Three-Way Orientation

Strategic management capacities are important to enable policy implementors to deal with the challenges of policy reform. Strategic management can be thought of in terms of a conceptual "shorthand" as capacity to (1) look outward, (2) look inward, and (3) look ahead (Brinkerhoff 1991).

Looking out. The tendency of managers to concentrate on the pursuit of day-to-day bureaucratic routines to the exclusion of taking action or being attentive to performance is widely recognized. Policy implementors need to build capacity to extend their focus beyond the boundaries of their individual organizations. This means becoming more aware of who and what is "out there" and figuring out how to respond appropriately. In essence, this calls for capacity in strategic planning and management. It includes the ability to identify key stakeholders; create opportunities for participation; forge partnerships among public, private, and voluntary sectors; set feasible objectives; build constituencies for change; and resolve conflicts.

Looking in. Efficient internal structures, systems, and procedures are important for achieving results. Critical to this kind of capacity are efficient and effective ways to design and implement programs; to set up and manage organizations; to hire, train, and motivate personnel; and to allocate, monitor, and account for financial and other resources. Without achieving some minimal level of operational efficiency, it is difficult to think or act strategically.

Looking ahead. The third capacity relates to bringing together strategy, structure, and resources to achieve policy goals. It includes attention to sustainability, which implies the capacity to be anticipatory and take the initiative, not just to be responsive and reactive. Dealing with what is critical today is not enough. Policy implementors must be capable of identifying and preparing for what will be critical tomorrow and the next day as well. This includes operational capacity in evaluation and monitoring, but extends beyond to those more intangible capabilities such as leadership, agenda-setting, and vision.

Strategic management consists of four guiding principles, presented here in terms of policy reform:

- *First, the strategic approach is oriented toward the future.* It recognizes that the environment will change. It is a long-range orientation, one that tries to anticipate events rather than simply reacting as they occur. The approach leads managers to ask where their organizations and their collaborators are at the present, where they want to be after a certain period, what they need to get there, how to develop strategies and the means, and how to manage those strategies to achieve their stated goals and objectives. It recognizes that the future cannot be controlled but argues that by remaining strategically focused and anticipating the future, organizations and their stakeholders can help to shape and modify the impact of environmental change.
- *Second, the strategic approach has an external emphasis.* It takes into account several components of external operating environments, including technology, politics, economics, and the social dimension. Strategic thinking recognizes that each of these can either constrain or facilitate the organizations involved in policy implementation. Politics will shape the policies that are to be implemented, economics will constrain the organization's level of resources, and social and political variables will influence who the policy's stakeholders will be. Some of these factors can be influenced by policy managers, but others will need to be treated as constraints and limits on action.
- *Third, the strategic approach concentrates on assuring a good fit between the environment and policy implementation organizations* (including their missions and objectives, strategies, structures, and resources) and attempts to anticipate what will be required to assure continued fit. Under conditions of rapid political, economic, social, and technical change, strategies can quickly become outmoded. Resources traditionally available to implementing organizations may dwindle or evaporate suddenly. The strategic approach recognizes that to maintain a close fit with the environment, implementation plans will have to be fine-tuned, functions may need to be reallocated among implementation actors, and implementors' capacities and performance will need to be assessed continuously as the policy reform evolves.
- *Finally, the strategic approach is a process.* It is continuous and recognizes the need to be open to changing goals and activities in light of shifting political, economic, and social circumstances. It is a process that requires monitoring and review mechanisms capable of feeding information to managers continuously. The process is not a one-shot approach—it is ongoing—and thus requires attention to

emerging needs and changing circumstances as they arise, and to the development of strategies to respond to those needs.

Unlike the traditional paradigms of public administration for routine service delivery and government functions, strategic management is ideally suited to the needs and challenges of policy change and implementation. It recognizes that a good technical policy solution is not enough to assure implementation. Its outward focus centers on the need for expanded participation of stakeholders, both internal and external. It seeks to fortify and strengthen new beneficiaries but soften the landing of those groups negatively affected by change. It recognizes the need for strengthening constituencies and for building alliances as a means to achieving changes and objectives. Strategic management actively seeks to find solutions to long-range needs; to develop and set priorities for plans, options, and strategies; and to match organizational structures and resources to assist in achieving results. Strategic management allows implementing organizations to be more adaptive and is thus more able to cope with challenges posed, for example, by demands for greater participation by civil society and for decentralization of government programs, which increasingly are features of the policy reform milieu in many countries. Finally, strategic management, through its outward-looking focus and emphasis on results, places a greater value on accountability and satisfaction of stakeholders.

Strategic management is more than set of tools. In essence, it is a mindset, a conceptual and attitudinal perspective on change and managerial action. Strategic planning and management tools embody a mental framework that goes beyond the application of one or more of the tools. Effective strategic management means that managers develop a strategic mentality that colors how they think about their responsibilities and actions. We stress the mentality aspect of strategic management because it is easy to become wrapped up in the tools. There are many skeptics who question the efficacy of strategic management tools and techniques, and rightly point out that empirical evidence linking their application and outcomes is scarce (see, for example, Goldsmith 1997). Any management tool, if used in a mindless and pro forma way, will generate nothing but empty documents and reports. In many situations strategic management exercises have consumed time and resources without contributing to progress with programs or policies, so the caveats are warranted.

How to Manage Strategically

Since strategic management is best characterized as a way of thinking, much of how to do it lies in the realm of inspiration, intuition, and informal problem-solving. As we warned, treating strategic management as a set of steps, checklists, and analytic techniques risks oversimplification and interference with creative thinking if applied mechanically or cosmetically. With that warning in mind, policy managers can usefully divide strategic management into four major steps: (1) developing agreement and setting objectives, (2) internal and external scanning, (3) developing options and strategies, and (4) implementing and monitoring. Table 2.3 shows the corresponding activities under each of these steps. These are listed sequentially, but in practice they form an iterative, cyclical process with important interactions and feedback. Several tools are also listed, most of which are discussed in later chapters of this book. Each is meant either to sharpen managers' information collection and analysis or to support the implementation of the corresponding step. As stressed above, the tools are meant to assist creativity and strategic thinking for policy implementation, but by themselves they constitute neither strategies nor strategic management.

- *Developing agreement and setting objectives*: This step entails identifying what needs to be accomplished, defining short and long-term objectives, and relating them to what the various implementing organizations need to do. The starting point is the policy to be implemented and where it stands in the sequence of six implementation tasks (see Figure 2.1). Some of the techniques or tools that might be employed in generating agreement and setting objectives include gap analysis (comparing current status on a set of indicators with where those indicators need to be to achieve results), conflict resolution (if actors are in conflict over objectives), and priority-setting. Mechanisms for using these techniques could be task forces, organizational retreats, or workshops.
- *Internal and external scanning*: This step includes inward-looking analysis of implementing organizations and groups to identify strengths and weaknesses affecting their implementation capacity, and outward-focused analysis to flag external opportunities and threats from the policy environment. This diagnostic is referred to as SWOT (strengths-weaknesses-opportunities-threats) assessment. Some useful tools for SWOT include stakeholder analysis, political mapping, various types of institutional capacity checklists, and/or political risk assessment.
- *Options and strategies:* Through the review of the SWOT analysis, policy managers and their implementing partners identify strategic issues and set priorities in terms of urgency and magnitude. They then design strategies and plans to address the key issues. Useful techniques and mechanisms for this stage include problem-solving workshops, scenario analysis, participatory planning, negotiation, lobbying, and conflict resolution.

Table 2.3 Steps, Activities, and Tools/Mechanisms for Strategic Management

Strategic management STEPS	Strategic management ACTIVITIES	Strategic management TOOLS/MECHANISMS
Developing agreement and setting objectives	1. Agreement on and initiation of strategic management process 2. Identification and clarification of mission, objectives, and current strategies	• Gap analysis • Conflict resolution • Organizational retreats • Task forces • Workshops
Internal and external scanning/SWOT	3. Assessment of internal strengths and weaknesses of the organization 4. Assessment of threats and opportunities from the external environment 5. Identification of key constituents, stakeholders, and their expectations	• Institutional capacity checklists • Political mapping • Political risk assessment • Force-field analysis • Stakeholder analysis • Workshops
Options and strategies	6. Identification of key strategic issues confronting implementation 7. Design/analysis/selection of strategic options and design of an action plan	• Problem-solving workshops • Scenario analysis • Participatory planning • Conflict resolution • Negotiation, lobbying
Implementing and monitoring	8. Implementing the strategy and action plan 9. Monitoring and review of the strategy and action plan's performances	• Coordination • Benchmarking • Performance indicators • Periodic strategic review

- *Implementing and monitoring*: In this step strategic plans are put into action, resources and commitments are mobilized, and organizational capacities brought to bear on the task to be implemented. Because factors in the operating environment are in constant flux (for example, budgets, political priorities, and policy constituencies), systems for monitoring and review of the chosen strategies should be put into place to allow policy managers to make appropriate and timely adjustments. These systems should provide feedback for day-to-day operations, and short-term adaptations, as well as informing the vision for reaching the long-term policy reform goals.

Policy managers can improve their own strategic management skills and capacities, and those of their implementing partners, in several ways. Skill-building can be accomplished through management training or through what is called process consulting (see Cooke 1998, UNDP 1994). Process consulting involves an outsider who specializes in coaching managers in the "how" side of strategic planning, participation, and decision-making. It is often combined with management training, either one on one, or in workshops and seminars.

For example, in Madagascar managers responsible for the implementation of priority environmental policies were provided training in strategic management for policy implementation, which helped them to deal with the interorganizational coordination issues they were facing. In South Africa, as provincial governments were transitioning to the new post-apartheid framework, training in strategic management assisted administrative heads in the development of a strategic plan to manage the transition. Training can also be productive if it is provided to those who train other managers. An IPC team provided training in strategic management and negotiation skills to the faculty of the Ukraine Academy of Public Administration, as well as assistance in curriculum development to create a new course in strategic management.

Building strategic management skills through process consultation actively involves people in problem-solving and working together on day-to-day tasks. For example, in Bulgaria, with the help of a long-term advisor, business associations became more effective advocates for policy reform. The advisor led them through a process of issue identification, constituency building, and policy dialogue using strategic management tools. The associations were able to continue to use these skills after the advisor left, and they have become active participants with government officials both in formulating policies that affect the private sector and in mobilizing the private sector to lobby for their interests (see Chapter 4).

Combining training and process consulting can be highly effective in developing strategic management skills. In Honduras, for example, training in strategic management helped the Economic Cabinet's Policy Analysis and Implementation Unit to develop a more externally and future oriented perspective in formulating policies to respond to Honduras's process of structural change. Through the introduction of skills such as stakeholder analysis and political and policy mapping, the staff of the unit became highly effective in identifying constituents, locating potential sources of obstacles, and developing mechanisms for reducing stakeholder opposition. Process consulting was used periodically to facilitate the unit's annual strategic review and to help the staff in maintaining a close environmental fit. As a result, the unit was able to work effectively under three different presidents. A second example comes from Tanzania, where a tax policy reform effort combined training with process consulting. Staff of the Tanzania Revenue Authority received strategic management training (in areas such as stakeholder analysis, political mapping, and some basics on lobbying and advocacy) that was followed up periodically by visits from a tax policy expert, who helped the staff apply what they had learned to keep tax reform on track. The results were increased collections and improved compliance.

Strategically Managing the Policy Implementation Tasks

What does strategically managing the policy implementation process involve? This can be illustrated by integrating the strategic management process into the policy implementation task model as shown in Figure 2.2. For simplicity's sake only one of the tasks shows this integration visually, but all of the six implementation tasks can be undertaken from a strategic perspective, balancing their looking-in, looking-out, and looking-ahead dimensions (recall Box 2.1). Figure 2.2a illustrates the application of the strategic management process steps to constituency building, but each of the other five implementation tasks should also be thought of as containing these steps. The cumulative result of taking a strategic perspective is a more effective management of the entire policy implementation task sequence. The strategic management process provides a useful framework for developing an overall strategic vision for implementing policies and for tackling the individual policy implementation tasks. Used effectively, strategic management will assist in developing a discipline that helps policy managers to look in, look out, and look ahead—precisely the sort of perspective needed to deal effectively with the uncertainty and complexity of policy implementation.

Figure 2.2 Strategically Managing Policy Implementation Tasks

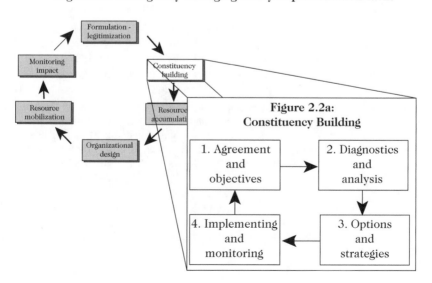

Box 2.2 provides an example of the application of the strategic management approach to the constituency building task shown in Figure 2.2a. It presents Ecuador's experience in building an effective constituency for

---

Box 2.2 Health Sector Reform in Ecuador: Strategic Management for Constituency Building

Health sector reform in Ecuador has remained a politically charged issue ever since it appeared on the political agenda as part of broader privatization reforms initiated in 1993. Developing politically acceptable reform measures and sustaining implementation across successive political administrations has been difficult, and progress has not always matched expectations. In 1998 USAID/Quito supported technical assistance in strategic management to help the Ministry of Health (MOH) reform team improve prospects for implementation. The Partnerships for Health Reform (PHR) project provided the assistance, with technical support from IPC, in using a variation of the stakeholder analysis and political mapping tools contained in Chapters 6 and 8 of this book. MOH policymakers identified a specific health policy around which to build a supportive constituency (Schmeer 1998). The policy chosen was new forms of resource allocation within the MOH, which included two main components: (1) deconcentration of the MOH, and (2) results-based resource allocation.

The MOH reform team conducted a constituency mapping exercise to develop recommendations and strategies that would help the MOH increase support for these policies in the context of the MOH's modernization and changing roles. The exercise targeted sources of support and opposition to the policies and ranked constituencies on a leadership and power scale. The team's findings included the following:

- The most influential stakeholders were, for the most part, outside of the MOH and included, for example, the powerful labor unions, doctors' and nurses' associations, and employers' associations. Provincial governors were also important.

- Stakeholders had relatively little knowledge of the policies' specific provisions, though they had more knowledge of and interest in deconcentrated forms of resource allocation.

- Stakeholders saw the MOH top leadership as opposing the policies and did not see the minister as a strong proponent for change.

- Stakeholders conditioned their support for policy implementation on several factors: clarity, transparency, and continuity of the policy implementation process; increased participation in the reform process; and demonstration of positive results in the short and medium term. Based on this analysis the reform team developed an advocacy strategy to increase the chances of effective implementation of the resource allocation policies. The strategy proposed the following steps:

  - Clarify and communicate the objectives and benefits of the new resource allocation policies to all stakeholders within the context of decentralization, privatization, and self-financing of health services.

> - Inform stakeholders more consistently on results achieved from the implementation of deconcentration measures and new resource allocation mechanisms.
>
> - Develop new modes of stakeholder participation to strengthen support from positive constituencies and reduce opposition from negative ones.
>
> - Empower current and potential supporters of the policies to become more active champions for reform.
>
> The strategy was operationalized in the form of specific policy communication and monitoring plans targeted on different categories of stakeholders. Although another change of government delayed progress on these plans, the reform team, with the help of donors, has continued to pursue implementation of the new resource allocation policies, as well as make some headway with other elements of health sector reform.

health policy reform. The case demonstrates the importance of communicating with stakeholders for crafting implementation strategies.

CHALLENGES FOR POLICY IMPLEMENTATION IN THE CONTEXT OF DEMOCRATIC GOVERNANCE

Across the developing and transitioning world, policy reforms are designed and implemented in contexts in which democratic governance frames how public officials and citizens interact. As Carothers (1999) reminds us, not all countries are proceeding uniformly or steadily along the democratization path. Yet governments everywhere, even in autocratic states, face pressures to open or broaden access to basic services and to enhance participation in political, economic, and/or social spheres. Policymakers and implementors must contend with groups that heretofore were excluded or were relegated to only a marginal role, and that now demand greater accountability from those charged with implementation. At the same time, elites and powerful interests remain important stakeholders, often holding the key to keeping regimes in power.[13]

As was noted earlier, no single government agency can fully take on and implement a complex policy change. Governments change, sometimes dramatically, both in terms of philosophy and in styles of leadership and operational management. Moreover, reforms that depend entirely on a single champion are likely to fail. In order to assure that reform moves forward, even if in a frequently interrupted way, demand and support for change need to be grounded in the new winners or beneficiaries of the proposed change. The participation of and support from these new constituencies is vital. But it is also essential that they be capable of articulating and transmitting demands to those charged with making decisions about how resources are to be allocated. Similarly, new mechanisms must be developed to process those demands. To assure that reforms are moving forward with the desired impact, the new constituencies must be capable of assessing the performance of the implementation agency and have the ability to hold the agency accountable should things not go well. These elements of the governance context for reform challenge policy managers in numerous ways: assuring broader and continuous participation, adjusting organizational mechanisms and capacities in order to leverage collaboration and coordination with other agencies and external groups, and developing policy management mechanisms that are accountable to newly empowered actors.

Opening the implementation process to new participants and stakeholders is desirable and important, but it raises serious management and democratic governance issues. How many groups should be taken into account? By what criteria should their participation be measured? How much support will be enough to get the policy implemented? While increased participation is at the core of democratic governance, policy managers in developing countries have only limited time and fewer resources to deal with and to satisfy demands of new participants. Managing participation thus becomes a challenge to successful policy implementation. We turn to these questions and issues in the following chapter.

As this chapter discussed, policy implementation frequently crosses agency lines and reaches beyond the public sector to private and nongovernmental entities. The challenge for policy managers is how to create partnerships that effectively combine the resources and capacities of other agencies, civil society, and the private sector with those of public implementing organizations to assure results—all in a context where no one is in charge. Chapter 4 examines partnerships and how to manage them.

The complexity of policy change creates challenges for coordinating actions at various administrative levels within government, as well as between government and external partners and stakeholders. With a multiplicity of organizations and actors involved in different aspects of policy reform, a premium is put on redesigning organizations to operate more effectively in multi-actor settings and on developing effective linkages among them. Assuring that the administrative machinery remains open to more inclusive participation in setting agendas and establishing priorities, while at the same time developing methods that permit a more participative review of performance and results achieved, is not be an easy task. But these mechanisms of accountability lie at the heart of policy implementation and democratic governance. Issues of organizational design, administrative linkages, and coordination are treated in Chapter 5.

NOTES

1. The clash between policy hopes and implementation reality is artfully captured in the subtitle to the classic treatment of policy implementation in the United States by Pressman and Wildavsky (1973): "How great expectations in Washington are dashed in Oakland; or, why it's amazing that federal programs work at all, this being a saga of the economic development administration as told by two sympathetic observers who seek to build morals on a foundation of ruined hopes."

2. In the U.S. policy literature this characteristic of policy change constitutes the essence of pluralist models, where policies are a function of interest group power and domestic politics. See, for example, two of the classics: Dahl (1961) and Lowi (1979). In the international development policy arena the international donor agencies loom large among the external actors, along with national economic and political elites. See Bates and Krueger (1993), Brautigam (2000), Haggard and Kaufman (1992), Haggard and Webb (1994).

3. While this feature of policy change is a basic premise of U.S. policy pluralism model, and of political economy models of international development, it was surprising the extent to which the sectoral policy specialists we worked with in IPC did not initially recognize policy's political aspects.

4. From the U.S. policy implementation literature, see Bardach (1977). A strategy frequently recommended to overcome or to get around resistance is the immediate implementation (or at least attempt) of reform measures, carried out before the entrenched opposition in bureaucracies and elsewhere has a chance to mobilize. Sometimes this can work in the short run, but initial success may give way to backsliding once opposition mobilizes.

5. As with the other characteristics of policy change in developing/transitioning countries, this one has long been noted in the U.S. policy literature. See the classic, Wildavsky (1974).

6. This is a key element in Mazmanian and Sabatier's (1989) policy implementation framework. Frequently, political dynamics limit the degree of specificity and coherence in policy goals, since maintaining some degree of vagueness allows larger numbers of stakeholders to support the policy.

7. Bryson and Crosby (1992) discuss the challenges of managing where no one is in charge. Pressman and Wildavsky (1973) documented early on the difficulties of managing the involvement of multiple agencies, noting the tendency for interference and delays to escalate seriously when increased numbers of actors are involved.

8. These are what Lowi, looking at the U.S. policy process, terms "iron triangles" (1979). The existence in developing countries of closed policy circles that reinforce the status quo has also been documented and analyzed (see, for example, Gulhati 1990). See also the policy economy literature cited in Chapter 1.

9. As our urban development image suggests and the discussion of the implementation task model that follows elaborates, our underlying assumptions about successful policy implementation fall within the camp of policy scholars who

contend that flexibility, managerial discretion, local ownership and coalition building, incremental learning, and participation characterize effective policy implementation. See Lipsky (1980), Winter (1990), Sabatier and Jenkins-Smith (1993), Ostrom (1990), Schneider and Ingram (1997).

10. In the U.S. policy literature one of the classics on these bureaucratic dynamics is Heclo (1977). In developing countries see, for example, Lamb and Weaving (1992).

11. Debate has been ongoing for many years regarding the equity and distribution effects of the International Monetary Fund's and the World Bank's lending programs. See, for example, Sarris (1990) and Zuckerman (1991). The latest debates have been taking place in the context of the World Bank's Poverty Reduction Strategy Papers. The anti-globalization protests in Seattle, Genoa, and Washington are another form of "debate" on the impacts of the multilateral lending institutions.

12. See the discussion of policy monitoring in Chapter 12.

13. The role of interest groups in democratic pluralist political systems and their impact on the policy process are topics of ongoing debate among political scientists. In the United States, among those critical of pluralist models, Lowi (1979) is one of the seminal works arguing that the dominance of interest-group politics that characterizes U.S. policymaking undermines broad-based democracy and the achievement of the public good (see also Pateman 1970). As Carothers (1999) points out, in thinking about democracy promotion and civil society strengthening overseas, we need to avoid overly rosy or simplistic notions of pluralism and democratic governance.

3

Citizen Participation
in the Policy Process

*The implementation energy of thousands, if not millions, of indepen-
dent agents is needed if the reform is to be more than words on paper.*
—Parity Commission for Education Reform, Guatemala

*Because of the participation of a large number of citizens in delibera-
tions with government officials on small and medium enterprises, our
SME policy not only built agreement on what to do, it was the most
democratically produced national strategy in the history of Bulgaria.*
—Member of the SME joint task force, Bulgaria

As these quotations from two of IPC's collaborators illustrate, participation is central to policy implementation. The first quotation highlights
the fact that implementation often requires actions by large numbers of
people in order to achieve results. Getting the right technical content
down on paper is only part of the answer for achieving policy results and
sustainable impacts. The second quotation emphasizes the importance
of the process by which the content of policies is formulated and the link
between participation and democratic governance. Participation and pluralist consultation are not simply features of effective policy processes;
they are integral elements of democracy itself. Throughout the developing and transitioning world over the past decade or so, citizens have increasingly organized to expand their influence in policy debates, to pressure their governments to be more responsive and accountable, and to
demand a greater role in governance. These trends toward empowered
participation and policy activism are present at all levels, from local, to
national, to international (see, for example, King, Feltey, and Susel 1998,
Blair 2000a and 2000b, Burbidge 1997, Florini 2000, Otto 1996).

Public officials in many countries find themselves under an obligation
to be more participative (see, for example, Montgomery 1988, Thomas
1995, Thompson 1995). For example, in 1994 Bolivia passed a law on

popular participation as part of a program of administrative decentralization and sectoral reform (Blackburn and de Toma 1998; see also Blair
2001). As a result, local civil society groups are empowered to participate
in policy and resource allocation decisions along with municipal government officials regarding infrastructure investments and service delivery
programs. Another example comes from Uganda, where during the period from 1995 to 1998 the government engaged in a broadly participatory policy analysis and planning exercise focused on poverty reduction.
Private sector representatives, civil society organizations, academics, the
media, and individual citizens participated in a national task force and
seven thematic working groups. The process produced an action plan,
which was vetted at a national conference, revised, and subsequently
endorsed by the cabinet in 1998 (Robb 1999).

Participation is a key component of the policy implementation task
model presented in Chapter 2. We argue that for almost all of the tasks,
participation is helpful, even essential. The link with citizen participation is especially salient for legitimization and constituency building—
for example, dealing with winners and losers—but there are also participatory aspects to resource mobilization and allocation, as well as
organizational arrangements and policy monitoring. Thus, stakeholder
participation is at the core of policy management and democratic governance.

However, participation is not a panacea for implementation success.
Serious questions can and should be raised regarding the expectations
for, and limits of, participation in the policy process. What are the objectives for increased participation, and when is it appropriate? Under which
circumstances does increased participation enhance or undermine democratic policy processes? How much participation is enough, how much is
too little, how much is too much—and how are these criteria defined?
What are the benefits and costs of expanding participation? What factors
constrain the expansion of participation in policy decision-making? And
are there certain preconditions or prerequisites that must be fulfilled if
efforts at expanding participation are to be fruitful?

This chapter explores these questions. We examine participation from
the point of view of public sector policy decision-makers and/or
implementors with an interest in sustainable reform and democratic governance.[1] However, much of the discussion is equally relevant to nongovernmental actors and to donor agencies seeking to assess the pros and
cons of participation from their perspective. We outline some practical
mechanisms to expand participation and offer guidance on balancing expanded input with getting decisions made and objectives accomplished.

The chapter is divided into five sections. The first examines current
concepts of participation, some of the objectives that managers might
achieve by expanding participation, and where participation fits within
our policy implementation task sequence. The second explores the

management of participation and its operational dimensions for policy managers. It explores the benefits of participation, recognizing that increased participation involves some costs, both for potential new participants as well as for decision-makers. These costs and the ability of the participating groups and policy decision-making structures to meet those costs place practical limits on the capacity and incentives of various actors to participate or for the decision-maker to encourage participation. The third section examines different mechanisms for participation, ranging from information-sharing to empowerment, offering some examples. The fourth section looks at the problem of relative balance between the supply of and demand for participation. We argue that citizen demand for participation opportunities cannot be effectively met without a corresponding increase in capacity of government to supply those opportunities and to respond to external stakeholder input. This section also reviews factors that appear to constrain or enhance participation supply and demand. The last section looks at the connections between participation and democracy, offering some caveats relating to frequently made assumptions about these links.

PARTICIPATION AND POLICY IMPLEMENTATION

Since participation can have different meanings for different people, we begin with some clarification of the term. *Participation* can be defined as "a process through which stakeholders influence and share control over development initiatives and the decisions and resources which affect them" (World Bank 1996: 3). This definition provides a starting point to look at participation in terms of its who, what, and how dimensions (see also Brinkerhoff with Kulibaba 1996).

Clarifying Participation: Who, What, and How?

The "who" question looks at the various stakeholders—the constituencies who are affected by a policy and who have the power to help it or obstruct it. For most policy reforms, participants can be divided into stakeholders in national government entities (for example, ministries, parliaments, and so on) and sub-national public sector agencies (for example, municipal governments, local legislatures, and so on). Beyond the public sector, participants include private sector actors, various organizations at national and local levels (for example, professional associations, think tanks, trade unions, religious organizations, youth groups, political parties, and so on), and citizens (especially poor and marginalized groups). Another category of participants includes the international donors that provide funding and technical assistance. Of concern for orchestrating policy participation is identification of the interests of each category of stakeholders, the resources they bring to the policy process, their motivation to use those resources, and their likely impacts (see Chapter 6).

The "what" question addresses the kind of participation being undertaken or considered. The kinds of participation that concern us here relate to the sequential steps in the policy implementation task model elaborated in Chapter 2. The options for participation in each one are detailed below.

The "how" question clarifies the qualitative aspect of participation. This dimension of participation can usefully be thought of as a range of options, from relatively more passive to increasingly active modes. These can be conceptualized as information-sharing, consultation, collaboration, joint decision-making, and empowerment. Box 3.1 defines these types and provides examples of each one.

Box 3.1 Types of Participation

- **Information-sharing:** one-way information flows. Information-sharing serves to keep actors informed, to provide transparency, and to build legitimacy. From government to the public, examples are dissemination of written material through official documents, newspapers, or magazines; distribution of documents from local government offices; press conferences; radio or television broadcasts; or establishment of websites. From the public to government, examples include responding to questionnaires and surveys, accessing toll-free telephone "hot lines," and providing various kinds of data, opinion surveys, or analyses.

- **Consultation:** two-way information flows and exchange of views. Consultation involves sharing information and garnering feedback and reaction. Examples are beneficiary assessments, participatory poverty assessments, town hall meetings, focus groups, national conferences, round tables, and parliamentary hearings.

- **Collaboration:** joint activities in which the initiator invites other groups to be involved but retains decision-making authority and control. Collaboration moves beyond collecting feedback to involving external actors in problem-solving, policy design, monitoring and evaluation, and so forth. Examples include public reviews of draft legislation, government-led working groups, and government-convened planning sessions.

- **Joint decision-making:** collaboration where there is shared control over decisions made. Shared decision-making is useful when the external actor's knowledge, capacity, and experience is critical for achieving policy objectives. Examples are joint committees, public-private partnerships, advisory councils, and blue-ribbon commissions or task forces.

- **Empowerment:** transfer of control over decision-making, resources, and activities from the initiator to other stakeholders. Empowerment takes place when external actors, acting autonomously and in their own interests, can carry out policy mandates without significant government involvement or oversight. Examples are local natural resource management committees, community empowerment zones, water user associations, some forms of partnerships, and civil society "seed" grants.

One issue that frequently clouds the "how" question is the tendency to interpret the types of participation normatively. Some see information-sharing and consultation as lower quality forms of participation and cite empowerment as the feature that distinguishes whether participation is "genuine" or not. However, the various types of participation are more usefully seen in instrumental terms, as serving a particular function or objective (see the next section) rather than in terms of "good" or "bad."

One reason not to make value judgments about the types of participation is that activities from information-sharing to empowerment tend to be connected in a hierarchy. Each subsequent type builds upon the previous ones. Therefore, it is more useful to think of these as interlinked rather than isolated or discrete alternatives. Information provision and transparency are the foundation for all stakeholder involvement in development tasks. Consulting with stakeholders is a means to improve the quality of information by creating a two-way flow of ideas with decision-makers. Consultation can blend into situations in which external stakeholders and beneficiaries either share decision-making power or actually make final decisions and assume responsibility for implementing them.

Objectives for Participation

In addition to thinking about what participation means, policy managers need to give some thought to the objectives to be achieved through expanded participation. Several interrelated objectives for expanded participation can be identified (Bhatnagar and Williams 1992). First, there are objectives that are primarily of benefit to the groups newly participating but that ultimately may increase the likelihood of implementation or sustainability of a new policy. These objectives flow from the revised role of the state where governance brings the public sector and citizens together for policy dialogue and problem-solving. These objectives relate to empowerment and increasing beneficiary capacity (Frischtak 1994). To the extent that groups feel empowered (to present demands or initiate actions aimed at solving those demands) and can gain capacity for managing resources or new tasks and processes, there is an increased likelihood of successful implementation and sustainability of the intended policy. Further, the chances that policy outcomes will respond to their needs and desires are enhanced. For example, a considerable amount of activity targeted at developing advocacy capacity among newly created community associations or NGOs is aimed directly at empowerment (Clark 1995, Carroll 1992, Bratton 1990).

A second set of objectives for expanded participation includes assuring or enhancing the successful implementation of a policy and better delivery of services (for example, Picciotto 1995). These objectives relate to effectiveness, cost-sharing, and efficiency. Expanding participation helps to assure greater responsiveness to the needs of the proposed beneficiaries, resulting in a better fit between needs and policy solutions, leading to increased service-user satisfaction. Evidence from a variety of development sectors—for example, health, education, infrastructure, and environment—shows that when target groups of policy reform participate in the decisions that affect them and in activities to implement those decisions, then better policy outcomes are achieved (see, for example, Brinkerhoff 2000, Ghai and Vivian 1992, McGee with Norton 2000, Rietbergen-McCracken 1996). Cost-sharing through the contribution of labor or capital by beneficiaries increases ownership, as well as providing incentives for maintenance of the services and facilities that the policy puts in place. Periodic consultation between implementors and beneficiaries can also increase efficiency by generating timely inputs and greater cooperation so that delays are reduced and smoother flow of services is achieved—resulting in more efficient use of resources and cost savings (see Alesina 1994).

A third set of objectives seeks to increase support, legitimacy, transparency, and responsiveness of a particular policy. This set relates closely to democratic governance. A key objective here is expanded information-sharing.[2] When policymaking is closed, suspicion may arise regarding the criteria used for deciding who gets what. Opening up the process and providing information helps to develop a sense of "nothing to hide" and bolsters legitimacy. When policy decisions are made transparently, acceptance can be more readily achieved, even among those who may lose as a result. Opposition is lessened, and there is greater likelihood of successful implementation (Hyden 1992). Incorporating the participation of target beneficiaries, for example in policy monitoring (see Chapter 12), increases transparency and responsiveness and contributes to greater accountability of public agencies and officials. Finally, expanding participation can reduce opposition to a particular policy. Inclusion of excluded or opposing groups may persuade them to support a proposed policy. Even when there is opposition, the inclusion of certain demands of those groups may serve to coopt potentially troublesome elements. By increasing participation, decision-makers will be better able to preempt or cope with opposition during the implementation process.

Box 3.2 offers some guiding questions that policy managers can use to select among policy participation objectives. It should be noted here that both the second and third sets of objectives discussed above provide clear incentives to managers to increase citizen participation. For the first set of objectives, however, the incentives are likely to be mixed in that increasing citizen empowerment, and thereby increasing demands on public officials, may make policy managers' day-to-day jobs more difficult and/or contentious even as the ultimate policy result attained may be more successful and more sustainable.

Box 3.2 Selecting Policy Participation Objectives

1. Is the participation objective to:

* Inform people about policy decisions that have already been made?
* Develop policies that meet people's needs and expectations?
* Give people a say in the design or implementation of the policy?
* Give people control over one or more of the policy's components?

2. Does the objective(s) remain the same for all participant groups being considered?

3. Are there differences in participation objectives among the various public agencies and/or nongovernmental groups involved in formulating or implementing the policy? What about conflicts?

Participation and Policy Implementation Tasks

As elaborated in Chapter 2, the policy implementation process can be viewed as a generalized sequence of tasks: legitimization, constituency building, resource accumulation, organizational design, resource and action mobilization, and monitoring. The sequence is launched by a stream of issues, agendas, priority-setting exercises, and analyses that inform policy formulation and decisions to proceed. As we noted, the policy process is iterative and multidirectional. This means that the cycle of steps repeats itself, reflecting the fact that policies emerge, evolve, and change incrementally over time, rather than making quantum leaps forward with no modification from their original specification. Each of the tasks has direct links to the others, as well as connections to the issues identification, agenda setting, and initial decisions that start the implementation cycle for a particular policy. For each task step of the cycle, various options for participation can be identified.

Policy Formulation and Legitimization

As part of the process of policy dialogue, a range of analyses, diagnoses, and positions are put forward. Initial policy formulation is informed by some preliminary analytic or diagnostic work, which lays out the rationale for the reform. This work is used by interest groups both inside and outside of government aimed at legitimizing the policy.

Participation options. Numerous options exist for external participation in policy formulation and legitimization. The most basic level of participation in this stage is where groups potentially affected by the policy simply provide information to technical specialists on their needs, desires, preferences, or prior experiences. Beyond information provision, participation that is more extensive can include consultation on these needs, desires, preferences, or prior experiences. Collaboration in policy formulation and legitimization implies involvement in conducting the analyses and lobbying campaigns, deciding upon which information is most important and upon information sources, participating in preparing action plans, and so on. Empowerment extends these collaborative activities to where the external groups take a leadership role, undertaking independent analyses and advocacy campaigns of their own.

Constituency Building

By definition, participation is at the heart of this implementation task. Creating reform constituencies means reaching out to stakeholders to bring them into the policy process.

Participation options. Options are wide open—and, in fact, are critical—for constituency building. Information-sharing, consultation, collaboration, and joint decision-making are all vital to making the policy content more understandable, creating commitment for change, and establishing supportive policy constituencies. To the extent that external groups feel empowered to take ownership for policies, implementation becomes easier and increases the chances for sustainable policy change.

Resource Accumulation, Organizational Design, and Resource/Action Mobilization

These implementation tasks involve pulling together the resources necessary to support policy action, putting in place new implementation arrangements and structures, modifying existing ones, and assuring that they function appropriately, smoothly, and effectively. Depending upon the type of policy, new implementation partners—such as NGOs, community groups, private sector service providers or professional associations—may be introduced.

Participation options. Entry points for external participation vary significantly depending upon the type of policy. Collaborating public agencies may provide creative alternatives for locating resources, designing new structures and procedures, and mobilizing actions. For many policies external groups can participate by pressuring legislators to allocate funding, and/or by lobbying policy managers to take implementation actions. Some sectoral policies, for example, offer opportunities for collaboration, shared decision-making, and empowerment through partnerships for service delivery, where external entities may take the lead through contracting out, delegation of authority, or community co-management (see Chapter 4). Some types of administrative reform policies introduce options for external consultation, such as decentralized public personnel policies that solicit input from local citizens on performance. Other policies, such as macroeconomic policies, have far fewer participation options beyond information-sharing and dissemination.

Policy Monitoring

This implementation task focuses on feedback that can be used to make adjustments, fine-tune interventions, adapt to changing conditions, and inform future iterations of the policy.

Participation options. The possibilities for external participation in monitoring (and eventually in evaluation) mirror those for policy analysis and diagnosis. External actors can provide information to policy monitors and evaluators, or they can be consulted for their opinions, interpretations, and analyses (see Chapter 12). They can collaborate in joint monitoring and evaluation, or they can conduct their own independent assessments and evaluations. These latter can serve as countervailing views on the policy from a range of alternative perspectives and as input to the broader arena of political dialogue and debate in a country.

MANAGING PARTICIPATION IN POLICY IMPLEMENTATION

Public participation can be instrumental to responsive and effective policy implementation, but unstructured and unmanaged participation leads to cacophony and confusion, not necessarily to good policy results. While there are solid technical, social, and political reasons for expanded citizen and civil society participation in the policy process, it is important to recognize that there are limits and trade-offs inherent in increasing participation. For example, if participation raises expectations that cannot be met, then policy implementors can find themselves in a difficult position. Even when managers actively seek to increase participation, the more groups that are brought in to participate, the more complex managing that participation becomes.[3]

From the point of view of policy managers, initiating participation, expanding participation to new sets of actors, or selecting among the types of participation in Box 3.1 can pose significant challenges. These make it all the more important to be clear about the objectives of participation (Box 3.2), the expected benefits versus the costs, the array of stakeholders who constitute current and potential participants, and the resources required. The other side of these challenges is the point of view of potential external participants looking for opportunities to be involved, to gain access to information and arenas for dialogue, and to increase their levels of participation. The same questions about objectives, benefits/costs, stakeholders, and resources apply to them. Taken together, the two points of view pose the management of policy participation in terms of supply and demand (Coston 1998a). We focus first on looking at participation from the perspective of public sector managers. Later in the chapter we turn to the demand side.

Costs and Benefits of Increased Participation

What should policy managers assess when considering expanded participation? Since, as noted earlier, there are trade-offs involved, managers need to clarify what will be gained or lost by involving a particular group, and how the group's participation will affect the chances for successful policy implementation. Box 3.3 offers a checklist of questions for participation's costs and benefits. Part II of this book offers help in coming up with the information to answer these questions. For example, stakeholder analysis and political/institutional mapping (Chapters 6 and 8) can assist in determining the level of support for a particular policy and in targeting efforts to increase it.

Box 3.3 Assessing the Benefits and Costs of Increased Participation

1. Will increased participation improve the technical content of the policy? enhance the legitimacy of the policy? increase ownership of the policy?

2. Is support from external actors required to adequately design or implement the policy? How much will be needed?

3. Will including new participant groups dilute the policy's objectives or compromise the intended impacts?

4. Can the organization(s) managing the participation process meet the participant groups' expectations? What level of participation will be required to satisfy them?

5. Are there actual or potential conflicts among the participation expectations and demands of the various participant groups?

6. How much additional time will be required to incorporate participation by the various groups into the policy process? Are there fixed deadlines and timetables that need to be considered?

7. Will the benefits of increased participation outweigh the costs?

Question 3 is especially important. If concessions resulting in alteration/modification of the policy under consideration are necessary, then benefits deriving from the policy may become more diluted (and therefore of less interest to some stakeholders) and may cause problems with other groups supporting the policy. This is a classic dilemma in coalition building; as more groups are brought into a policy constituency, the increased breadth of interests that the policy needs to incorporate can diminish the original policy objective substantially.[4] Adding new participants complicates the policy process, because more groups will need to be satisfied before actions can be taken. Technical specialists may be tempted to cling to the optimal policy solution and resist making any modifications, but sometimes settling for a second- or third-best option that a broad coalition of stakeholders buys into will lead to a more implementable and sustainable outcome.

Once the door to participation is opened to one group, then others may be tempted to try to gain access as well (Whitely 1995). This can create problems for policy managers to cope with and respond to the new demands. Questions 4, 5, and 6 address the response capacity issue. The ability of managers to deal with demands is limited by the time, skills, and resources available. When limits are approached, the risk of overload arises. Corporatist participation (discussed later in this chapter), in which the government interacts with a selected set of stakeholders, for example, trade unions and the formal private sector, is one approach governments use to set limits on external input to the policy process. Corporatist arrangements are common under one-party regimes and some authoritarian systems, but variants are also found in democracies. If insufficient resources and capacity are available to process and satisfy demands, the government may simply choose to ignore some groups.[5] However, should the number of groups rise to unmanageable proportions, if demands turn strident or threatening, or if the chosen means of expression by the petitioning group are unacceptable to decision-makers or important sectors of society, then the government may close the door or begin to repress participation. This outcome is highly undesirable, both in terms of its negative impact on the prospects for policy implementation success and on democratic governance. Responsible management of participation can, in most cases, avoid the need to resort to drastic measures.

Transactions Costs of Participation

A key aspect of answering Question 7 has to do with the transactions costs of participation, not all of which may be apparent at the outset. Despite the evidence that greater participation improves the likelihood of more effective implementation, those benefits may be perceived as marginal once lined up against the costs that will be incurred for both parties (those well-experienced in participatory policy advocacy generally acknowledge that participation costs more).

The benefits derived from increased participation for external constituencies and implementing agencies will always have costs associated with them (see, for example, Picciotto 1995). For citizens and civil society organizations the costs will be in the form of time, effort, and/or other scarce resources, or in extreme circumstances, the dangers of repression.[6] Stakeholder groups attempting to increase their participation will have to invest in information collection and analysis, and, depending upon what outcome they are seeking, in preparation of an advocacy strategy (see Chapter 10). They may have to invest resources for transportation to the capital to talk to decision-makers. Their members may risk their status and authority should they fail to achieve a favorable decision. Further, the groups may run the risk of negative repercussions from competing groups, or of rebuff or even repression from the state if their tactics or message appear threatening. If the groups' leaders decide to make concessions to achieve a compromise, they may risk friction with members opposed to such concessions.

While success may breed encouragement to try again with other issues, failure may cause them to give up entirely. Perceived experiences of failed participation may have a negative effect on other groups' efforts at involvement. However, as Hirschman (1984) documents, groups can also take what they learned from failure and apply the lessons later in subsequent efforts to organize, advocate for, and pursue their interests.

For public agencies, transactions costs derive from time and funds expended or opportunity costs, from the loss of exclusive control or dominance in their particular area of competence, or from the administrative burden of handling increased participation. Pressman and Wildavsky (1973) were among the first to document the delays and diversions introduced into policy implementation as the number of actors increases, and many others have examined these issues in developing and transitioning countries.[7]

Besides the transactions cost of managing a participatory process, public agencies also face, as previously mentioned, risks of raising expectations and not being able to deliver, whether for lack of resources, administrative capacity, or political reasons. In some cases these failures can lead to public protests by negatively affected stakeholder groups (see, for example, Alesina 1994).

Who Should Participate?

This issue has much to do with the objectives for expanded participation in the first place (Box 3.2). Should more groups have access to the process and under what circumstances? How many groups should participate, for how long, and in what ways? If more groups or interests are included, how can policymakers be sure that implementation does not veer off track such that the public good is "hijacked" by private interests?[8] Box 3.4 offers some guidance that can help to establish some criteria for choosing participants. Obviously, in a democracy, public officials are limited in the extent to which they have individual discretion to select participants in the policy process. A country's political system, legal framework, and governance structures set the parameters for participation. In most advanced democracies opportunities for citizen input are legally mandated through public hearings, so-called sunshine laws that require open meetings and information dissemination, and citizen consultation and review processes at various levels: national, state, local, and municipal. These structures and processes are essential to accountable and transparent policymaking and implementation. In democratizing settings the issue is often more one of opening up the policy process beyond a relatively closed circle of interlocking elites, and increasing government responsiveness to citizens, rather than figuring out how to limit participation.

Box 3.4 Selecting Participant Groups

1. Who are the policy's stakeholders (winners and losers), and what are their interests?

2. What does each participant group have to offer? New and important support? New insights or technical information?

3. Will support or input offered by the group significantly improve the quality of policy formulation or implementation?

4. Will the group's participation attract other groups to support the policy? reduce opposition?

5. Will failure to include the group and respond to its demands cause implementation problems, policy failure, or problems in other quarters (for example, criticism in the media, social unrest)?

6. What will be the costs of incorporating a new group into the policy coalition? Can the group's expectations and demands be balanced with other interests supporting the policy?

Stakeholder analysis (Chapter 6) can be useful in answering these questions, as well as informing the answers to those posed in the previous box. In Box 3.4 most of the questions are directed at trying to determine what a group brings to the policy process and how much difference the group might actually make. It also raises questions regarding the costs and the benefits of bringing in a new participant. Questions are also aimed at determining the level of participation that will be required by the group. Force-field analysis, discussed in Chapter 8, can be used to determine the balance of support and opposition to a particular issue and can be helpful in showing the impact of a particular group's support on that balance.

It should be noted that the questions in Box 3.4 assume that the rationale for policy participation relates to effectiveness of implementation. We recognize, though, that the policy process is highly political, and objectives other than effective policy implementation are at stake. For instance, it is not at all uncommon that a decision-maker will get enough support on a policy to win the day in the congress or another arena only to discover later that too many promises had been made (whether unintentionally or cynically) to too many groups and too many expectations raised. Indeed, politicians often have self-serving objectives beyond the implementation of a given policy to increase participation. Broader participation by stakeholders may also provide the decision-maker with a larger base of support, perhaps leading to a wider degree of responsibility, authority or advantage on other decisions, or increased political power. As elections near, politicians frequently invite larger participation, but once the election passes, access begins to close up. The influence of the ebb and flow of politics on opening and closing opportunities to pursue reforms and involve various interest groups in the policy process is well recognized (see, for example, Haggard and Webb 1994, Grindle and Thomas 1991, Schneider and Ingram 1997). A particularly thorny problem for long-term policy reform is maintaining a sufficiently robust policy coalition so that over time political tides do not gradually wash away support for change (Nelson 1989).

When participation is expanded, the coalition supporting the policy grows, again with the expectation that the expanded coalition will enhance the implementation of the policy. However, additional partners will condition their support on the basis of concessions made to their demands. Thus, for the decision-maker it is important to assess whether expanded participation is affordable. The cost of satisfying the new partner's demands must be offset by improved implementation prospects and future support on other related initiatives. Box 3.5 offers a checklist for examining the resources necessary for participation.

Box 3.5 Finding the Resources for Increased Participation

1. What kinds of financial, human, and organizational resources are required to manage the policy participation process effectively and efficiently? How much is needed of each kind?

2. Do the various organizations managing policy participation have sufficient resources and capacity? Will capacity building be needed?

3. If the organizations do not have enough resources or capacity, are other sources available?

4. What resources and capacity do the external participant groups command? Will some groups need financial help or capacity building in order to participate?

5. Can some groups provide resources to assist in policy design, implementation, or monitoring?

PARTICIPATION MECHANISMS

Selecting among participation mechanisms relates directly to the objectives for participation. The menu of mechanisms mirrors the different types of participation (Box 3.1). Moving toward empowerment offers increasing degrees of power and control to external actors, while decreasing the unilateral and autonomous decisional authority of public sector managers. From an instrumental point of view, these higher forms of participation are not automatically better. (As we said above, the continuum of types of participation is not normative.) However, experience shows that the type of participation invited can influence stakeholders' motivation to participate and their satisfaction with the process. Civil society groups, for example, often consider that the lower forms of citizen involvement are not "genuine" participation.[9] The following discussion offers some guidance and illustrations of mechanisms ranging from information-sharing to empowerment.

Information-sharing Mechanisms

Information-sharing is the most basic level of participation, and the one that offers the least active involvement for external stakeholders. Control over the information to be shared remains with the policy managers and their organizations, governed by laws and regulations. Nonetheless, information-sharing is crucial to policy implementation for a number of reasons. First of all, for implementation to be conducted according to democratic governance principles, accessible and widely disseminated information is key. Second, as noted earlier in this chapter, all the higher levels of participation and their associated mechanisms depend upon participants having information. NGOs and private sector actors cannot engage in effective consultation or collaboration without information. Neither can they pursue joint decision-making or empowerment if they do not have information. However, it is common knowledge that in many developing and transitioning countries, public agencies do not routinely share basic documents on policies, procedures, regulations, or planned interventions. Historical legacies of secrecy and information-hoarding remain strong.

New information technologies are, in some cases, making inroads into these legacies. For example, in South Africa, in an effort to break the apartheid pattern of limited information flows, the Johannesburg Metropolitan Council created a website for council members and, later, local community members through which much of its business is now conducted. As a result, council processes and outcomes have become more transparent and participatory, with a wider range of citizen involvement in municipal governance (Benjamin 2001).

Third, information-sharing is necessary in order for public agencies to elaborate and communicate the rationale behind policy decisions. Policy communication is critical to building reform constituencies and support for change (see, for example, Frischtak and Atiyas 1996). Providing stakeholders with information on the potential benefits of policy change and laying out a vision will help to prepare for collaboration and consultation.

Fourth, and related to the third reason, for the process of policy implementation to be carried out in a transparent, responsive, and accountable way, citizens need information. In order to exercise demand effectively, citizens need to know what public authorities are supposed to do, what they plan to do, what they are currently doing, and what the results are. Thus information-sharing mechanisms are instrumental for basic democratic governance as well as higher levels of citizen participation. Such mechanisms can be relatively simple.

In Bulgaria, for example, USAID supported the compilation and publication by the National Parliament of a simple registry of parliamentarians. The booklet included names, photographs, addresses, phone numbers, and so on. In addition the National Parliament set up a public information office, complete with documents and videos. Another example comes from Uganda, where the government, with donor support, is implementing a broad decentralization policy. To increase transparency and accountability in decentralized management of resources, advertisements are placed in the press indicating amounts disbursed to each district by sector. In the education sector, budget allocations for schools are posted on school notice boards so that citizens can inform themselves regarding what is supposed to be spent on education and can compare that with what they observe (Mugambe and Robb 2000).

Consultative Mechanisms

Here, stakeholders are invited to offer their views on a given policy. Ideally, consultative processes should identify all major stakeholders and encourage their participation. Consultation works best when stakeholders are provided with sufficient opportunities to develop an understanding of the issues to enable their informed involvement. Administrative mechanisms should be in place to process input in a timely manner. Input can be broadened and enhanced by participation of groups with experience in the intended policy areas, for example, professional associations with sectoral expertise. It is important that public agencies employing consultation convey the message that they are sincerely interested in stakeholder views, not simply looking for "rubber stamp" approval of decisions already made. External groups can quickly sense when consultations are pro forma exercises in public relations rather than serious efforts to incorporate their input and perspectives into public policy decision-making.

In a number of countries successful economic development outcomes have been linked to consultative policymaking and implementation, where civil society, labor, and private sector actors have had opportunities for input and oversight. For example, in East Asia, public-private deliberation councils—such as Korea's monthly export promotion meetings,

Thailand's National Joint Public and Private Consultative Committee, and the Malaysian Business Council—have provided mechanisms for feedback, information-sharing, and coordination (World Bank 1997). In Chile the government consulted business associations extensively on trade and economic policy, resulting in a new economic policy regime and strengthened ability of Chilean firms to compete in world markets (Perez-Aleman 2000). In Honduras the Economic Policy Analysis Unit (UDAPE), attached to the president's economic cabinet, carried out a series of consultative stakeholder workshops aimed at channeling sector producer input toward both the development and generation of support for a public sector rural investment strategy (see Chapter 5).

Country governments working with donors are increasingly using policy and planning frameworks that rely heavily on participation through consultation. For example, the World Bank's Poverty Reduction Strategy Papers (PRSPs) are intended to be comprehensive poverty diagnostic and action planning exercises that will trigger debt relief.[10] The guiding principles for PRSPs are that the process of their development should be country driven, based on extensive consultation between government and civil society, and should lead to national consensus on policy priorities and programs. The PRSP experience base is limited at present, though in several cases, civil society groups have complained of superficial and inadequate consultation. For example, in Bolivia citizens viewed the official participatory process for the PRSP as insufficient, and the church and civil society organizations took the lead in organizing a successful Foro Nacional out of frustration with the official Dialogo Nacional (Eurodad, 2000). This example demonstrates that organizing policy consultation is not restricted to top-down, government-initiated efforts, but can be bottom up as well. The case also serves as a warning to public officials that inadequately organized or insincere efforts at consultation are likely to backfire.

Collaborative Mechanisms

Collaborative mechanisms allocate policy design, implementation, or monitoring responsibilities to external groups, while government retains ultimate decision-making authority. Collaboration is applicable when the public sector cannot achieve particular policy goals without bringing in the capacity and knowledge of external partners (see, for example, Gray 1989). This type of participation takes place through the formation of joint committees with stakeholder representatives, joint working groups and task forces, and joint work with intermediary organizations and other stakeholder groups. Such mechanisms can be formalized procedures for external involvement in setting policies and regulations or informal structures that are more ad hoc and temporary.

Successful consultative mechanisms often grow into collaboration over time. In Uganda, for example, the National Forum evolved from a periodic consultative meeting to more of an ongoing collaborative mechanism during the course of about three years. Initially, in the early 1990s when IPC helped with start-up, the Forum was organized as a conference to bring together government officials and members of the private sector to discuss changes in policy to promote private sector growth. The success of the initial meeting, which President Museveni attended, led to the establishment of a National Forum working group to develop a shared policy agenda for further discussion and development. Technical subgroups formed to undertake joint policy analysis and develop options. In these subgroups, private sector actors played a critical role in providing the necessary technical expertise for developing feasible policy options and implementation strategies.

Another example is the Regional Livestock Trade Reform project in the West African Sahel. It illustrates a collaborative partnership focused on developing and implementing a specific set of policy reforms regulating the cross-border trade of livestock among three countries. The partnership operated through a set of public-private task forces/committees with cross-sectoral membership including public sector officials and private associations representing operators involved in cross-border trade. It combined an emphasis on technical problem-solving with advocacy on the part of the private sector associations involved. A collaborative scheme of participation was imperative since the private sector partners had the technical expertise to work out the details of viable policy implementation, and they were in a position to block any reform not to their liking (see Chapter 4).

Shared Decision-making Mechanisms

Shared decision-making, as Box 3.1 indicates, entails collaboration where control over decisions is not held unilaterally by public officials but is shared. This type of participation begins to address the power differentials among the collaborating parties, which is an important aspect of making it work effectively (Brown and Ashman 1996). Shared decision-making mechanisms allow stakeholders not simply to develop policy options but to engage in the choice of options and participate in carrying them out. Joint decision-making reinforces commitment and ownership. This kind of participation may take place through the periodic use of temporary structures, such as workshops, discussion forums, or task forces where discussion centers on the determination of priorities, solving conflicts, seeking agreements, and developing ownership (see Chapters 5 and 9). Or it may take place through more permanent structures that persist over time, such as partnerships (Chapter 4).

In Bulgaria, for example, an IPC-supported partnership that assembled government, business associations, and independent think tanks illustrates the effectiveness of shared decision-making. The sectoral focus of the partnership was on small and medium enterprise reform (SME). Joint activities involved policy dialogue to set a reform agenda and collaboration to develop draft legislation. The business associations and think tanks shared decision-making with public officials on both the content and the process of legislative development. The SME Act was accepted by the Council of Ministers at the end of 1998, submitted to the National Assembly, and then finalized by the Economic Commission of the National Assembly. The law was subsequently passed and officially promulgated in September 1999. As the quotation at the beginning of this chapter indicates, participants in the SME task force heralded the process as a step forward for democracy in Bulgaria (see Chapter 4).

Another example comes from Southern Africa, where the Southern Africa Transport and Communications Council (SATCC), supported by IPC, used a series of local, national, and regional stakeholder workshops to hear demands, debate ideas, create ownership, and flesh out the operation details of seven regional protocols in the areas of transport, telecommunications, and postal services. Over one thousand people participated in fourteen major workshops, at which thirty-four protocols were developed and agreed to (Billings and Miller 1995). The protocols were later ratified by the member countries of the Southern Africa Development Community, and public officials affirmed that implementation proceeded smoothly in large part because the affected stakeholders had played a role in making the decisions affecting the policies in each of the areas addressed.

Empowerment Mechanisms

Beyond shared decision-making, empowerment means that public officials enable external stakeholders to achieve their own objectives by providing space for independent initiation and pursuit of actions, increasing capacity, and delegating decision-making authority. It entails a more equitable sharing of power and a higher level of political awareness and strength for disadvantaged groups. Empowerment includes capacity building of stakeholder organizations, strengthening the legal and financial status of stakeholder organizations, and supporting initiatives conceived independently by stakeholders. Empowerment also relates directly to accountability in that increasing the power of external actors serves to enable them to exert more clout in their interactions with public officials to assure that policies are adhered to and services delivered.

Empowerment's contribution to policy implementation is widely recognized in community-based natural resources management. In many countries, governments, in recognition of the failure of command-and-control strategies, have delegated resource management responsibility to local communities. The communities exercise delegated authority to establish and enforce rules governing their resource base, within a broad environmental policy framework (see Western and Wright 1994, Brinkerhoff 1999b). Empowerment is also a mechanism used in the health sector, particularly in primary health care. For example, in maternal and child health policy in Nepal, government's willingness to empower NGOs and community groups to develop and implement programs contributed to a turn-around with the policy, which had been adopted by the government in 1993, but not implemented. The NGOs and communities formed a Safe Motherhood Network, which clarified the policy in operational terms, built consensus, and lobbied government health officials. The network then worked with the public health system to carry out the program (Putney 2000).

It should be noted that empowerment is not necessarily something that policy managers provide to external stakeholders. By definition, government actors are not in control of this type of participation, since power is delegated to external groups. As our previous discussion, both in this chapter and in others, makes clear, to a large extent empowerment derives from governments putting in place the features of democratic governance that offer citizens the space to play an empowered role in the policy process. Further, reaching the level of empowered participation in policy is often the result of civil society's independent organizing and advocacy efforts (see Hansen 1996, Burbidge 1997). Here, empowerment relates to the creation and application of countervailing power on the part of citizens regarding the role and actions of the state. In a democracy, empowered participation is less something that public officials "give" to external actors on a discretionary basis, than it is a right or a demand that citizens exercise in their relations with government.

SUPPLY AND DEMAND:
PRACTICAL DIMENSIONS OF POLICY PARTICIPATION

Participation in the policy process has both a supply and a demand side. The supply side of the equation is made up of state institutions and their designates.[11] These entities take the lead in developing and implementing policies, providing public goods and services, and allocating resources for these activities. As the discussion in this chapter makes clear, public officials can play a major role in creating opportunities for and in shaping participation. If participation is to be effective, then the supply side must be receptive to and capable of accommodating external involvement aimed at affecting policy decisions and service delivery. The ability of the supply side to handle participation depends on the transparency, openness, and accessibility of the policy decision-making structure; the capacity of decision-makers to process and respond to demands; and the extent of administrative and political decentralization. Many countries face serious problems on the supply side. Legislatures do not work well and are often inexperienced in handling participatory processes. Courts are frequently nonfunctional, with staggering caseloads, lack of administrative staff, and an inability to enforce compliance even in judgments faithfully rendered. Executive agencies are often unable to meet even minimal demands for external participation due to lack of funds and/or managerial capability.

The demand side of participation is largely composed of members of the private sector and civil society and ranges from individual citizens, to informal associations, to formally established interest groups. The extent and effectiveness of their voice in policy decisions and demand-making are conditioned by the enabling environment for participation, the existence of a tradition of participation, the political economy of government–interest group relations, and the capability of civil society groups to organize and to articulate their demands. Numerous countries face problems with the demand side as well as supply. Particularly in societies that have semi-authoritarian governments or that are newly democratized, civil society tends to be weak, fragmented, and under-organized, and the private sector split between a well-connected elite of large business people and small and informal entrepreneurs.

Since supply and demand are both necessary elements for participation, there must be some rough equilibrium between the two (see Coston 1998a). While the lack of capacity on the part of civil society is a constraint to interest aggregation and participation in many cases, governments may be unable or unwilling to hear or act on demands, even if articulated clearly and coherently. In these circumstances, bolstering the capacity of the demand side with no attention to supply will likely produce little, if any benefit, at least in the short run, and may contribute to social unrest or instability. We now examine some of the practical dimensions to increasing participation on both the supply and demand sides.

Increasing Participation: Supply Issues

As the checklists in the various boxes presented above indicate, supply-side issues for increasing participation center upon the structural, procedural, and administrative constraints of the organizations that policy managers operate within. These constraints produce incentives that, along with individual and cultural attitudes, shape whether managers can, or want to, pursue participatory policy implementation. For external participation to function effectively, the constraints that discourage participation should be dismantled and the factors that facilitate participation need to be encouraged. Mechanisms capable of capturing demand for policy change from the environment need to be set up and multiple channels of access created. Obstacles to existing channels of access need to be removed.

Lack of "Processing Capacity"

A serious constraint to participation is the inability of decisional structures to process multiple demands. Low processing capacity means that some citizen demands will not receive adequate attention or will simply be ignored. In newly democratizing countries, policymakers are frequently new to government and have yet to master the peculiarities of their particular policy area and/or organization. Expertise and skill to handle citizen input, to separate legitimate demands from special interest pleading, and to weigh the quality of proposed alternatives are acquired only in the long term (Lamb 1987, Silverman 1997). Sometimes, when public officials feel ill-equipped to make judgments, they may choose to hide their ignorance by refusing to listen to anyone, or to rely only on the advice of those closest to them or of trusted constituencies.

Increasing processing capacity faces the same dilemma that confronts most capacity building efforts: to create a new entity or to reform an existing one. When new organizations or organizational units are created, they usually have only a limited capability for receiving and responding to demands. They may have few and/or inexperienced staff, their roles may not be clearly articulated or accepted as valid, and/or they may not have well-developed procedures and operating routines. When organizations are merely reformed to open them to a larger number of stakeholders, developing adequate capacity may in fact be more difficult than in a new institution due to the legacy of ingrained exclusionary or anti-participatory practices (Grindle and Thomas 1991, Thompson 1995). Top-down procedures and arrogance of officials are common residuals of traditionally closed governance systems. Trying to change the behavior of officials and staff accustomed to ignoring demands of petitioners can be frustrating.

Besides attitudinal constraints and top-down procedures, routine administrative practices can inhibit processing capacity. For example, rigid schedules for public meetings, inadequate lead time in announcing consultations, and acceptance of input only in particular formats or in official languages can all be hindrances to participation.[12] Another core aspect of processing capacity is the availability of resources. If agencies have no funds to disseminate information, hold public hearings, send their staff outside of urban centers to meet with citizens, then supplying participatory opportunities to external stakeholders is highly problematic. For example, these kinds of "nuts and bolts" issues are among those that PRSPs are confronting in several countries.

Openness of the Policy Process

An open policy process and multiple venues for dialogue, debate, and decision-making are key to expanding participation (see, for example, Cernea 1992). Where policymaking is narrow and concentrated in a very few hands, access will be difficult, and participation, particularly by groups without privileged access, such as the poor, will be restricted. In authoritarian systems decision-making is a closed and elite-dominated process; there are few alternative centers of decisional authority (see Brinkerhoff with Kulibaba 1996). For example, under some of the more personalistic regimes in Latin America and Africa, such as Nicaragua under Somoza or Malawi under Banda, virtually all policymaking was concentrated at the top. While other institutions (legislature, courts, municipal councils) had nominal decisional authority, in practice they had very little.[13] Without access to the top leader, the chances of a societal group getting a fair hearing were practically nil.

As countries move toward democratic governance, the policy process has the potential to open up to a wider range of citizen input and participation. For example, if legislatures evolve from merely ratifying executive decisions to functioning as true alternative sources of policy debate and decision-making, then they may be more likely to serve as effective avenues for participatory policy debate. This is a long-term process, obviously, hampered in part by the dearth of experience of most developing country legislators. In El Salvador's Legislative Assembly, for example, the average tenure of members of the budget committee is less than three years.

In the executive branch, collaborative policy implementation partnerships in a variety of sectors are opening up governance structures to increased participation and more democratic practices (Brinkerhoff 2000). These efforts multiply the access points of civil society groups and individual citizens for participation, thereby expanding their ability to interact with public officials, exercise voice, and—importantly—hold them accountable. Obviously, caution is called for because political and administrative systems change slowly, and there can be a risk of mistaking participatory "window dressing" for the real thing.[14]

Decentralization

Another constraint, related to openness of the policy process, is that in many countries both the administrative and the political systems are highly centralized, although as Manor (1999) points out, increasingly countries are experimenting with various forms of decentralization. Administrative centralization limits policy and program decision-making to a small and select set of actors occupying the top positions in official hierarchies. For example, when education policy is set by a ministry of education (the norm in many developing countries), avenues for participation are determined at the center, and opportunities for participation by external stakeholders can only be pursued at that level assuming ministry officials are open to input. However, where policy and operational responsibilities are decentralized to the regional or local level, opportunities for participation can increase dramatically.[15] Educational reform in Chile took this path when the central ministry greatly increased school autonomy at the local level. As a result, school officials, teachers, and parents in local communities were able to work together effectively to improve educational quality and effectiveness (Angell 1996).

Political decentralization increases the opportunities for citizens to lobby local officials and to hold officials accountable through the ballot box in elections and through voice in public hearings. Participation is expanded to greater numbers of citizens, and there are many examples of increased responsiveness in service delivery and better public sector performance (see Crook and Manor 1998). Empowerment can result when citizens run for office and are elected as representatives. For example, USAID's studies of democratic local governance revealed several cases (Bolivia, Philippines, Mali, India) in which women and minority groups have gained representation on local government bodies, thereby increasing their participation in policymaking (Blair 2000a, 2000b). While decentralization is no guarantee that participatory opportunities, especially for the poor and disadvantaged, will automatically increase, there is evidence that it is an important factor in contributing to the supply side of participation. Decentralization can contribute to setting the incentives that reinforce local government bodies' willingness to incorporate citizen participation (IPC 1996).

Increasing Participation: Demand Issues

On the demand side, focusing on increasing civil society's participation in the policy process, there are numerous and varied obstacles, most of which are not susceptible to quick fixes. These include laws and customs limiting participation, lack of tradition of participation, the political economy of interest group relations with government, and a lack of capacity to articulate demands by civil society. Each of these, by itself, will be difficult enough to overcome. However, most developing and transitioning countries face more than one of them.

The Enabling Environment

The enabling environment for participation includes laws and customs that set the "rules of the game" for participation (see Foley and Edwards 1996). The development of flexible legislation regulating NGOs, advocacy groups, or other associations is considered key to creating a conducive environment (see ICNL 1997). However, in several instances governments have increased restrictions on participation through creation of laws regulating associational activity. In Egypt NGOs must first meet strict requirements to organize and then are directly regulated by the Ministry of Social Welfare. New laws in South Africa and El Salvador permit greater state intervention in NGOs through regulations on the organizations' financial operations. These have met with stiff opposition from civil society.

Besides laws, however, the enabling environment comprises the larger political and institutional framework that establishes the competitive and cooperative relationships of society and norms that constrain the behavior of organizations and individuals (see, for example, North 1990, Ostrom 1990). For example, a fundamental norm that supports participation is tolerance of diverse opinions. In extreme cases, such as Taliban Afghanistan, the Balkans, and parts of Central Africa, such tolerance is in short supply.

Another factor influencing the enabling environment for citizen participation is the openness of the decision-making system, discussed above. Multiple centers for decision-making and significant decentralization can increase the likelihood of participation. They also can reduce the chances of state capture by dominant groups. Where power is centered in a narrow elite, or where little if any decisional capacity is delegated or devolved to local government or authorities, what little opportunity there is for participation will be highly circumscribed and highly competitive. The historical experiences of the disenfranchised can discourage their participation; where participation has been repressed, even though the system now may be open, there will be reluctance and even fear on the part of the formerly repressed to participate. In some cases these situations contribute to the perpetuation of patronage relations between the powerless and marginalized and socioeconomic elites.

Tradition of Participation

The extent of civil society participation varies widely around the world. In some countries there is little tradition or history of participation, while in others participation is both common and longstanding. Even in societies that appear relatively closed, such as in formerly apartheid South Africa, the growth of civil society groups stems from a much older tradition in African society. For example, in the former Soviet republics and in Eastern Europe the dominant role and power of the communist state allowed almost no space for the development of an independent civil society. Citizen participation was state-led (see, for example, Siegel and Yancey 1992, Reisinger et al. 1995). In the United States the long history of democratic philosophy and governance has created a strong tradition and practice of citizen participation (for example, Dahl 1971). In western

Europe, as Putnam (1993) argues, the shape of today's civil society owes its roots to historical patterns of social development in the medieval period.

The primary advantage of a tradition and history of participation is its contribution to social capital formation (see Uphoff 1998). Through the practice of participation, groups become more capable of organizing themselves independently from the state, articulating their demands, maneuvering successfully in various policy arenas, and interacting with public officials and agencies. The more experience groups have at participating, the more likely they are to develop enduring patterns of mutual trust, to mobilize around issues, to engage in collective action, and to be successful in securing a place in the policy process and in influencing outcomes in their favor. Social capital and its contribution to empowerment and socioeconomic development are the topic of a growing literature (see, for example, Evans 1996, Pretty and Ward 2001, Tendler 1997, Woolcock 1998).

However, enduring traditions of participation are relatively rare in the developing world.[16] In Latin America for example, the notion of broad citizen participation is relatively new, although there are some exceptions (see, for example, Jelin and Hershberg 1996). In part this may be due to the hierarchical and centralized nature of most Latin American societies, stemming from the colonial period. There is a single highly centralized church (though some Protestant sects have made inroads during the last twenty years). Education policy is dictated from the center; local boards of education, where they exist, handle some minor aspects of implementation and routine functions. In the private sector, firms are privately held and managed from the top down. Such lack of tradition and history for participation helps to explain why the growth of interest groups in Latin America has been slow and why they remain relatively ineffective.[17]

The Political Economy of Government–Interest Group Relations

Governments everywhere tend to rely upon particular societal groups, usually the most powerful and influential, for support to remain in power (see, for example, Grindle 1999, Lowi 1979). To keep this support, governments create policy regimes that favor these groups, and in many developing/transitioning countries they maintain their power base through patronage.[18] As a result, strong vested interests develop, and politico-bureaucratic dynamics lead to either overt or covert efforts to protect the status quo and to exclude groups interested in change. As noted above, in certain Latin American countries a variety of official groups were created to represent different sectors (particularly the professions) in deliberations with government. As officially established bodies, they monopolized the ear of government decision-makers, effectively precluding wider participation (see, for example, Schamis 1999, Zapata 1998). As is widely recognized, the political economy of policymaking is not restricted to the formal structures and procedures of the policy process; informal relations are also influential or even predominant (see, for example, Good 1996, Gulhati 1990). Efforts on the demand side to increase popular participation of new stakeholders, such as the poor or other marginalized groups, can founder if these dynamics are not recognized. Entrenched interest groups and "cronies" of those in power are unlikely to welcome efforts of others to gain access to decision-makers. In order to achieve their own ends, these groups may do everything possible to assure that others cannot or will not participate.

Strengthening the demand side can combat cronyism and the closed circle of elite domination by contributing to the diversification of interest groups. By creating diversity and fostering competition among groups, a balance of interests becomes more likely and state capture by a narrow set of privileged interests less of a threat (assuming the availability of political space for civil society to organize, which is limited in many countries). This is desirable both for promoting the principles of democratic governance and for assuring that policies reflect the needs of broad segments of citizens, not simply of minorities.

For civil society groups seeking to participate in reforms, dealing with competition among interest groups is integral to building effective demand-making capacity. One strategy is to create coalitions, though making them work effectively is rarely a simple matter. Interest groups seek to form the smallest possible coalition in order to retain control and assure that the majority of their interests are satisfied. To the extent that a larger coalition is necessary to prevail in the policy process, the less control there will be for any single participant group (Haggard and Kaufman 1994, Frischtak and Atiyas 1996). Large and diverse coalitions are difficult to manage and run the risk of diluting already scarce resources, as well as suffering free-rider problems (Olson 1965).

Lack of Capacity to Articulate Demands

Citizens and civil society groups need to learn the skills necessary for effective participation in the policy formulation and implementation process. First of all, they need to have the ability to listen to their members, to represent their views accurately, and to aggregate those views into a credible policy position. To articulate policy positions requires analytical and presentation skills. A group must be able to collect and process information that will reinforce its position, and it must be able to present that information in an accessible manner to the appropriate people. To know whom to present information to implies a solid grasp of the workings of the policy process. To get a message across requires advocacy capacity. It is unlikely that a group that has recently begun to try to voice its demands will have a very clear grasp of how the policymaking process works. Groups that have worked with government policymakers before will not necessarily know how the process works for another issue, since actors will change and the number of steps in the process might vary as well.

When legislatures are introduced or become true alternative decision-making centers, stakeholder groups may be unable to take advantage of the new opportunities presented simply because they are unfamiliar with how legislative processes work, how to approach legislators and their staff, and which members to approach.[19] For instance, the committee system in El Salvador's National Assembly provides for hearings with testimony from invited organizations or individuals, but according to observers, such committees are rarely used by groups or individuals to argue their point of view. It takes time for stakeholder groups to learn how the system works and at which points they can intervene.

When a country shifts to more democratic and transparent processes of policymaking, those accustomed merely to employing a few key contacts may suddenly find themselves struggling to access the new process (see Ribot 1995). These groups must assess their resources and learn which ones will be the most helpful in presenting their demands so that their participation is effective. When groups are new, they may be unable to formulate or articulate their demands in a way that catches the attention of the policymaker and therefore go unheard. Limited capacity in any of these areas will ultimately affect the quality of participation of a given group. Capacity and availability of resources clearly affects the quality and effectiveness of participation. Some groups, typically influential ones and those close to powerholders, have considerably larger pools of resources (funds, but also contacts, political clout, analytic savvy, and so forth), thereby giving them a stronger competitive edge over others in both developing persuasive analyses and in the advocacy processes required for convincing decision-makers.

Civil society groups need to understand how policy decisions are made to become contributors to the policy process. Capacity building with a focus on "how to play politics" can be valuable. Techniques such as policy characteristics analysis can assist in improving the presentation and articulation of their interests and concerns (see Chapter 7). Grounding in techniques such as political mapping can bolster their understanding of the decision-making system, its leverage points, and how to access decision-makers (see Chapter 8). Training centered on policy analysis and organizational skills will also help provide resources to help civil society groups compete in the policy marketplace. Finally, training focused on strengthening advocacy and lobbying skills can assist in developing strategies for presenting their views and gaining influence (see Chapter 10).

PARTICIPATION AND DEMOCRACY

In this chapter we have sought to clarify participation's role in policy implementation and to offer policy managers some guidance on realistically weighing participation's pros and cons. We close the chapter with some selected caveats regarding participation and democracy. Participation has been on the development agenda for many decades and has been both widely studied and widely practiced in the context of projects and programs. While the state of knowledge about what works and what does not has increased, there is still a significant amount of simplistic thinking and excessive expectations surrounding participation. Some of this is associated with participation's connections to democracy and democratization.

More Participation Means More Democracy

While it is certainly true that participation is a necessary component to democratization, it is not true that more participation always leads to democracy. To cite a couple of extreme examples, both fascist and Marxist regimes tend to be highly participative but, of course, not very democratic. In many if not all Marxist regimes, sector organizations were developed to represent virtually all interests (professionals of various types, women, youth, farmers, labor, business, and so on). Vertically, party and other local organizations, such as "neighborhood defense committees," were designed to reach down to the block level in urban areas. However, membership was often mandatory and activities described as voluntary were actually obligatory. In most jurisdictions these organizations had resources available to them and some limited discretional authority, and were hence capable of satisfying limited demands. At the same time, local sector organizations (such as women's or farmers' groups) were often influential in the decision-making process of the local committees. In a similar manner, particular interests could have their influence felt up the line to the national level through the various strata of the sector organization and sector representatives were frequently prominent members of the policy decision-making apparatus. However, participation through sector organizations was both highly structured and monopolistic. And although people were free to participate in as many organizations or sectors as they saw fit (while there were generally no sanctions for nonparticipation, often there were substantial rewards for doing so), there were no competing groups to join or which could represent the same interests.

Participation may also be corporatist, where government designates certain groups as the representatives of sectoral interests (usually labor and business) for participation in policy dialogue, usually excluding other competing groups from the same sector. In certain cases membership in such organizations is obligatory, as, for example, business associations in several Latin American countries and in the francophone states of West Africa. When a business registers its existence, it is required to join the mandated employers' association or sub-sector chamber association and is usually taxed to provide resources for the association. In some countries governmental policy and decision-making bodies have established guaranteed seats for certain sectors. Sector representation (especially of the private sector) may be accorded on regulatory boards and other quasi-governmental decision-making bodies, but these seats are frequently ceded to particular ("official") organizations. Representative bodies such as legislatures also may have seats reserved for sector organizations. However, representatives are often appointed and not necessarily representative of the whole sector but perhaps only a particular sub-sector. The Philippines has recently incorporated sector representation into its legislature, which, while assuring participation for some societal representatives, effectively precludes access to decision-making by alternative groups. Another example is the "panchayat raj," or local governments of India, where a quota system for the participation of women and scheduled castes has been set up. However, because of dominant patronage systems, many if not most of these representatives are hand-picked by the local chiefs and vote their bidding (see Blair 2000b).

Participation Is Positive

Participation is regarded primarily as a positive act. It is easy to overlook the fact that participation can also be a negative force, one which blocks and rejects rather than positively contributes to policy decisions and implementation (recall Pressman and Wildavsky 1973). Negative participation is, in fact, one of the main methods by which governmental and nongovernmental actors classed as "losers" in policy decisions will intervene. NGOs may use mechanisms such as protests, strikes, demonstrations, or the like to manifest their disagreement with a chosen policy (see Hirschman 1970). Governmental actors (such as executive agencies or legislature) who lose resources or are otherwise negatively affected by the new policy have several mechanisms for negative participation at their disposal. They may simply choose to be passive and not act on the new policy directives, they may reject orders from superiors, or they might block implementation of the new policies by refusing to authorize needed resources. As Colburn (1989, cited in Brinkerhoff with Kulibaba 1996) notes, strategies of noncompliance (including foot dragging, feigned ignorance, false compliance, or sabotage) provide a means by which stakeholders outside and inside government can "critique" policy without drawing the government's wrath.

Negative participation may frustrate or cause fear among public officials, but it is not necessarily bad. For losers or opponents of policy who do not have a forum, this may be their only means of participation. And depending on the policy, negative participation may be very good from a democracy perspective. Certainly the civil disobedience movement led by Ghandi in India in the 1940s and the civil rights movement in the United States in the 1960s are eloquent reminders of the important role that can be played by negative participation.

More Participation Leads to Greater Equity

While increasing participation brings more players to the table, legitimate questions can be raised regarding the extent to which increased or expanded participation actually serves the interests of greater pluralism or equity (recall Lowi 1979). It should not be automatically assumed that because there are more participants the greater collective effort is actually equal to or coterminous with the "public interest." The politics of the policy process may in fact favor special interests over the public good or over pro-poor policies (see Echeverri-Gent 1992). Groups that are anxious to participate and respond to openings in the policymaking process are those that wish to have certain demands satisfied—but they are mostly interested in having their own demands satisfied, not those of others. That is the nature of politics, and the policymaking process is, of course, highly political. Societal groups differ in their access, resources, and capacity to voice their demands. Well-organized and well-connected groups have the advantage, while under-organized and/or marginalized constituencies (such as the poor) are rarely the best at mobilizing clout and participating without assistance.

Civil Society Is Participatory

Sometimes there is a quasi-automatic assumption that civil society organizations are, or should be, democratic and participatory in nature. Civil society is often promoted as a sort of "incubator" for democracy. Yet civil society organizations should not automatically be assumed to be democratic (see Ottaway and Carothers 2000). Rather, this assumption needs to be posed as a topic for investigation. Bratton's questions apply beyond Africa, about which he asks: "Is there internal democracy in the organizations of civil society? Or do these structures mirror and reinforce the personalistic and authoritarian patterns of rule that prevail at the political center?" (1989a, 430). While participatory and egalitarian civil society groups certainly exist, many groups in fact are exclusionary and focused on advancing their own narrow interests. Thus, a dilemma for participatory policy managers is how to structure state-citizen relations so that one set of clientelist relations is not simply replaced with a new one, where the clients are the most powerful civil society groups rather than the old elites (see Rothchild 1994). A related question for policy managers to ask is, Do the civil society groups seeking to participate pursue objectives that contribute to the public good? For example, some groups advocate racial or ethnic messages (for example, the Ku Klux Klan in the United States, or Serbian nationalists in the Balkans) that are contrary to principles of tolerance or democracy.

CONCLUSION

In this chapter we have argued that participation is a key issue in policy implementation. It relates to both the technical and process aspects of implementation. The role of participation in technical matters of policy content is widely recognized; for example, local input is often critical to designing and carrying out policies and programs that work. On the process side, first, participation is central to the state-society realignments associated with democratic governance. These changes influence the political and organizational settings that policy implementors operate within, increasing pressures for transparency, accountability, and responsiveness to citizens. Second, for a particular policy, participation issues emerge as part and parcel of the development of an effective implementation strategy. The guidance provided in the various boxes, and elaborated in our discussion, can help policy implementors to work out action strategies in collaboration with those who either have a direct stake in the policy outcomes or who play pivotal roles in the implementation process.

These stakeholders come not just from within the country; policy managers are subject to pressure for expanded participation from members of the international community. These include so-called transnational civil society, that is, NGOs and other informal advocacy groups involved in a variety of capacity building, collaboration, service delivery, and lobbying efforts (see Florini 2000, Otto 1996). The interaction patterns among these groups are multiple: North-South, South-South, North-North, between them and national governments, between them and donor agencies and other international organizations (such as the United Nations, the World Trade Organization, and others). The pressures also come directly from donors, who have become increasingly insistent on the need for wider participation in the design and implementation of the projects or policy change programs they finance. The World Bank's PRSPs are just one example. These combined pressures make it all the more important for developing and transitioning country decision-makers to understand clearly participation's benefits and costs and how to manage citizen participation in the policy process.

NOTES

1. While cynics might question the existence of such public officials, we have in mind the category of civil servant that Dominguez (1997), in his study of Latin American leaders, calls "technopols" (part technocrats, part politicians, who understand that democratic politics can best shape and assure long-term economic development). Leonard (1991) profiles African civil servants with this same orientation to their responsibilities. See also Grindle's (1991) discussion of public-minded government officials.

2. Development of information technology has vastly expanded the possibilities for information-sharing. In many countries, including some developing and transitioning economies, citizens have much greater access to knowledge about what government agencies are doing and planning than was previously possible. Electronic participation is opening new horizons for citizen engagement in policymaking, policy implementation, and governance. See, for example, Heeks (2001a, 2001b). For a warning against overoptimism regarding African e-governance, see Berman and Tettey (2001).

3. One lesson from the World Bank's experience with participatory development strategy formulation relates to the time and resource requirements for participation (see Clarke and Dorschel 1998).

4. In addition to diluting the original objective, the problem of "free riding" arises. This occurs when actors associate themselves with a particular group and gain benefits from that association but do not contribute resources to the group to help achieve its objectives. See Olson's (1965) classic study on collective action. He argues that because of the free-rider problem, large coalitions are inherently unstable and unsustainable. See also Burki and Perry (1998), and Ostrom (1990).

5. Recall Lowi's (1979) analysis of "iron triangles," where exclusive relationships with government decision-makers privilege special interests.

6. A number of analysts have focused on the costs to citizens associated with various types of participation. Among the classics is Hirschman (1970). His concepts of exit, voice, and loyalty have been applied in numerous studies of citizen-government interaction; see, for example, Paul (1992). The institutional economics literature also addresses these costs, looking at the citizen-government relationship as a principal-agent problem, in which citizens (as principals) incur costs (for example, searching for information, assessing performance) in order to assure that government actors (agents, acting for citizens) perform the tasks delegated to them (see, for example, Burki and Perry 1998, Klitgaard 1991, Meier 1991, Ostrom et al. 1993, Picciotto 1995).

7. See for example Honadle and VanSant's (1985) study of integrated rural development, or Bryant and White (1982, chap. 10).

8. As stated above (in note 1), we assume that there are policymakers and public managers with a sincere interest in the public good, despite the incentive issues posed by "iron triangles" and bureaucratic dysfunction. The developing/transitioning country counterparts that we worked with in IPC over the ten-year life of the project confirmed the existence of such individuals.

9. For an analysis that blends the normative with the instrumental perspective on participation, see Gran (1983). Although nearly twenty years old, much of what Gran has to say remains relevant today. See also the chapters in Korten and Klauss (1984), and for a more recent reference see Burkey (1993).

10. For more on PRSPs, see <http://www.worldbank.org/poverty/strategies>. See also CIDA 1997.

11. At times, NGOs and private firms can also become part of the supply side of participation. This takes place when they have been delegated functions by government, either at the national or the local level. See, for example, Lewis and Wallace (2000).

12. This is an area in which information technology is making some changes. See Heeks (2001a, 2001b) and Berman and Tettey (2001).

13. While the constitutions of many countries spell out relatively decentralized systems, quite often the local structures are very poorly equipped to make decisions, mostly because resources remain controlled from the center.

14. See Dominguez and Giraldo (1996) and Zakaria (1997) for interesting discussions of the persistence of closed systems within democracies or democratizing countries and the difficulty of creating true alternative decision centers.

15. However, as Charlick (2001) points out (examining African cases), local government reform does not automatically lead to more options for citizen participation. Without strong local civil society groups, local elites tend to dominate these opportunities.

16. There are certainly exceptions to this generalization; for instance, many of Africa's traditional societies were highly participative. The imposition of colonial rule and subsequent independence movements and institutions of government dramatically eroded such participation; however, traditional structures have been tapped to increase participation in policy implementation, for example in the environment sector (for example, Ribot 1995, Brinkerhoff 1999b, Pretty and Ward 2001).

17. There are some interesting exceptions to this. During the 1930s and again in the 1950s the organization of the labor movement surged in Latin America. However, most of these organizations represented only relatively small proportions of the overall sector. Where they became effective, it was largely because of corporatist affiliations, such as the "sindicalista" movement in Argentina under Juan Perón, the COBOL in Bolivia during the first Paz Estenssoro government, and Mexico's PRI-affiliated Confederación de Trabjadores Mexicanos (see, for example, Buchanan 1995, Collier 1996, Zapata 1998).

18. There is a longstanding debate whether interest groups are part of the problem in development or part of the solution (see, for example, Brautigam 2000). Our view is that sustainable citizen participation cannot be separated from interest group–government political dynamics. Recall that this is also an issue in U.S. political science (see Lowi 1979).

19. In one Latin American country the leader of the most prominent business chamber could not accurately describe how a piece of legislation moved through the congress because prior to that time one only needed to gain the assent of the president, and the congress would merely follow that lead. However, with democratization of the country, the congress took on a stronger role.

4

Policy Partnerships

At first we thought that trying to change the government's policy [on cross-border livestock transport levies] was utopian and hopeless, but now that we are organized jointly and can dialogue together with them [public officials], we see that change is possible.
—Member of the national coordinating committee for livestock trade, Côte d'Ivoire

My advice to you [head physicians of newly created private entities to provide family care] is to form an association. You will need to be strong to work together with government as an equal partner.
—Director of the oblast [region] health department, city of Zhezkazgan, Kazakhstan

Around the world there is wide recognition that the socioeconomic problems that policies address cannot be solved by governments acting on their own, nor are they the exclusive domain of one sector. The first quotation, from a member of a committee that joined government officials with business association representatives to address barriers to livestock trade in West Africa, illustrates this point. In fact, one of the key features of policy implementation is that it is multi-organizational; rarely does a single agency carry out all the tasks associated with implementation. Beyond government actors, as the size and scope of the state has shrunk, the role of NGOs and the private sector has expanded (see Salamon 1987). With the addition of new actors, pressures for more responsiveness to citizen demands, and shrinking resources, governments are looking for new ways of structuring policy implementation. This search has led to, among other trends, increased experimentation with collaborative and cross-sectoral structures and processes, which have been termed partnerships. The second quotation, from one of the Central Asian republics that initiated a partnership to implement health sector reform, illustrates two important issues related to making partnerships work: sufficient capacity and the balance of power between state and non-state partners.

85

Managing policy partnerships leads to an expanded set of linkages that connects government to other public agencies, private firms, NGOs, community associations, and so on. Administrative reality is defined by mutual interdependence and negotiated joint action rather than by top-down direction and supervision. Democratization influences these linkages due to the growth of newly empowered citizens' groups advocating a reframed relationship between government and the governed (see, for example, Sachikonye 1995, Uphoff 1993).

In this chapter we examine cases of policy formulation and implementation in which governments and civil society groups, NGOs, and the private sector are jointly involved, and we offer some guidance relating to (a) the situational variables that constrain or facilitate cross-sectoral partnerships for policy reform; (b) effective mechanisms and processes for bringing together diverse groups to cooperate around a policy issue; and (c) the applicability of strategic management techniques and tools for supporting cooperative action. We also offer some steps that governments, donors, NGOs, and the private sector can take to enhance the use of policy partnerships.[1]

CLARIFYING CROSS-SECTORAL POLICY PARTNERSHIPS

In broad terms these partnerships can be defined as cross-sectoral interactions whose purpose is to achieve convergent objectives through the combined efforts of both sets of actors, but where the respective roles and responsibilities of the actors involved remain distinct. The essential rationale is that these interactions generate synergistic effects; that is, more and/or better outcomes are attained than if the partners acted independently. This definition suggests a set of factors that partnership arrangements need to address in order to contribute effectively to policy implementation. These include specification of objectives and degree of convergence, mechanisms for combining effort and managing cooperation, determination of appropriate roles and responsibilities, and capacity to fulfill those roles and responsibilities.

Specification of Objectives and Degree of Convergence

The starting point for any partnership is the purpose that brings the partners together. Two features are important. First is that the goals constitute objectives that individual partners cannot achieve on their own. Contributions from all parties are necessary for success. Second is the extent to which the goals pursued are compatible and convergent. Setting partnership objectives in developing/transitioning country contexts can be problematic for a variety of reasons. First is the multiplicity of actors and their broad range of interests. National governments, international NGOs, local NGOs, international donors, and other civil society organizations all have differing agendas. Development experience is replete with stories of the difficulty of reaching agreement on policy and program objectives, and on the roles each partner should play. Sometimes the compatibility of objectives is more apparent than real; over time the hidden agendas often work at cross purposes with the ostensible ones.

Second is the power differential among the various actors, which arises as a function of differences in resource levels, operational capacity, and political clout. When governments partner with local NGOs, they are in a significantly more powerful position. A similar situation holds in cases where international donors fund the implementation of programs and projects and/or where Northern NGOs work with Southern NGOs and local civil society groups (see Lister 2000, Brown and Ashman 1996). The objectives of the relatively stronger partners tend to prevail, and the weaker partners are accountable to the stronger ones, but not the reverse.

Third is the tendency for partners' individual objectives to shift and potentially diverge over time, apart from the goals of the partnership. Policy implementation is an extended process, and the interests and purposes of the actors involved can change. A classic illustration is when local NGOs initially involved as service delivery conduits begin to want more of a say in policy and resource allocation decisions (see Smith 1987, Fisher 1998). Or, a new government is elected, and the officials assuming power have a different agenda from their predecessors. These changes can mean that the partnership's objectives will have to be renegotiated.

Mechanisms for Combining Effort and Managing Cooperation

Making cross-sectoral, multi-actor arrangements operate effectively is key to the success of any policy implementation partnership. Managing interdependencies is the sine qua non of both policy management and of state-civil society collaboration. Several factors appear critical: participation, decentralization, and incentives. These are interrelated.

As noted in Chapter 3, participation is an essential aspect of building policy constituencies. For partnerships, participation is an important factor for two main reasons. First, from the instrumental perspective of improving the quality of policy formulation, planning, and implementation, participation has the following benefits. Participation leads to better policy targeting, that is, a closer fit between the needs and demands of beneficiaries and the design of policy objectives and modalities. As a result of improved targeting, policy solutions can be achieved more effectively and at a lower overall cost. Participation also can build ownership for policy solutions among beneficiaries and implementors; this means that these actors feel that they have a hand in defining and carrying out the solution and that they are committed to the policy objectives. Ownership can lead to higher use rates of policy goods and services, reduced maintenance and operating costs, and better conformity between policy intent and outcomes. Over time, participation facilitates greater sustainability of policies and programs (see, for example, Thompson 1995).

Second, participation is significant from a democratic governance perspective because of its empowerment potential. Increased participation of civil society groups and beneficiaries in policy implementation partnerships can be one of the means by which the accountability, transparency, and responsiveness features of democratic governance are operationalized and reinforced. Through participation civil society partners can expand their degree of influence, for example, in decision-making for policy planning and in implementation; under other policy formulation/implementation arrangements this power resides solely with government. Citizen participation in policy oversight and service quality monitoring is another example of empowerment. Tendler (1997) illustrates this kind of empowerment in her analysis of improved governance in Brazil, where citizen involvement in performance monitoring coupled with central government shaping of task parameters and job incentives for local public employees led to significant increases in policy/program effectiveness in several sectors, such as community health and agricultural extension. These cases demonstrate the potential for participatory partnerships to generate synergy and increase societal problem-solving capacity.

Decentralization in its various forms—deconcentration, delegation, devolution, deregulation and privatization—can be both an enabling condition for the emergence of partnerships and a means to establish them. Decentralization redefines the relationships between national and subnational entities (regional, state, and local), and between those entities and civil society and the private sector. By allocating authority to regional and local levels, decentralization assures that non-state actors will have someone to enter into partnerships with (Fiszbein and Lowden 1998; see also Teune 1995). This expands the number of potential partnerships; if only national-level partnerships exist, fewer people will be involved. Decentralization through privatization in essence creates partnerships with private sector actors by narrowing the scope of government's role in goods production and service delivery, and opening up the playing field to private business (Rondinelli 1998). To the extent that decentralized relationships already exist that support and promote local autonomy and cross-sectoral collaboration, partnerships can more easily form and operate effectively. In situations where administrative and service delivery structures remain centralized, partnerships are a way of experimenting with different forms of decentralization, demonstrating which forms work best under particular conditions and/or providing operational capacity at the local level in cases where it is nonexistent or weak (see, for example, Brinkerhoff 1995).

It should not be overlooked that central government has an important role to play in making decentralization and participation effective, beyond the initial steps of deconcentrating, delegating, devolving, and empowering (see Manor 1999). The center creates the parameters within which a particular partnership operates, shaping the scope and nature of the interactions between the state and non-state actors involved, as the Brazil cases cited above illustrate (see Tendler 1997). This activity can include, for example, development and communication of a consistent message regarding the policy reform that the partnership addresses, determination of rules that limit clientelist behaviors at the local level, and/or promulgation and enforcement of uniform quality standards for citizen consultation or for NGO service delivery. Such parameter-shaping efforts lead directly to a consideration of incentives.

Incentives are the essential lubricant that makes partnerships possible. Positive incentives provide the stimulus that impels partners on both the state and non-state sides of the equation to work together; negative ones discourage them from doing so. For civil society groups, one positive incentive for partnering is increased participation and empowerment, which can mean that policies and programs more effectively meet their needs. If the partnership involves resource transfers, say to NGOs for service delivery outreach, then the acquisition of those resources is an important incentive. On the government side, an incentive for partnering is the ability to make scarce resources go farther and achieve greater impact than would be possible by acting alone. A negative incentive for all members of a partnership is the loss of control and autonomy that comes from shared action. Decentralization links to incentives because, as noted above, it changes traditional administrative relationships and encourages new forms of cross-sectoral interaction at the local level (see Blair 2000b, Crook and Manor 1998). Incentives are fundamental to the feasibility of using partnership mechanisms for policy implementation and to the sustainability of policy outcomes.

Determination of Appropriate Roles and Responsibilities

In the developing world the state, until recently, assumed major responsibility for policy formation and implementation. Resource constraints, advice and pressure from the international donors and multilateral development banks, international market forces, and citizen demand for democracy have all combined to force a fundamental rethinking of the appropriate roles and responsibilities of the state from the former

Soviet Union's economies in transition to the incipient democracies of sub-Saharan Africa (see Frischtak 1994, Migdal 1988, Kooiman 1993, Turner and Hulme 1997, World Bank 1997). The thrust here has been on limiting and circumscribing the role of the state so as to create space for other actors. Politically, this has meant creating a legal and institutional framework that establishes civil liberties and public accountability. Economically, the major vehicles for reducing the role of the state have been market liberalization and privatization. In combination, these measures define a role for the state in policy formulation and implementation in which the state (1) undertakes the direct provision of a limited set of essential goods and services and (2) facilitates and encourages the engagement of civil society and the private sector across a wide range of social and economic sectors.

The scope of civil society's role in policy formulation and implementation, then, is highly dependent upon the discretion of the state, at least initially. Political and economic liberalization establishes new state–civil society boundaries and interaction patterns, and it opens the door to institutional pluralism, which creates potential opportunities for a larger role and new responsibilities for civil society (see Brinkerhoff with Kulibaba 1996, Coston 1998b, Fisher 1998). Over time, interactions between government and civil society actors can reshape those boundaries and enlarge (or shrink) civil society's role and responsibilities. Vis-à-vis the state, civil society has a central role to play in accountability and responsiveness of the state to citizens, although getting beyond simplistic solutions requires delving into the political economy of state–civil society relationships. Especially at the level of local government, clientelism, where local officials and elites dominate decision-making and resource allocation, means that government is responsive to a narrow slice of society. Determination of appropriate roles for civil society in policy formulation and implementation needs to take account of these dynamics.

Within the broader civil society category of non-state actors, NGOs can play a number of roles in policy formulation and implementation: service deliverer, project manager, intermediary and spokesperson, information disseminator, impact analyst and monitor, dialogue promoter, and/or advocate and lobbyist. In many developing countries, particularly at the local level, NGOs fill a service delivery void, often operating relatively independently in the absence of government services (see McCarthy et al. 1992). They also participate more directly with governments through service co-production arrangements, building on their comparative advantage for efficient and effective service delivery. For example, NGOs work with public sector agricultural research institutes to transfer technology to farmers in many African countries (Farrington et al. 1993) and provide HIV/AIDS services through government contracts in Brazil (Connor 2000). Concern for impact has led some NGOs to focus more strongly on the policy advocacy role, though fewer numbers of NGOs function in this mode than in the service delivery one (see Bratton 1990, Korten 1990, Fernando and Heston 1997).

In many developing countries, however, the determination of appropriate roles and responsibilities is contested territory, with significant differences in points of view among governments, NGOs, and international donors. For example, African governments are often uneasy about the political implications of service delivery partnerships with relatively autonomous NGOs, whose grassroots activities can lead to challenges to state authority (see, for example, Bratton 1989b, Ndegwa 1993). In Latin America many governments view NGOs with suspicion, given past links to liberation theology and insurgency movements (Pearce 1997, Fiszbein and Lowden 1998). In Central Asia governments are wary of both the private sector and civil society, distrusting their objectives and concerned about their political motives (Hensher 1999). Donor agencies, by favoring programs with NGOs when the commitment and capacity of government to pursue reform are in doubt, can exacerbate state–civil society tensions when governments perceive themselves to be in competition with NGOs for scarce resources. NGOs sometimes view collaboration with government with suspicion, concerned about loss of autonomy or interference. Private sector groups tend also to be suspicious, seeing government as anti-business, overly controlling, and/or inept.

Capacity to Fulfill Roles and Responsibilities

To tap the full potential for policy implementation of NGOs and civil society means addressing capacity issues on both the state and civil society sides of the equation. For partnerships to function effectively, the state needs both the willingness and the capacity to respond effectively and appropriately to input from civil society (Coston 1998a, Migdal 1988, Tendler 1997). As Fiszbein and Lowden indicate, "Partnerships should not be seen as a substitute for conscious efforts directed toward the strengthening of public sector capacity. . . . For the partnership to achieve its full potential private actors require effective public partners" (1998, 73).

However, building management capacity in the state alone is an incomplete strategy for promoting partnerships for policy implementation. On the civil society side, non-state actors must possess the capability to participate in the policy formulation and implementation process (see Chapter 3). Enhancing the effectiveness of partnerships is linked to fostering the ability of civil society groups to address both supply and demand issues. The supply side deals with capacity to handle the managerial and technical tasks involved in implementation partnerships, including issues such as service delivery efficiency and effectiveness, or expanding local efforts to regional or national levels—scaling up (see Edwards and Hulme 1992, Fowler 1997, Korten 1990, Lewis and Wallace 2000). Demand-making capacity relates to advocacy and policy dialogue functions, as well as policy monitoring and ability to interact with policymakers and public sector implementors to promote responsiveness, accountability, and transparency.

FIVE CASE ILLUSTRATIONS

This section briefly presents five cases of cross-sectoral society partnerships.[2] The literature distinguishes two broad categories of interaction between government and civil society regarding democratic governance: partnerships that focus on advocacy and responsiveness/accountability to civil society; and those that focus on policy planning, implementation, and service delivery. Of the five cases reviewed here, three fall primarily into the policy advocacy/accountability category and two mainly into the policy reform planning/implementation category. These groupings, however, are not mutually exclusive, and to varying degrees all of the cases combine advocacy and implementation.

Sahel Regional Livestock Trade Reform

In the African Sahel the efficiency of commercial livestock trade was significantly constrained by the prevalence of corrupt practices associated with government regulation of cross-border trade. In 1991 the World Bank and USAID jointly financed the formulation of an action plan to improve the efficiency of livestock trade in the central corridor of the Sahel by lowering administrative and procedural barriers to inter-country commerce. The draft plan was subsequently distributed to African governments, regional organizations, and international donor agencies for discussion. In March 1992, at a conference jointly sponsored by two regional organizations, representatives of twelve nations in the Sahel and coastal West Africa adopted a modified version of the action plan and recommended that Mali, Burkina Faso, and Ivory Coast implement a pilot effort to promote regional economic integration.[3]

The plan presented an integrated approach to reform that built upon the convergent interests of government, whose leaders wanted to see their economies grow, and civil society actors, who were the direct beneficiaries of reform. These latter included livestock producers and traders, professional organizations, private transporters, and the consumers of livestock products in each of the three target nations. The plan addressed a politically charged topic (reducing corruption) in the context of a universally accepted objective: the promotion of regional economic integration.

Its proposals to reduce corruption focused upon limiting opportunities for rent-seeking through reduction of regulation, rather than upon sanctions to discourage it.

To implement the plan, a partnership with a committee structure was created. National coordinating committees were established, made up of government officials from a variety of ministries or agencies and civil society actors representing stakeholder groups in all three countries. While the partnership arrangements were at first largely informal, ad hoc forums for the discussion and elaboration of a reform agenda, in less than a year the committees obtained legal recognition through governmental decrees that established the committees as deliberative bodies with official convening and operating authorities. Thus the partnership took on a formal identity.

Progress in implementing the reform agenda took place during a period characterized by major changes, including advances toward democratization and greater public sector accountability in each of the three countries and, in January 1994, a massive devaluation of the region's common currency, the CFA franc. The dynamism in the environment required a high degree of flexibility from the partnership's coordinating committees. Building an inclusive coalition for reform to mobilize the numerous stakeholders having an interest in political and economic outcomes of efforts to reduce the costs of corruption placed a premium on strategic skills. These were important because progress on reforms often engendered countermeasures aimed at recovering lost revenue or privileges, which then needed to be dealt with by the reformers. For example, in Burkina Faso the suppression of one set of quasi-official levies was met by efforts to reimpose those same fees under another rubric. Similarly, in Mali, when livestock traders contested the imposition of fees for services provided by customs brokers, the brokers organized an effective political defense of their interests. Unable to obtain suppression of the brokers' levy, livestock traders shifted tactics and organized a campaign to broaden and improve service delivery by customs brokers.

However, despite some setbacks, through the national coordinating committees the partnership enhanced the prospects for reform success by ensuring that the principal stakeholders—winners and losers alike—played a structured role in the policy implementation process. Although demand-making and advocacy were not an explicit focus of the partnership, the committees proved to be an effective counterweight to the tendency of African governments deliberately to exclude or marginalize non-elite civil society groups from the policy process. The USAID-supported technical assistance to facilitate the functioning of the committees built civil society actors' capacity to lobby effectively for change while increasing public sector actors' ability to listen to constituencies and engage in policy dialogue.

The West African Enterprise Network

The idea of creating a network of business persons from both anglophone and francophone West Africa emerged from a 1991 conference jointly sponsored by USAID and the OECD's Club du Sahel.[4] The conference focused on the business climate in West Africa, and one of the issues raised was the need to modify the policy environment to make it more supportive of business. Many countries have policies, regulations, and procedures that hamper private sector operations. African conference participants recommended the establishment of some sort of coalition among members of the region's private sector to work on advocacy for policy reforms and to explore ways of interacting with governments to pursue reform agendas. USAID initiated a project to set up such a network with the dual objectives of improving the business climate in member countries and promoting regional cross-border trade and investment.

The Enterprise Network started with twenty donor-selected representatives from eight countries; by 1999 it comprised around three hundred locally designated members in thirteen countries. Network members were typically second-generation entrepreneurs, between thirty-five and forty-five years old, who returned to Africa from overseas in the 1990s to set up businesses. Generally educated abroad with a preexisting set of international contacts, members invested their personal equity in their enterprises, often in conjunction with other family members. Most had not visited another country in the region before joining the network but quickly became convinced of the potential of regional trade integration. They tended to be innovative, aggressive, and impatient with the pace of change in their countries, and willing to finance their participation in the network out of their own pockets.

Initially the national networks were informal entities, but between about 1994 and 1996 most of the networks formalized their status as registered NGOs or nonprofit corporations. As part of their strategic planning process, each national network identified policy reforms, articulated policy positions, and undertook actions to promote the reforms. In most of the networks these action plans began with internal mobilization around a policy agenda, followed by lobbying of government and donor officials. Later, however, national networks engaged in partnership activities, such as participation with government officials in joint task forces to explore policy options, organization of policy debate forums and round tables, and provision of comment and review of proposed legislation and regulations. Besides national-level consultative partnerships in individual countries, the Enterprise Network as a regional entity participated in a variety of joint collaborative efforts with regional organizations. For example, these included working with the West African Monetary Union on harmonization of investment codes, and with the Central Bank of West Africa on private sector financing.

Some national networks were more dynamic than others. Differences emerged in the effectiveness of network leadership, the relative strength of members' participation in planned activities, and the relative progress of country governments toward democratization and open governance. Among the West African countries the networks in Ghana and Mali made the most progress. In Burkina Faso, where the government has authoritarian tendencies, the network members proceeded gingerly with the pursuit of an advocacy agenda. The state–civil society partnership potential of the Enterprise Network was limited by government mistrust both of the private sector specifically and of civil society groups generally. The state viewed organizing autonomously for any purpose as a possible threat. The state-dominated, corporatist sociopolitical systems that historically dominated post-colonial Africa impeded the development of formal associational activity (see Bratton 1989a, Bratton and van de Walle 1997), but as civil society has gained strength these dynamics have changed to some extent in many countries.

SME Policy Reform in Bulgaria

The transition from command-and-control to open-market economies in Central and Eastern Europe launched fundamental changes on the part of both government and citizens, but the countries in the region are at various stages of this change process. The collapse of Bulgaria's communist dictatorship in 1989 instigated political freedoms and constitutional reform. However, it did not result in any significant change in economic policy. A succession of governments consistently failed to restructure the economy, and it sank progressively into stagnation, inflation, and recession. By 1996 an estimated 90 percent of the population lived in poverty. One of the key components of USAID assistance to Bulgaria focused on nurturing private sector development, particularly of small and medium enterprises (SMEs) in recognition of their importance to economic growth in the region. SME-focused objectives included increasing the availability of financial services and equity financing, strengthening the capacity of a selected set of individual firms, and improving laws and policies that promote competitive private sector growth. To support the third objective USAID targeted assistance to creating a policy dialogue process involving the stakeholders in Bulgaria's SME sector.

During Bulgaria's democratic transition, civil society organizations blossomed, including the formation of a number of business associations (cf. Siegal and Yancey 1992). USAID sought to help with establishing a partnership that could build on the vibrancy of Bulgarian civil society to engage government in policy dialogue and reform related to SMEs. This effort began in early 1997 in collaboration with a new organization, the Bulgarian Association for Building Partnership (BAP). The BAP, with USAID assistance, developed an SME action plan and a coalition building campaign that led to a coalescing of support for SME reform nationwide from over fifty private sector groups. In the meantime public outrage over the failure of government led to the collapse of the socialist government, and a reformist government came to power in the spring of 1997. The new regime was much more open to change and subsequently adopted the BAP platform as part of its economic restructuring package, which was submitted to the National Assembly in the summer of 1997.

The success of the coalition-building campaign and the new openness of the government led to the formation of an SME policy reform partnership that linked civil society and the state. A "trialogue" strategy evolved, bringing together three categories of actors. The first two were civil society entities: business associations and policy research/advocacy think tanks. The third group was composed of members of the public sector: government officials and parliamentarians. The three nodes of the partnership pursued a diverse program that concentrated on (a) effective interest aggregation among SME stakeholders, (b) high-quality technical information and policy analysis, and (c) open and receptive public administration.

Interest aggregation took a huge leap forward with the formation in mid-1997 of a national coalition of business associations called the National Forum, intended to be a policy advocacy entity with the capacity both to lobby government and cooperate with it in the development of critical legislation. At its organizing meeting a structure was developed and voted upon. The BAP, chosen as coordinator, subsequently oversaw the establishment of a working group to develop a strategic plan. During 1997–98 the National Forum began to strengthen its capacity to engage in a targeted campaign of policy dialogue and legislative lobbying.

Work on policy analysis focused on support to local think tanks to undertake analyses and develop position papers. The think tanks worked in close collaboration with the members of the National Forum and built linkages with government that gave them a seat at the table for policy discussions while preserving their independence. The think tanks participated actively, along with business associations, in the development of the National Strategy for SME Development.

On the public sector side of the partnership the range of actors included the Public Information Working Group of the Council of Ministers, the Economic Commission of the Bulgarian Parliament, the Bulgarian National Assembly, the Agency for SMEs, the Foreign Investment Agency, and the Agency for Mass Privatization. The unifying theme of their activities was increasing openness, access, and participation. For example, during the summer of 1997 members of the Public Information Working Group undertook a study tour to the United States to increase their capacity in public relations and information dissemination. The Economic Commission organized a round-table discussion on the Law for Foreign Investment. The National Assembly put together and promoted a handbook containing biographical data and contact information for members of parliament, a list of parliamentary commissions, lists of constituencies and parliamentary groups, and names of National Assembly leadership.

In the fall of 1997, as part of the process of developing the National Strategy for SME Development, the Economic Commission convened a series of seven participatory regional town hall meetings around the country to bring together SME stakeholders, government officials, and parliamentarians to discuss policy issues and strategy. These public forums were managed by a joint civil society–government working group. A team drawn from the working group drafted a policy paper, building on the outcome of the town hall meetings. The draft strategy was reviewed by a cross-sectoral joint committee in January 1998, revised and finalized, and then a national summit was organized by the Economic Commission and the Agency for SMEs, attended by nearly three hundred participants from government, civil society, the private sector, and international donors. This type of participatory structured policy debate was a first for Bulgaria. Following the summit a small cross-sectoral working group drafted legislation for SMEs, which in July 1998 was submitted to and accepted by the Council of Ministers. Further "trialogue" among members of the partnership was planned for the future, building on the successes achieved.

Natural Resources Co-management in Africa

Sub-Saharan African economies are heavily dependent upon their natural resource base, yet many of those resources are being degraded and/or exploited at an unsustainable rate. Turning these trends around is critical to the survival and well-being of the people of sub-Saharan Africa. With assistance from international development agencies and NGOs, Africans have rethought approaches to environmental and natural resources (ENR) planning and management. Traditionally throughout Africa, ENR policies have been considered the responsibility of the state. Yet the track record of public sector ENR policy implementation is uniformly poor. Across Africa ENR policy design and implementation reflect two trends. The first is less reliance on control-oriented policies, which involves a move away from centralized regulation and proscriptive policies and toward positive incentives and increased participation of NGOs and local communities. The second is a mismatch between the new tasks associated with ENR policy innovations and the old organizations charged with their implementation.

These two trends form a general pattern, referred to as co-management, which can be defined as the integration of local and state-level ENR management systems in partnership arrangements where power and responsibility are shared between the government and local resource users. Co-management offers the possibility of developing viable common property resource management strategies that combine centralized state control with local-level self-management. Co-management calls for a changed relationship between government and natural resource users. Because co-management involves government-civil society partnerships, delegation of authority to the local level, and responsiveness of government to citizens, ENR policy reforms are closely linked to issues of democratic governance.

The configuration of ENR partnerships features a division of responsibilities between central public sector agencies, NGOs, and local resource users. Policy formulation, elaboration of regulations and incentives, and technical/scientific tasks are reserved for the state agency(ies) with statutory authority for the ENR sector. However, field-level implementation functions are devolved to NGOs and/or NGO associations, which then undertake participatory resource conservation and protection activities in concert with local communities. One of the major forces pushing for public–civil society partnerships is the above-mentioned lack of government capacity to implement ENR programs effectively. While some ENR policy functions must necessarily reside with the state, others can be accomplished by nongovernmental entities.

Often the NGO partner serves as the guarantor of the community's ability to manage the resource and as the source of technical assistance to strengthen community resource management capacity. For example, in Mali, CARE, with USAID funding, supported a village self-help organization—the Ogokana—to manage forest resources on a contract between the Ogokana and the Malian Department of Water and Forests. In Zimbabwe the Communal Areas Management Programme for Indigenous Resources (CAMPFIRE) created a partnership between two government agencies, the Forestry Commission and the Department of National Parks and Wildlife Management (DNPWM), and local communities. A local NGO, Zimbabwe Trust, supported by several international NGOs, worked with the local communities and served as an intermediary with the Forestry Commission and the DNPWM. CAMPFIRE distributed wildlife resource management between the DNPWM and local communities, and the Forestry Commission developed mechanisms to involve local residents in determining ways to provide access to gazetted forest areas. Villagers and bureaucrats became partners in protection and sustainable use.

In the Zimbabwe case a specific example illustrates how the partnership operated: the DNPWM provided technical assistance to communities participating in CAMPFIRE. DNPWM technical experts established the game quota parameters within which the community made its decisions. If DNPWM determined that an offtake of eight elephants was appropriate, the community would then decide how many would be reserved for sale to a safari operator and how many would be allocated to local hunters. Department staff would then assist in the negotiations with the commercial organizations to help the community receive benefits such as higher fees, employment and training for community members, and low-impact hunting practices to preserve the physical surroundings.

Health Sector Reform in Kazakhstan

Kazakhstan and the other Central Asian republics inherited a health system from the Soviet Union that was centralized, hierarchical, and standardized. Policies, practices, and treatment norms were all developed in Moscow and passed to each republic for implementation by the health ministry, which in turn issued directives to oblast (province) health departments that oversaw city- and county-level administrative units. The system emphasized tertiary care and specialty services. Hospitals and polyclinics received most of the resources, while primary care was under-funded and served mainly to refer patients upward to specialists and hospitals.

Kazakhstan's health sector reform has the following features: (a) cost reduction, (b) rationalization of health facilities, (c) a health insurance fund to introduce cost-consciousness and performance incentives, and (d) separation of payment from service provision. The reform also emphasizes training of physicians and other medical personnel both to upgrade and broaden clinical skills and to focus on strengthening primary health care. Faced with declining economic conditions, budget crises, and shrinking expenditures in the social sectors, the government turned to the private and nonprofit sectors as partners in health care delivery. Primary care was delegated to newly privatized units called Family Group Practices (FGPs). New NGOs, Family Group Practice Associations (FGPAs), were established to serve as intermediary institutions between government and the FGPs.

Reform implementation began in the 1990s in four oblasts that set up a health insurance fund, a new provider payment system, and development of a basic benefits package. FGPs were created to provide primary care through contracts with the fund. The first FGPA was established in the city of Zhezkazgan, one of the original experimentation sites where one of the most forward-thinking health administrators in the country began testing new approaches. Working closely with government health services, the FGPA participated in direct service provision and in health status monitoring and reporting. It played a minor role in health policy advocacy. The FGPA's relationship with its members centered on capacity building to help the FGPs make the transition to viable private providers of quality primary care services to families. The association was instrumental in obtaining donor resources, through grants, for FGP strengthening. Besides the FGPA's involvement in service delivery and support to FGPs, devolution of some regulatory functions and shared approaches to quality assurance and monitoring brought them new roles and responsibilities in setting quality-of-care standards, monitoring performance, and accrediting health care providers.

Following Zhezkazgan's example, other oblasts created FGPAs to partner with their public sector health agencies. A national FGPA was established in late 1998, and its founders focused immediately on resolving the legal and organizational issues concerning its relationship to local-level FGPAs. During 1999–2000 the national FGPA developed a program of activities, concentrating on building membership and deciding upon a policy platform.

Donor resources and technical assistance were instrumental in allowing FGPAs to fulfill their new partnership roles and responsibilities. These were important in providing the means to enable the associations to demonstrate to government officials that they could be effective partners in health sector reform. Although nominally the FGPAs' roles included representing the interests of their members and lobbying for policy and procedural changes in support of those interests, this role did not induce much advocacy activity. The associations for the most part avoided advocacy and lobbying in favor of capacity building and participation in service delivery. Given the authoritarianism of the Kazakh state, it is unclear to what extent the FGPAs will emerge as health policy advocates and representatives of citizens' health needs in policy dialogue.

SITUATIONAL VARIABLES
INFLUENCING CROSS-SECTORAL POLICY PARTNERSHIPS

Several basic situational variables condition both the emergence and the degree of success of cross-sector policy partnerships. We review four here.

Regime Type

A fundamental variable is the type of regime, which influences the nature of the state; state relations with civil society; and the "space" available to civil society (Fisher 1998, Frischtak 1994, Rothchild 1994, Salamon and Anheier 1997). The ability of civil society to play a role in either service provision or advocacy and mobilization/expression of demand depends on the larger politico-bureaucratic setting. As a rule, democratic political systems offer a more supportive enabling environment for state–civil society partnerships than authoritarian or limited democratic (so-called pseudo-democracies) forms of government (Diamond 1994). As Foley and Edwards observe,

> Where the state is unresponsive, its institutions are undemocratic, or its democracy is ill designed to recognize and respond to citizen demands, the character of collective action will be decidedly different than under a strong and democratic system. Citizens will find their efforts to organize for civil ends frustrated by state policy—at some times actively repressed, at others simply ignored (1996, 48).

The five cases support this observation. The Sahelian livestock coordinating committees depended upon the willingness of the three governments involved to remain open to civil society input to the policy implementation process. As noted above, the West African Enterprise Network members experienced more or less success in organizing and pursuing a dialogue with the state depending upon the degree of democratization and government openness to citizen input, with Ghana and Mali at one end of the spectrum and Burkina Faso at the other. The effort in Bulgaria began under a government that was relatively unreceptive and unresponsive to citizen involvement; little progress on the partnership was made until a reformist administration came to power. ENR co-management has progressed furthest in countries such as Botswana, Zimbabwe, and—more recently—Mali. All three are characterized by relatively democratic regimes. Kazakhstan is an authoritarian state, despite its leadership having been elected. In the health reform partnership the state holds the vast majority of power, and the FGPAs and FGPs have been docile and cooperative (see Hensher 1999).

However, as the Kazakhstan case shows, the pursuit of partnerships does not have to wait until democratic regimes have come to power. As noted above regarding participation and decentralization, partnerships can serve as demonstration efforts that help to "push the envelope." This is one of the ways that sector-specific partnerships can contribute to encouraging democratic governance (see Brinkerhoff 2000). Further, as Coston points out: "Governments are not monolithic. Regimes of all types may incorporate agencies and actors that are more cooperative or repressive than the overall regime" (1998b, 364). This means that, while regime type is important, especially for scaling up of partnerships and for their sustainability, finer-grained assessment is called for to determine the degree of receptivity and responsiveness of the particular public sector entities that could be potential partners.

Level of Trust

Partnerships are on occasion uneasy collaborations, both from the government and the NGO/civil society sides (see, for example, Farrington et al. 1993, Hulme and Edwards 1997, Lewis and Wallace 2000). The level of trust among the partners influences their willingness to initiate joint activities and to work together over time. State actors tend to be concerned that the very features that give civil society organizations and NGOs their grassroots advantages also provide a potential springboard for political activity. In some cases governments are sensitive to the presence of NGOs in service delivery and technical assistance roles as implicit criticism of their lack of capacity to fulfill those roles and are resentful of the donor resource flows going to NGOs instead of to ministries. On the other hand, governments frequently cite concerns about lack of NGO capacity, particularly for programs that involve a significant expansion of activities initially begun as pilot or experimental efforts. As one eighteen-country assessment found, African governments are not uniformly receptive to NGO participation in ENR management (Brown et al. 1993). As noted above, Latin American governments' perceptions of NGOs are often colored by their past association with populist insurgency movements.

From their side NGOs are often suspicious of government intentions, particularly in the case of regimes with limited commitment to poverty reduction, ENR protection, private enterprise development, and so forth. Further, NGOs are rankled by government attempts to monitor and control their activities, often perceiving such efforts as unwarranted interference. For some NGOs partnership arrangements can appear too constricting compared to the relative freedom of independent grassroots development projects and programs. NGOs are also concerned that over time partnering with government will jeopardize their autonomy, discretion, integrity, and ability to pursue their own mission (Fowler 1997, Hulme and Edwards 1997).

The trust issue emerges as important in each of the cases. The experience of the national coordinating committees in the Sahelian regional livestock case illustrates a "two steps forward, one step back" pattern, in which trust levels rose and fell, and then had to be renegotiated, with the technical assistance team playing the role of neutral brokers to the process. In the West African Enterprise Network case the caution exhibited by the founders of the national networks in keeping their structures small and informal during start-up reflected their concern for building trust with their government interlocutors. Network members were careful to maintain their focus on private sector policy issues and to engage public officials in problem-solving discussions rather than attack government as the source of problems. This helped to build trust. National networks formalized their structures into full-fledged NGOs only when they were convinced that government did not perceive them as potential political threats. In Bulgaria both sides of the partnership were initially wary of the motives and intentions of the other; the shared experience of collaborating led to greater trust among the partners. In the ENR co-management partnerships, state lack of trust in community capacity to manage resources and community mistrust of government were mitigated by having international environmental NGOs serve as intermediaries between state and community. In Kazakhstan the FGPAs and FGPs wanted to focus on quality service delivery in part to build trust of their capacity with their government partners and funders. Over time, the experience of working together increased the comfort level of both state and non-state participants in these partnerships.

Legal Framework and Regulation

The presence of a supportive legal and regulatory framework is another important factor conditioning state–civil society partnerships.[5] This factor is related to the other two. Nondemocratic regimes tend to have restrictive regulations applying to NGOs and local associations. Even in democratizing countries there are often legal impediments to innovative partnership arrangements, for example, limitations on the ability of local organizations to be recipients of public funds or onerous accounting requirements. Such regulations reflect a lack of trust in NGOs; they are often implicitly designed to limit political activity by NGOs although ostensibly justified as safeguards against corruption and financial malfeasance (see Clark 1995).

This factor is central to the Sahelian livestock policy case in that a major focus of the partnership was on revising the legal and regulatory framework for regional trade in order to make it more open and responsive, and less susceptible to rent-seeking. It emerges in the Enterprise Network both as a target of the networks themselves and as an influence on the development path of the networks, whose members sought initially to remain small and informal so as to avoid legal and regulatory problems. In the Bulgaria case the legal framework for SMEs was an explicit focus of the partnership's joint efforts, along with a new and more participatory approach to policy and legislative development. The factor is important across Africa in ENR policy implementation because often a barrier to co-management arrangements is lack of legal recognition for local forms of resource management structures (see, for example, Bragdon 1992). In Kazakhastan, as in the other Central Asian republics, the legal framework has been problematic for the emergence of viable NGOs, and the FGPAs had to focus considerable energy on their legal status.

However, it is not simply laws and regulations applying to NGOs and community groups that are important. The legal framework for the organization and operation of the public sector is critical to the ability of government actors to enter into partnerships. This can be at the macro level, for example, in cases where new democratic governance procedures mandate citizen involvement in public decisions through various consultation mechanisms. Or it can be at the more micro level of individual agency operations. For example, in the Sahelian livestock policy case a key target of reform was the rules governing how the public sector interacts with private sector interests and NGOs. Another example concerned the laws and procedures relating to decentralization, which set the parameters of central-local government responsibility and authority. These parameters condition the extent to which local public entities can raise and retain revenue, use funds without excessive central oversight, enter into service-delivery partnerships, and so forth. In the ENR case, the public sector legal framework in most African countries created a highly centralized system resulting in weak or nonexistent local public sector presence and capacity. This has been a factor in creating the space for a role for NGOs and community groups in resource co-management.

The Nature of the Policy to Be Implemented

The potential for successful state–civil society partnerships is also influenced by the characteristics of the policy that the partnership deals with. Policies vary in terms of the degree of technical expertise required, the time frame within which results and impacts occur, the array of interests affected, and their distributive consequences (Lowi 1979, Grindle and Thomas 1991). These features shape the determination of appropriate roles and responsibilities of the partners, and are important for capacity and incentive issues as well (see Chapter 7).

For example, regarding the degree of technical expertise, the civil society participants in the Sahel livestock policy committees consisted of members of livestock herder and transport associations, marketing groups, and butchers' associations. They all possessed in-depth knowledge of the technical issues involved, in some cases to a greater degree than their government counterparts. Thus, civil society participation in the committees contributed greatly to the success of the reform implementation not simply by representing demands to public officials but by assuring the technical correctness of proposed solutions.

Another example of the technical expertise demands of a policy comes from ENR policy implementation partnerships. Local groups have several advantages here. They have detailed knowledge of the resource base, and they often know how to adapt technologies to exploit those resources, because they depend directly upon them for survival. For some aspects of ENR policy, however, in-depth technical expertise beyond what community members possess is required. As the CAMPFIRE example reviewed above shows, specialists located in public agencies can provide vital technical information that local groups can then use for ENR management. Farrington et al.'s study (1993) of government-NGO partnerships for agricultural development further illustrates the allocation of different components of policy implementation to the partners involved, capitalizing on their strengths: basic research and technology development to government research institutes, and extension and field applications to NGOs.

In the Bulgarian case the partnership's formulating and vetting the National Strategy for SME Development illustrate how the technical expertise of the business community was brought into the process. Further, the participatory arrangements assured that the policy's formulation addressed the panoply of stakeholder interests as part of the development process.

For Kazakhstan's health reform the FGPAs were key to building expertise among the FGPs in primary health care and in operating their practices as viable businesses. The associations' close links with their membership assured that they were in tune with their members' needs and could seek the resources, both from the government and from donors, to help meet those needs and build capacity. The FGPAs also mobilized capacity from health professionals in the country and facilitated their cooperation.

The Sahelian livestock policy case illustrates the influence of the array of interests and the distributive aspects of policy. Livestock policy touched on a broad range of stakeholders, both inside government and in civil society, and, because livestock trade is an important component of the economies of the three countries involved, the distribution of benefits and costs was a critical concern. Two important issues over the life of the partnership arose: how to manage a policy dialogue and planning process with a large number of participants, and how to keep the process on track when various interest groups sought to bend (or in some instances hijack) the process to fit their particular purposes.

The interest array factor also emerged in the Enterprise Network case in terms of the incentives for organizing around a particular policy agenda. The formation of the national networks required a flexible approach to agenda-setting to galvanize members and to stimulate and maintain their commitment to pursue policy advocacy and enter into partnerships. Because the civil society side of partnerships often involves voluntary collective action, successful policy implementation partnerships must pay attention to crafting an agenda and actions that solicit and hold the interests of the non-state partners, whose contribution is usually noncompulsory and nonremunerative. Structurally, the Enterprise Network addressed the incentive question by creating sub-networks around specific interests, such as auditing and accounting, export marketing, and private sector finance/investment.

EFFECTIVE PARTNERSHIP MECHANISMS AND PROCESSES

The case examples summarized here illustrate variations on the two major categories of partnerships between governments and civil society: policy advocacy and service provision. However, the cases are in no way representative of the full range of cross-sectoral partnership possibilities. Nevertheless, a few general points regarding partnership mechanisms and processes emerge from the discussion as tentative guidance and lessons.

Ad Hoc Versus Formal Mechanisms

The Bulgarian SME policy reform and the Enterprise Network cases illustrate a pattern of ad hoc and relatively informal partnering mechanisms at the start of the partnership. This informal approach appeared to be successful in engaging state actors for purposes of policy dialogue, advocacy, and design with civil society. It permitted a "testing of the waters" of cooperation by both sides without committing either one to a formal path until trust and agreed-upon modes of interaction could be developed.

The ENR case illustrates the use of more formal mechanisms from the start. Government agencies—departments of forestry and of wildlife management—entered into formal agreements, in some cases actually specified in contract-like documents, with NGOs and/or local communities for resource management. These agreements clarified at the outset the roles and responsibilities of the partners, the terms by which the partnership would be evaluated, and criteria for continuation. The partnership, in essence, constituted a delegation of authority and responsibility for ENR policy implementation from the state to civil society actors. Similarly, the Kazakhstan health reform partnership began as a formal arrangement based on FGPs contracting for services with the health insurance fund and a clearly specified and formal intermediary role for the FGPAs.

The Sahelian livestock case is an intermediate one. The partnership emerged in response to the need to implement the action plan, and thus it began with a set of preset objectives. However, much remained to be elaborated in terms of the details, and the partners were relatively wary of each other at the outset. Thus the partnering mechanisms began as ad hoc but quickly became formal once interaction among the partners started up.

A preliminary conclusion is that formal partnership mechanisms appear to be more appropriate for partnerships whose objectives focus on implementing predetermined policies and programs. Such objectives can more easily be clarified and negotiated at the point of partnership creation, thereby allowing for a more formally structured approach. The informal, ad hoc mechanisms appear more suited to partnerships with initially more diffuse objectives, or in those where the ultimate path of the partnership is not initially clear. This pattern characterizes the partnerships that emphasize policy advocacy and policy design.

Initiation of the Partnership

In none of the five cases reviewed here did the government initiate the partnership independently. The major impetus for the creation of the partnerships came from international donors. However, in two of the three advocacy/demand-making cases, the Sahelian livestock action plan and the Enterprise Network, the initiative quickly passed to the civil society actors involved, and it was they who pressed ahead to define their agenda and make progress. In the case of the Bulgarian SME policy reform, initial donor-supported work with business associations laid the groundwork for the partnership, which once the reformist government came to power was supported by all sides of the "trialogue." The ENR case tells a somewhat different story; throughout Africa partnerships for ENR co-management have been brokered by multilateral and bilateral donor agencies, often in collaboration with international environmental NGOs, such as the Worldwide Fund for Nature or the International Union for the Conservation of Nature. Kazakhstan's health reform, including its privatization and partnership aspects, was designed with significant donor input and has been implemented with an important level of donor resources.

The cases discussed in this chapter confirm the fact that governments in the developing world and in transitioning economies are, for the most part, still relatively mistrustful of civil society and tend to retain vestiges of old attitudes concerning the primacy of the state. Governments, left to their own devices, do not tend to seek out partnership arrangements with civil society and in many cases view NGOs at least with suspicion, if not hostility. Democratizing regimes, however, are more disposed to respond to demands from civil society groups for more involvement and thus may be less likely to resist partnership arrangements. Acceptance of the desirability of partnerships is increasing, however, and governments in some countries have shown progress in reaching out to the nonprofit and private sectors for collaboration.

Coordination and Linkages

State–civil society partnerships are prime examples of interorganizational activities in which success depends upon coordination of effort
and effective linkages among the actors involved (see Chapter 5). Getting
groups to work together across organizational boundaries is not easy, and
a significant amount of analytic effort has focused on this question (for
example, Alexander 1995, Brown and Ashman 1996, Kooiman 1993). In
Bulgaria the partnership operated with relatively diffuse linkages, and
the various partners tended to use the technical assistance team as a sort
of informal coordination hub. The Sahelian livestock action plan and
Enterprise Network cases illustrate the complexity not simply of cross-
sectoral coordination but of cross-national coordination. Critical to moving the livestock action plan forward were the efforts of the national coordinating committees in the three participating countries to orchestrate
the efforts of their members to reach agreements, resolve disputes, and
implement agreed-upon steps. Similarly, the Enterprise Network supported
both individual national networks and a regional set of actors to engage
in policy dialogue. These two cases suggest the value of informal coordination and linkages as appropriate to deal with a fluid and evolving policy
dialogue process.

Service delivery partnerships also pose coordination problems, as the
ENR co-management case illustrates. Here the lack of trust and the differing agendas of the partners often find expression in conflicting interpretations of coordination and linkages. For example, in Madagascar local communities with support from both international and local NGOs
implemented small ENR projects through contracts. Those contracts were
designed and coordinated by a quasi-governmental agency attached to
the Department of Forestry. The agency interpreted its coordination mandate to mean close supervision and contractual oversight, insisting that
weaknesses in local management capacity warranted this degree of control. The NGOs rejected this perception, complaining that their flexibility was being limited and their autonomy impinged upon. From their perspective, coordination did not signify hierarchical supervision but rather
collaborative interaction among equals.

As this example indicates, governments frequently want much tighter
and more formal coordination arrangements than do their NGO and community partners (see Brinkerhoff 1996a). Increased decentralization is
one way of addressing these problems, as is a broader mix of informal
linkages that allow for greater flexibility and participation (see Schubeler
1996, Thompson 1995). In Kazakhstan, because the FGPAs were initially
government created, coordination links were tight and top-down. Over
time the FGPAs began to loosen those government controls and strengthen
their links with their FGP members. Observers noted that the flexibility,

autonomy, and responsiveness of the FGPs and FGPAs working together made a difference in the speed and effectiveness of primary health care services reform.

STRATEGIC MANAGEMENT FOR PARTNERSHIPS

Making partnerships work effectively depends, as noted above, on the capacities of all of the partners involved. The strategic management steps overviewed in Chapter 2, and the tools presented in Part II, can be useful for the planning and implementation of policies through cross-sectoral partnerships. Here is how the elements of the tool kit were applied in the cases we presented above.

IPC provided technical assistance to the Sahelian livestock action plan coordinating committees and other groups working with them. Starting in late 1992 and continuing through 1997, a small team of consultants, both American and African, supported the committees on an intermittent basis. This support focused on introducing stakeholder analysis, political mapping, lobbying techniques, and workshops for promoting, coordinating, and implementing reforms in each of the action plan countries. With IPC assistance the committees developed strategies and workplans for (a) identifying alternatives to existing policies, procedures, and regulations; (b) developing legitimacy for the alternatives and building constituencies for change; (c) designing organizational structures and procedures to coordinate effort; and (d) mobilizing resources and actions in each of the three countries. The technical assistance team provided ongoing coaching to the committees, articulated around meetings that brought together various groupings of the actors involved for progress reporting, discussion, conflict resolution, and negotiation.

Similar assistance through IPC was provided to the West African Enterprise Network during 1993–98. A two-person team worked with each of the national networks and with the regional structure. On average, each of the eleven national networks was visited two to three times a year by the team. Early in the capacity building effort the team held strategic management workshops for network leaders that gave them skills in SWOT analysis, stakeholder analysis and political mapping, and lobbying. Using the skills acquired in these workshops, each network analyzed its own strengths and weaknesses, developed strategic plans, and, with the plans as a guide, pursued advocacy and lobbying efforts and joint policy dialogue with government officials. Networks focused explicitly on legitimization of private sector policies and on building constituencies for reforms, using evidence-based policy arguments. In Ghana and Cote d'Ivoire they also undertook monitoring and analysis of specific policies and produced independent white papers as input to policy dialogue. As the regional

Enterprise Network became more organizationally complex, its leaders used the strategic management and policy implementation skills they had acquired to modify their structure and procedures, creating the sub-networks around particular interests.

From January 1997 through 1998 Bulgaria had an IPC team composed of a resident advisor and short-term consultants, both local and expatriate. Assistance focused at first on civil society, through business associations, helping them with issue identification, stakeholder analysis, political mapping, policy agenda setting, and lobbying and advocacy. With the coming to power of the new government in the spring of 1997, public-sector actors began to express openness to input from civil society and the private sector, reaching out for such input on their own initiative. This change expanded the target of IPC technical assistance in strategic planning and policy reform to public sector partners as well. A major focus was on legitimization of new policy options and constituency building, both with government and within the private sector, followed by re-source accumulation. The technical assistance team helped both private sector and government actors to use policy dialogue workshops during the multi-city round of town meetings that gathered input for the SME strategy. The policy implementation task framework served as an informal guide to the committee that drafted the SME strategy upon which the law was based. The IPC assistance helped to support the participatory democratic values that the Bulgarian participants found so striking about the strategy development process.

IPC's work with ENR policy implementation was more analytical than technical assistance, although some training workshops for ENR managers were held. The analyses conducted highlighted the importance of strategic management techniques and flexible processes in making ENR partnerships work effectively when critical issues revolve around the interaction of governments and civil society groups in confronting how to control access to and judiciously manage natural resources. Examples of such issues include the extent of delegation of regulatory enforcement authority to non-state actors, the appropriate mix of resource conservation versus exploitation measures to be undertaken, and the time frame for assessing implementation progress of partnerships.

In Kazakhstan the health reform technical assistance team used a number of strategic management tools. Consultants provided training for FGP and FGPA staff in stakeholder analysis, strategic planning, and policy lobbying and advocacy, and assisted in developing action plans for the partnership and capacity building. Other assistance was provided in analyzing the legal framework for nongovernmental association status and in determining appropriate registration procedures. As with the other cases, legitimization and constituency building proved essential, first of all to bring suspicious public officials on board with the reforms, and second, with members of the health establishment unconvinced of the need for change. The FGPAs also focused strongly on resource accumulation and mobilization as essential implementation tasks. Further, policy monitoring was one of their specifically articulated roles in quality assurance and health status monitoring.

ENHANCING PARTNERSHIPS

In recent years experimentation with partnerships has exploded in both number and scope (see, for example, Smillie and Helmich 1999). The cases reviewed here illustrate just a few of the possibilities. Making partnerships work involves actions by all partners. Increasingly, partnerships include direct participation by private sector firms as well, including private sector and NGO partnerships (see Heap 1998).

Steps for Governments

What can governments do to enhance both the opportunities for engaging in cross-sectoral policy partnerships and the possibilities that partnerships, once entered into, will be effective and successful? The state occupies both a privileged and challenging role in partnerships—privileged because it holds the legal prerogative of creating the rules of the game, and challenging because unless state actors at all levels respect and abide by those rules, the potential success of the partnership can be undermined.

To assure the success of partnerships that can capitalize on the synergies of joint action, governments need to undertake the following steps:

- Establish the legal framework necessary to enable civil society organizations and the private sector to engage in partnerships with the public sector. This involves such actions as legal recognition and tax exemptions for non-state entities of various types (NGOs, interest group associations, and so forth), establishment of financial and contracting mechanisms to allow funding for partnership activities, and so on. These mechanisms should go beyond standard contracts to focus on shared authority and joint decision-making between the potential partners.
- Create the administrative structures, procedures, and mechanisms that will facilitate the establishment and operation of partnership arrangements. Primary among these is decentralization, which will allow for many more partnerships to be formed. However, full-scale decentralization is not a prerequisite. Other examples of these administrative measures include, for example, increasing information

dissemination, expanding opportunities for civil society access to government officials (see Chapter 3), establishing venues for dialogue (for example, town hall meetings, public hearings), forming working groups, and so on.

- Build the institutional capacity of public sector agencies and staff to work effectively with civil society and the private sector. Such capacity building includes providing agencies with the resources and incentives to interact with citizens' groups and NGOs, for example, funds to hold meetings and to travel outside of major cities and towns, and recognition and rewards for officials who solicit civil society participation and engage in dialogue.

- Develop monitoring programs to assure adequate oversight of partnerships and to reduce the potential for clientelism (special interest monopolies of government services) at all levels. This can include ministry reporting systems or support to legislatures to undertake reviews and hold hearings on nonprofit and private sector involvement in policy and program implementation. This step represents a particularly important function for central government to undertake as a contribution to making partnerships effective.

- As a corollary to capacity building, provide training to public agency staff. This could be, for example, in the areas of strategic management, policy implementation, community relations and outreach, negotiation and conflict resolution, stakeholder consultation, accountability, and/or service quality assurance and monitoring.

- Develop communications and public relations strategies for informing civil society, and the private sector, regarding government intentions and plans for partnerships, and for assuring stakeholder participation in partnering arrangements and the policy process. Make decision-making related to partnerships, whether formal or informal, more transparent. An important legislative accompaniment to this step can be the passage of sunshine laws that mandate such communication and participation.

Steps for NGOs and Private Firms

With the worldwide expansion of partnerships, many NGOs and an increasing number of private firms are undertaking these steps:

- Network among potential partners, and broker partnership arrangements. This is a major focus of the work of the Prince of Wales Business Leaders Forum (PWBLF), for example. Another example is the International Medical Services for Health, an NGO that builds partnerships with local agencies and pharmaceutical firms for health reforms and service provision. These kinds of networking and brokering can help to deal with the power asymmetries inherent in many partnerships.

- Promote capacity building, particularly policy advocacy, constituency building, and implementation capacity. This kind of activity is going on all around the world. A number of the U.S.-based NGOs that are active in partnership capacity building efforts include, for example, CIVICUS, CARE, and Pact. Outside of the United States, for example, the Regional Environmental Center for Central and Eastern Europe, based in Hungary with local offices in fifteen other countries in the region, encourages cooperation and partnerships for environmental decision-making. Another example is the International Forum for Capacity Building (IFCB), an association of Southern NGOs that is active throughout the developing and transitioning world.[6]

- Undertake research and analysis on partnerships. NGOs can do this independently or in cooperation with donors and/or governments. In the United States CIVICUS is an example of an NGO that focuses on research and analysis as well as capacity building. An example from India is PRIA, the Society for Participatory Research in Asia, an umbrella NGO with affiliates throughout the country. PRIA is an active member of the IFCB.

Steps for Donors

As noted earlier in this chapter, donors have been important catalysts in getting government, NGOs, and, more recently, private sector partners together to pursue partnerships. The steps described here are all currently being pursued by a number of donors and are in fact expanding rapidly as partnerships become more widespread organizational mechanisms for policy and program formulation, implementation, monitoring, and evaluation.

- Support analysis, dialogue forums, and learning activities that contribute to developing knowledge about the formation and management of cross-sectoral partnerships. Because of the popularity of the partnership concept, it is important to understand where and how partnerships work best, what constraints they face, and what constitutes best practice. USAID's New Partnership Initiative, begun in 1995, and the more recent Intersectoral Partnerships effort promote learning as well as providing support to partnership operations.[7] The World Bank has established the Knowledge Resource Group (KRG), one element of its Business Partners for Development (BPD) initiative, to collect, analyze, and disseminate lessons learned about partnerships involving business, government, and civil society. The World Bank works with CIVICUS and the PWBLF on the KRG.

- Support organizations that specialize in brokering partnerships. For example, USAID supports Pact's work with the PWBLF to link civil society and private firms in development partnerships. The Bank's BPD supports and promotes selected strategic cross-sectoral partnerships in countries around the world.
- Provide direct capacity building support to potential partner organizations, both funding and technical assistance. As the case examples presented in this chapter show, donors can assist governments, civil society organizations, and private sector groups in coming together in partnerships for policy formulation and implementation. For example, USAID's Office of Private and Voluntary Cooperation (PVC) provides direct support to efforts made by the U.S. NGO community and its local partners to forge cross-sectoral partnerships.

CONCLUSIONS

This chapter shows that, appropriately structured and managed, partnerships can produce improved technical policy solutions and outcomes. Thus, from an instrumental/technical viewpoint, policy partnerships make sense. The synergies generated can help both state and non-state actors to achieve objectives beyond what each can accomplish by acting on its own. These synergies, in turn, lead to higher levels of policy impacts and improvements in people's lives. Such positive outcomes, however, are by no means a foregone conclusion; effective partnerships require a minimum set of facilitative conditions and government actions, which we have sought to detail above.

Beyond these direct policy results, policy partnerships can potentially fulfill a broader function of promoting more responsive, transparent, and accountable government. They can facilitate increased citizen participation in public affairs, empowerment of local groups to take charge of their livelihoods, and capacity to advocate for policy reforms with public officials and political figures (see Chapter 3). Again, these are not guaranteed outcomes; political dynamics, social conflicts, and power differentials can all intervene. Nonetheless, partnerships offer one operational avenue for strengthening democratic forms of governance.

NOTES

1. This chapter draws substantially on Brinkerhoff (1999a).

2. Four of the cases are drawn from the IPC Project's experience and one from the Partnerships for Health Reform Project.

3. The sponsoring organizations were the Comité Permanent Inter-États de Lutte Contre la Sécheresse dans le Sahel (CILSS) and the Communauté Economique du Bétail et de la Viande (CEBV); that is, the Permanent Inter-State Committee to Combat Drought in the Sahel, and the Economic Community of the Livestock and Meat Sectors.

4. The Club du Sahel is a donor consortium and counterpart to the CILSS. Club membership is comprised mainly of bilateral donors—Austria, Belgium, Canada, Denmark, Italy, Japan, Switzerland, France, Germany, the Netherlands, and the United States—and a few multilateral donors—the European Union, some of the U.N. specialized agencies, and the World Bank. It serves as a forum for discussing and analyzing development issues with Sahelian state and civil society partners and as a means of coordination among the donors. The Organization for Economic Co-operation and Development serves as the host organization for the Club du Sahel.

5. For an informative elaboration of legal principles applying to NGOs, see the World Bank's handbook on NGO laws, prepared for the World Bank by the International Center for Not-for-Profit Law (ICNL 1997).

6. For information on these organizations, visit their websites: <http://www.civicus.org>, <http://www.care.org>, and <http://www.pactworld.org>. For the Regional Environment Center, see <http://www.rec.org>. For the International Forum for Capacity Building, see <http://www.alop.or.cr/ifcb/ifcbupdate.htm>.

7. For the New Partnership Initiative, see <http://www.info.usaid.gov/pubs/npi>. For the Intersectoral Partnerships activity, see <http://www.info.usaid.gov/pubs/isp>.

5

Coordination for Policy Implementation

We talk and talk about the need for better and more efficient policy at our cabinet meetings, but the ministers keep forwarding the same poorly prepared dossiers. Are we not part of the same team? We need better coordination.
—Staff member of the Cabinet Office, Zambia

There are many groups involved in environmental policy in Madagascar, and we all need to work together. Everyone wants to coordinate, but no one wants to be coordinated.
—Staff member of the National Office of the Environment, Madagascar

Throughout this book several managerial topics have emerged consistently from the discussion of policy implementation, citizen participation in the policy process, and partnerships. First is that the issues facing developing/transitioning country policy managers, whether they deal with macroeconomic or sectoral policies, inevitably call for solutions that cross individual agency boundaries and, in many cases, extend beyond the public sector to incorporate private sector and nonprofit entities. Policy implementation brings together multiple organizations and groups that are intended to work in concert to achieve a set of objectives. As the previous chapter illustrated, multi-actor structures for policy implementation can usefully be examined as partnerships.

Second, in these multi-actor settings, no single entity is "in charge" in the traditional sense, where it is assumed that responsibility and authority are combined in one place to a sufficient degree that top-down management structures and procedures will function effectively. For many policy objectives, the tendency remains to establish a hierarchical locus of authority and build outward and downward to accomplish what needs to be done (Landau 1991). However, for most of the process tasks of implementation—legitimization, constituency building, accumulating resources and mobilizing action—using a hierarchical approach will not work well.

Even for organizational structuring and policy monitoring, hierarchy is only one among several options, and may not be well suited for most implementation situations, particularly when managers are trying to operate in a participatory way in interaction with non-state actors.

Third, and closely related to the second topic, is that strategic management in multi-actor policy implementation is not a question of command and control. Managing policy implementation is about developing shared vision, influencing and persuading supporters and opponents, negotiating agreements, resolving conflicts, cooperating with a wide array of stakeholders, devising work programs in participatory and collaborative ways, and so on. The case examples of policy partnerships in Chapter 4 clearly show that managing them is a shared endeavor with linkages that largely extend laterally, with relatively little recourse to top-down management.

Common to each of these three topics is coordination, which is the focus of our discussion here. As the quotations at the opening of the chapter illustrate, coordination is often a thorny and potentially conflict-provoking problem. In the sections below we discuss what coordination is and some of the issues involved in designing and managing coordination for policy implementation. We offer some guidance on different coordination options and some solutions for coordination problems. The chapter then turns to an exploration of coordination mechanisms that can help different groups to work together.[1]

GETTING SPECIFIC ABOUT COORDINATION

The multi-actor, cross-sectoral, nobody-in-charge features of policy implementation create linkages among the various organizations, civil society groups, NGOs, and private sector entities with a role in the implementation process. These linkages distribute functions to those involved in ways that establish varying degrees of interdependency among them (Hjern and Porter 1981, Gage and Mandell 1990). These interdependencies create requirements for coordinated action in order to achieve policy objectives. For example, in the Kazakhstan health policy reform case presented in Chapter 4, the public sector health departments (at the national, regional, and municipal levels), the new health insurance fund, the private service providers (Family Group Practices), the Family Group Practice Associations, citizens, and donor agencies all needed to work together to make the reform effective.

Coordination is a term that is frequently called for as a solution to implementation problems. To say that a policy or program is uncoordinated means in a general sense that its elements are somehow incongruent, that they do not interact smoothly to produce desired results, and that the connections among them create excessive friction or conflict. However, improving coordination is rarely elaborated in an operationally meaningful way beyond a vague notion of building more harmonious linkages. Getting specific about coordination for policy implementation leads to asking questions about the nature of the linkages among the various actors involved. What do they need from, and provide to, each other in order to fulfill their respective functions and contribute to achieving results? How can these exchanges be orchestrated effectively?

One way to think about coordination is in terms of three types of activities: information-sharing, resource-sharing, and joint action (Honadle and Cooper 1989). Information-sharing essentially involves communication, one agency or subunit letting another or others know what it is doing. This can be done through distributing written reports, public hearings, holding meetings of various sorts, or setting up information units. Information-sharing can also take place through the media or on the Internet.

Resource-sharing means that resources controlled by one organization or group are allocated to another for particular purposes. Examples here are loans, grants, contracts, and/or secondment of personnel. Resources can also be in the form of public support for a policy, so here resource-sharing involves actors creating legitimacy and lending their status and credibility in the service of reform. This relates to the implementation tasks of legitimization and constituency building. As Chapter 6 on stakeholder analysis emphasizes, the notion of resources includes a broad range of items, not simply money, personnel, and equipment. It can include knowledge, motivation and commitment, capacity to mobilize others either for or against change, and so on. All of these constitute "currencies" that actors can spend or withhold (Cohen and Bradford 1990). By recognizing the full range of resources at their command, actors frequently find that they can play a stronger role in policy implementation than a first glance might reveal.

Joint action entails two or more entities collaboratively undertaking some activity together, either sequentially, reciprocally, or simultaneously (Alter and Hage 1993). Joint activities could include planning, data gathering, service delivery, monitoring, training, and/or supervision. Each of these types of coordination implies greater or lesser degrees of linkage among the organizations involved.

MAKING COORDINATION WORK

For coordination to be effective, it must deal with three interorganizational problems: (1) threats to autonomy, (2) lack of task consensus, and

(3) conflicting requirements from vertical and horizontal linkages (Brinkerhoff 1991). Each of these problems imposes transactions costs, which combine political issues with organizational ones.

Threats to Autonomy

A core dynamic in most organizations is to try to maintain as much independent control over inputs, outputs, and operations as possible. To the extent that coordination requirements impinge upon its independence, an organization will be reluctant to coordinate. These threats are increased in situations in which stakeholder interests are diverse, cooperating agency operational procedures are different, resources are scarce, and linkages among agencies are multiple and interlocking. Some of these linkages are task driven; that is, the nature of the actions to be undertaken requires significant degrees of information and resource exchange, collaborative planning, and joint task accomplishment. Others are administrative, driven by bureaucratic oversight, reporting, and accountability requirements.

For example, in Madagascar, implementation of environment and natural resources policy under the umbrella of the National Environmental Action Plan (NEAP) exhibited all of these features. The NEAP implementation network created numerous threats to autonomy among the actors involved. Among these were conflicts between the semi-autonomous agency responsible for managing protected areas (known as ANGAP), which operated through grants and contracts to local entities, and its grantees and contractors in the field over the appropriate degree of autonomy they should exercise. Similarly, tensions between ANGAP and the government's forestry department, which oversaw ANGAP, revolved around the same issue (Brinkerhoff 1997a).

Lack of Task Consensus

Task consensus means agreement on what the policy is intended to achieve and how to reach its objectives; this includes the client groups to be targeted, the actions to be undertaken, the services to be provided, the methodologies to be employed, and so on. Because many of the technologies for socioeconomic development are only partially understood or are site specific, lack of agreement on what to do, for whom, and how is highly likely. Without some minimum level of agreement, however, cooperation and coordination are difficult. In this area as well, diversity among stakeholder perceptions and interests, political considerations, multiplicity of linkages, and scarcity of resources aggravate the coordination problem. Resolving lack of agreement can be an ongoing issue, with high transactions costs imposed by the need for continuous communication, negotiation, and renegotiation to forge a workable consensus.

To continue the Madagascar NEAP example, there was overall agreement on the general policy goals, a moderate degree of consensus on target groups and their needs, and vastly diverging views on how best to carry out programs to achieve the NEAP's objectives. Much debated was how to blend conservation-oriented efforts for the long term with development interventions designed to deal with immediate economic survival needs. The first five years of NEAP implementation concentrated strongly on conservation, but this shifted during the next five-year period to blend conservation and development in light of limited conservation results and public pressure for access to natural resources for economic uses. Environmental policy became highly politicized, with some Malagasy groups accusing donors and the National Office of the Environment of caring more about the welfare of endangered species of lemurs than about the poor and disadvantaged.

Also hotly contested among the NEAP implementation actors was the task of coordination itself. Most of the actors had some form of coordination role, yet there was little consensus on what it meant for them operationally. The public sector actors tended to interpret coordination as close programmatic monitoring and control, a view not shared by the intended subjects of this scrutiny. The NGO actors thought of coordination much more in terms of information-sharing and joint learning about community-based resource management strategies.

Conflicting Vertical-Horizontal Requirements

Most implementation actors belong to a variety of networks, some formal hierarchies in the case of sectoral ministry units, or more informal and lateral systems, for example, in the case of civil society groups or community associations. Frequently, coordination places actors whose actions are to be coordinated in a situation in which they are subject to conflicting demands. The most common conflict is between the requirements for participating in lateral coordinated activities at the field level and in vertical sectoral hierarchies. Some of the difficulties here arise from legal constraints imposed by enabling legislation and administrative statutes that place limits on an agency's margin for maneuver. There can sometimes be restrictions on the use of funds that can hinder coordination. For example, in many countries' public administration systems, spending authorization is required prior to utilization of funds, and approvals are often subject to long delays. These requirements can significantly constrain an agency's ability to operate flexibly in cooperation with others, since coordination does not always allow for predictability in the use of funds.

Diversity of stakeholders contributes to vertical-horizontal strain; for example, agency stakeholders may resist coordination if it diverts resources from activities they are interested in maintaining. The potential for this conflict is high where resources are scarce, because agencies have little slack available and the costs of coordination are rarely factored into budgets. Complex and diverse linkages also heighten the probability of conflict, because so many connecting threads exist that some degree of working at cross-purposes becomes inevitable. The transactions costs of trying to satisfy these various stakeholders can be a disincentive to coordination, which is often reinforced by political factors (for example, when one set of stakeholders is significantly more powerful than others).

For example, among the organizations created to implement Madagascar's NEAP was the National Office of the Environment (ONE), which initially occupied a department-level position in the Ministry of Agriculture and Rural Development, yet its mandate called for a significant cross-ministerial role in coordinating policies and programs. In the strongly hierarchical Malagasy public sector, ONE's mandate led to "turf" battles within the ministry and with other public agencies. To deal with these conflicts, ONE was later removed from within the agriculture ministry and administratively attached to a supra-ministerial body.

IMPROVING COORDINATION: WHAT TO DO?

To implement policies successfully, managers need, first of all, to clarify what forms of coordination are appropriate, and second, to address the three obstacles to coordination, including their political dimensions. Table 5.1 examines the relationship between the three types of coordination and the obstacles, and provides an indication of where potential difficulties may arise.[2]

As the table shows, information-sharing generally imposes the least burden on an individual organization from the standpoint of coordination. Threats to autonomy are low because the organization is not necessarily obliged to modify its actions but simply to provide information on them. Lack of task consensus poses potential problems, because if actors cannot agree on what is to be done, then deciding what kinds of information should be shared becomes an issue, particularly if what is requested requires the organization to collect and analyze information that is new and different. Vertical-horizontal conflicts are on the low side, since it is usually possible to negotiate to provide variations on the same information to lateral partners and hierarchical superiors.

Table 5.1 Problem Areas for Interorganizational Coordination

Types of coordination	Obstacles to coordination		
	Threats to autonomy	Lack of task consensus	Vertical-horizontal conflicts
Information-sharing	Low	Medium-high	Low
Resource-sharing	Medium-high	Medium	Medium
Joint action	Medium-high	High	High

For resource-sharing, the degree of potential difficulties posed by each of the coordination obstacles falls in the medium to medium-high range. Sharing resources in most cases entails a significant increase in degree of interdependence among implementation actors over simply sharing information. For example, if service providers depend upon government funders for their budgets, then it is clear that those public agencies will have a relatively strong say in what the recipients can do with the funding, which poses threats to their autonomy in the use of the funds. Similarly, if funders and recipients do not agree on what tasks should be undertaken, problems can arise, though their degree is likely to be somewhat lower since most grantees and contractors tend to be reluctant to accept funding if they do not agree with the uses to which it must be put. Vertical-horizontal conflicts may arise, particularly when, as noted above, resources are scarce.

Joint action is clearly the most intensive form of coordination, with the highest degree of potential problems for all three obstacles. This is logical, because working together on policy implementation requires an individual organization to make numerous adjustments in how it plans its activities, allocates its resources, manages actions, and interacts with other partners. Joint action can pose real challenges when organizations are brought together that do not have a history of working together and/or have very different operating procedures or organizational cultures.

For example, in Mali, when community-based natural resource management policies were first introduced, forestry agents, rural development workers, NGOs, and community groups were all supposed to collaborate in joint resource management activities (Brinkerhoff 1995). The forestry agents came from a government department that was organized like a police force. They distrusted all the other actors, who also distrusted them, and in the case of local communities, feared and hated them. Particularly when the policy was first promulgated, most forestry agents did not agree with it at all (lack of task consensus). Further, they did not like working jointly with their NGO and community partners (their autonomy was threatened), and their hierarchical agency culture was at odds with the partnership ethos of collaboration and with the democratization sweeping Mali, which deeply affected state-civil society relations (vertical-horizontal conflicts). It took many years and much effort for these actors to deal with the obstacles to coordination, and while improvements have been made, some of these problems persist.

Policy managers can use Table 5.1 as a guide to analyze their particular interorganizational implementation settings to pinpoint where they might be experiencing problems currently or to flag potential problems in the future. The next step is to decide what to do to address the problems identified. There are two general categories of coordination improvement strategies. The first is to examine the types of coordination to see how they fit the implementation components of the policy. It is clear from the table that, in general, joint action poses the highest degree of interorganizational difficulties, and that, in contrast, information-sharing is much easier. So one option, for example, is to see whether some coordination functions could be handled through resource-sharing or information-sharing. The second strategy is to select among the obstacles the one (or ones) that is most critical and target it for managerial attention to reduce its strength and negative effects on coordinated effort. This option will be especially needed if it is not possible to reduce the level of coordination toward the less difficult information-sharing end of the spectrum. For example, if implementation partners are dependent upon each other for resources, policy managers may want to hold a workshop that brings together the various partners and representatives of their supervisory entities to discuss, and reach agreement on, the tasks to be accomplished and the balance between vertical and lateral communications, reporting, and resource availability. The following suggestions offer some options that can help address coordination problems.

Concentrate on Developing the "Rules of the Game"

Because, as we have noted previously, no single actor is "in charge" of policy implementation in the sense of being able to command compliance from other actors, achieving objectives will ultimately result from the various actors pursuing activities in ways that contribute to (rather than impede) progress. Whether coordination involves sharing information, sharing resources, or programming joint action, linked implementation actions will only operate effectively when governed by an accepted set of rules. This suggests the need to focus on developing agreed-upon "rules of the game."[3]

The types of rules that need specification and negotiation include determination of who is eligible to make which decisions in which areas;

what actions are allowed, required, or proscribed; what procedures must be followed; what information must be provided, to whom, and when; what benefits and costs are to be assigned to organizations (or groups) as a result of their actions; and how monitoring and enforcement will be undertaken. Some of these rules will already exist in formal laws, regulations, public sector procedures, and donor assistance packages. Other rules specific to the new policy will need to be developed; some of these will be formal, but others will be informal and thus will resemble "understandings" among the actors more than codified practices. All of these rules, both formal and informal, create incentives and organizational cultures that influence how implementation partners interact with one another. We should remember that rules are ineffectual unless the actors they affect know of their existence, agree to them and see some benefit in compliance, expect that the rules will be used to monitor behaviors, and anticipate sanctions (formal and/or informal) to be applied for noncompliance (Ostrom 1990).

Reduce Excessive Interdependencies and Control

Because of the tendency to equate coordination with supervision and control, excessively high degrees of linkages among implementation actors are often established. This situation can also emerge when implementation actors do not trust one another, as can happen, for example, when public agencies work with NGOs (recall the Mali forestry policy example above). Overly tight interdependencies risk hampering progress, because the closeness of the linkages means that delays or capacity problems affecting one member of the policy implementation network will have an impact on everyone. Too many interdependencies also can be a source of friction and conflict, particularly when some actors are not convinced of the need for coordination. Further, they raise the transactions costs of coordination. Since interdependencies tend to be reflected in rules and regulations, this issue also relates to the specification of the "rules of the game."

Reducing interdependencies and control can be accomplished through less frequent formal reporting or supervision, more operational autonomy once cooperative agreements (or contracts) and workplans are approved and there are fewer requirements for ex ante approvals, more reliance on informal collaborative arrangements, and/or less information required for existing reporting frameworks. It can also be achieved by reducing the extent of joint action, and replacing it with more resource-sharing or information-sharing; actors would pursue actions relatively independently, while perhaps participating in a joint oversight committee to exchange information, discuss progress and problems, and so on. One way of deciding where joint action can be reduced is through a close specification of the policy and program tasks to be accomplished, which can reveal which implementation partner may be best suited to carrying out the task at hand. Looser linkages will have the benefit of reducing most of the threats to coordination as well, thereby increasing the likelihood of cooperation.

Decentralization is one way of reducing interdependencies and control because it allows for more discretionary action at the local level, thus allowing implementation actions to be taken more freely by those in the field (assuming, of course, sufficient devolution of resources and decision-making authority). For example, in Chile's education sector reform in the first half of the 1990s, decentralizing management of the reform from the central to the provincial level and introducing flexible administrative procedures were credited as important factors in the success achieved (Angell 1996). Rather than having local activities dependent upon direction and approval from the Ministry of Education at the center, provincial supervisors had the autonomy to work with local schools in carrying out improvements. The policy reform did not start out with decentralized and flexible management, but it evolved in the early years of the program as excessively tight interdependencies and control emerged as problems.

Search for Win-Win Opportunities for Coordination

Among the members of a policy implementation network, shaping consistent and synergistic action on everyone's part can be extremely difficult because the three threats to coordination (threats to autonomy, lack of task consensus, and conflict between vertical and horizontal linkages) operate internally within an individual organization as well as across the various organizations. The risks of implementation gridlock and divisive conflict are very real, but the temptation to pursue additional hierarchical authority to deal with these problems must be resisted. In highly complex and interdependent situations, management based on hierarchical monitoring and control often sets in motion a downward spiral of minimal compliance and declining performance. Multi-organizational coordination that relies heavily on formal mechanisms enforced by a central unit is rarely successful. A wide range of experience shows that formal and centralized coordination creates excessively complicated procedural requirements and slow response (see Chisholm 1989, Peters 1998). In these situations frustrated managers often seek to circumvent formal coordination channels, leading to the development of parallel communication channels, evasion of official procedures, pro forma fulfillment of formal requirements, and so on.

Alternatively, coordination solutions can sometimes emerge from a process in which implementation actors can address how to develop mutually beneficial relationships, for example, in start-up workshops or annual review sessions (see Chapter 9). In essence this means negotiation and bargaining so that all parties feel that they gain something (win-win) rather than issuing top-down directives. This connects to the development of the "rules of the game" in that effective coordination is based more on principles of joint benefits and value-added than on negative sanctions and hierarchical policing. A key feature of successful multi-actor policy implementation networks is that they provide a way of processing differing views and dissent, articulating points of agreement and airing the rationale for policy decisions, and jointly developing management strategies (see Lowndes and Skelcher 1998).

An example of how win-win strategies for interorganizational coordination can work comes from monitoring and evaluation (M&E) systems. Most policy reforms contain an M&E component, often assigned to a specialized unit. The traditional approach is for the M&E unit to develop the system and then issue reporting instructions to implementation partners on what information is required and when it must be submitted. This kind of top-down, one-way information-sharing tends to generate resistance on the part of those whose collaboration is required to collect, prepare, and submit the information. It also can lead to a heavy burden of information collection at the field level; resentment by field staff, who may not see the information collection task as important to their work; and information overload at the higher levels. For instance, this situation occurred at the start of Madagascar's NEAP, where the M&E design required the NGOs working at the local level to provide huge amounts of reporting information to central authorities, little of which ever made its way back out to the field. Eventually the NGOs complained and the system was modified.

A win-win approach to M&E development, which is the norm among information system specialists, focuses on participatory system development and operation, so that all implementors have a role in deciding on the system and in assuring that it fits their needs and constraints. The result is a system in which all parties agree on what needs to be done for coordination (information-sharing) and perceive that they will benefit from the system. As discussed in more detail in Chapter 12, the policy-monitoring system should not overshadow or excessively constrain the business of carrying out the reform components that will lead to results and impacts for policy beneficiaries.

Shorten Policy Implementation Planning Horizons

As we have noted, one of the key characteristics of policy change is that it is long term. Policy targets usually take years to achieve, and given the complexity and uncertainty of implementation environments, it is difficult to plot in advance a clear course toward success. Indeed, this is one of the reasons that the strategic management approach presented in Chapter 2 is helpful. However, in many countries bureaucratic requirements for excessively detailed and long-term action plans, some of which derive from national policy and planning frameworks and some from international donor requirements, can lead policy managers to prepare blueprints for reform (Brinkerhoff 1991). Over time, these blueprints will become less and less accurate guides for action, and the gap between plan and reality will begin to pinch implementation partners. In terms of coordination, actors begin to lose their margin for flexibility and responsiveness as they are pushed to meet the planned targets while coping with changed circumstances.

Experience shows that shorter planning horizons strengthen flexibility and potential for adaptation to uncertain and changing conditions, and result in a better fit with the challenges of the policy implementation. Further, they can help deal with some of the threats to coordination. Actors are more inclined to collaborate if they are not held to what often seem to be increasingly unrealistic planning time frames. Planning in smaller increments can increase task consensus by making it easier to agree on what to do in the short term, subject to refinement based on the lessons of experience. The increased ability to fine-tune activities in the short term makes achievement of long-term policy reforms more likely.

Particularly in policy areas in which solutions to problems are unknown and uncertain and depend upon a high degree of experimentation and learning among a large number of stakeholders, a shorter planning cycle and looser coordination can speed up the learning and lead to better results. This is one of the lessons of experience with environment and natural resources policy (see Chapter 4, Brinkerhoff 1999b, Western and Wright 1994). It is an emerging lesson for HIV/AIDS policy as well. Countries around the world are experimenting with multi-sectoral policies and programs to discover the most effective blend of social mobilization, prevention and treatment, and protection for vulnerable groups (see, for example, Stover and Johnston 1999, USAID 1999).

COORDINATION VENUES FOR POLICY IMPLEMENTATION

In the multi-actor, nobody-in-charge world of policy implementation, reformers need to facilitate linkages but not rely solely on hierarchy or formal authority to get the coordination job done, whether it is information-sharing, resource-sharing, or joint action. What kinds of venues are available that can help different actors to work together? Building on Bryson and Crosby (1992), we see four options on the interorganizational "landscape." Each one can serve useful functions in leading and managing policy reform in a coordinated way. The options can be classified as follows:

- *Forums*. These are events such as round tables, discussion or planning meetings, and policy seminars.[4] Forums exchange information and opinion, promote dialogue, identify issues, foster analysis, and debate (previous or current) policy results. In the policy process, forums create shared understanding and agreement through discussion, debate, and deliberation. They are useful for shaping issue agendas that lead to policy decisions, developing legitimacy for new policies, and building constituencies for support. They are often broadly participatory, assembling government officials, politicians, and members of civil society to air their views on the impact of current policies or the desired shape of future policies. Forums may take many forms including town meetings, seminars, ad hoc dialogues, conferences, and other assemblies.
- *Arenas*. These are venues where policy decisions are made and decisions about allocation of resources taken. They differ from forums in that at least one of the actors involved has the power and authority to make binding decisions. Policy arenas can include such entities as executive cabinets, legislative public hearings, parliamentary committees, regional or local governing bodies (for example, municipal councils), and/or inter-ministerial commissions. They can also include less formal entities vested with decision-making authority and control over resources, such as temporary task forces.
- *Agencies*. These are the entities charged with taking policy implementation actions. They may include line ministries, special commissions, NGOs, community groups, or private sector firms. All have some operational role in transforming policy decisions into action. Their organizational structures, procedures, cultures, and past experience strongly influence how they will operate in a multi-actor setting.
- *Courts*. These are venues for judging and evaluating policies and/or implementation actions in relation to laws, agreed-upon rules, planned outcomes, and/or impacts. As part of their function they include settling disputes. While formal courts, such as supreme courts, tribunals, and so on immediately come to mind, other entities can serve "court" functions. These include public agencies charged with accountability mandates, such as auditing agencies, regulatory bodies, or parliamentary account committees. "Courts" may also be embodied in civil society watchdog organizations or professional associations with licensing and sanctioning authority. Internally, implementing organizations may fulfill a "court" role through their M&E functions.

Why should policy managers pay attention to the distinctions among these structures and venues? The reason is that each of them is directly related to one or more of the policy implementation tasks outlined in Chapter 2. As we discussed there, successful implementation depends upon addressing each of the implementation tasks. Forums are the primary venues for policy legitimization and constituency building and are essential for the orchestration of participatory policy implementation (see Chapter 3). Arenas can also contribute to constituency building but are central to decisions regarding resource mobilization and allocation and to developing strategies for mobilizing action. For example, as the Sahelian livestock trade policy case in Chapter 4 illustrates, the national coordinating committees served as arenas for the governmental and private sector actors to make decisions about resources, responsibilities, and actions.

Agencies are directly concerned with the implementation tasks of resource allocation and mobilization, organizational design and structuring, and mobilizing actions and actually carrying them out. To a lesser extent agencies can serve constituency building and legitimization functions, particularly with their staff, who need to be committed to the policy change (recall the Malian foresters). As the previous discussion in this chapter makes clear, implementing agencies will need to make adjustments in how they operate in order to coordinate with other implementation actors. To function effectively they need to become more outwardly focused, more open to external input, more collaborative, and less control oriented. When existing formal organizations are given responsibility for reform actions, the challenge is often for them to become less hierarchical and inward looking (see Box 2.1 on strategic management). In many cases meeting this challenge means a significant departure from prior mission, values, procedures, and processes.

"Courts" play a vital role in monitoring the effectiveness of implementation strategies and actions, the sixth task in the policy implementation task framework. This means looking at "due process" as well as outcomes and impacts. "Courts" play a vital role in assuring that policy objectives are achieved and in detecting and correcting errors. Here they can support the implementation task of policy monitoring. They can be particularly useful in responding to the demands of losers or those negatively affected by the policy change process. These venues contribute to making coordination among implementation actors more effective by providing space for negotiation and arbitration of disputes (see Chapter 11). As part of this contribution they will adjudicate decisions about resources and allocation of implementation functions among the actors involved. In this way, "courts" are useful to the implementation tasks of resource mobilization and organizational design.

Further, related to democratic governance, "courts" are critical to accountability, transparency, and responsiveness to citizens. One of the dilemmas of coordinated policy implementation is the difficulty in determining who did what and in holding them accountable (Peters 1998). "Courts" of both the formal and informal varieties can be useful to sort out responsibility, enforce accountability, and resolve conflicts.

Box 5.1 contains a set of questions policy managers can use to review the status, appropriateness, and quality of the various venues that are, or could be, available for policy implementation. These questions are not intended to suggest that managers need to undertake system-wide institutional analysis and reform in order to proceed with implementation. Rather, the questions can serve as a guide for selecting where to begin, if it appears that problems with interorganizational venues will impede coordination. The answers to the questions can serve as input to the implementation task of organizational design (see Chapter 2).

Box 5.1 Reviewing Policy Coordination Venues

For each category of policy coordination venues (forums, arenas, agencies, and "courts"), the following questions will assist policy reformers to assess their interorganizational landscapes.

1. Does the venue have credibility in the eyes of key officials and policymakers?

2. Do stakeholders in the private sector and civil society see the venue as legitimate and appropriate? Is there significant divergence of opinion among the stakeholders?

3. Does the venue have a clear mandate to address the policy issue in question?

4. Do those who exercise functions within the venue have the capacity, motivation, and resources to take the actions necessary to deal with the policy issue?

5. How does the venue rate in terms of accessibility, accountability, and transparency? Do some stakeholders dominate the venue, and are others excluded?

6. If the answers to these questions indicate problems, what steps might be taken to improve the situation?

In the next sections we look at some examples of these multi-actor coordination venues, drawn mainly from IPC's experience. These cases clarify how forums, arenas, agencies, and "courts" have worked on the ground.

REFORMING TRANSPORTATION AND COMMUNICATIONS POLICY IN SOUTHERN AFRICA: REGIONAL FORUMS FOR POLICY DIALOGUE

In 1994 the Southern Africa Transport and Communications Council (SATCC) was charged with the development of regional protocols that would harmonize the conflicting and disjointed policy and regulatory frameworks affecting roads, ports, air transport, customs, meteorology, postal service, and telecommunications (see Miller and Billings 1995). SATCC's governing body, the Southern Africa Development Council (SADC), recognized the detrimental impact on economic activity of the hodge-podge of policies, rules, and regulations of its member states. Previous efforts at reform had taken a technocratic approach, in which SATCC sector specialists assembled proposals for changes and passed these to SADC to be voted on. But member states consistently failed to approve them. The SATCC director discovered that one of the main reasons for failure to make progress was that the constituencies in the region most affected by the regulatory chaos were disorganized and did not communicate their concerns to their national representatives to SADC. The director decided that the solution lay not in keeping the reform effort within the organizational boundaries of his council and SADC, but in bringing together technical specialists, national and regional policymakers, and the groups in the member states with roles in these transportation and communication sub-sectors. This included both public officials and members of the private sector, for example, truckers associations, customs officials, shipping agents, air-traffic controllers, postal workers, and so on.

He wanted to build a public-private constituency for uniformity and harmonization of regulations affecting economic activity that would reach agreement on proposals for what changes were needed and that would coalesce into an interest group in support of reform. A forum was needed that brought the stakeholders together at both the national and regional levels for dialogue, discussion, consensus, and the formulation of draft protocols. SATCC, with some technical assistance from IPC, designed a highly consultative process to serve as this forum.

The process consisted of three major consultation venues designed to develop shared understanding of the issues and support for change: (1) regional consultations (1 to 1.5 days each) with representatives from each of the SADC member countries held for each of the seven sub-sectors to determine a list of issues to be treated by the protocols; (2) half-day national stakeholder consultations for each of the sub-sectors in each country; and (3) a final, three-day omnibus session for each of the sub-sectors with the participation of designated, official representatives from each country. All these events took place in the first seven months of 1995, organized and managed by a team within SATCC. Interest in the various forums was high, and the management team could not accommodate all the people who wanted to participate—eloquent testimony to the value stakeholders saw in the process. Local media reported on several of the national workshops, but the most intense coverage was devoted to the omnibus session held in July in Lusaka, Zambia. In all, fourteen participatory forums were organized with approximately two thousand people engaged in the process.

From the dialogue, debate, and deliberation that culminated in the Lusaka forum emerged consensus on a framework for each of the sub-sectors. A working group then used that framework to develop draft protocols by September 1995, which were then transmitted to SADC. The process mobilized a significant constituency for policy change. This mobilization of support created a burden of accountability for SATCC, and then SADC, to develop and ratify the protocols. SADC voted approval of the protocols the following year, 1996.

ECONOMIC POLICY IMPLEMENTATION IN BOLIVIA AND HONDURAS: AD HOC ARENAS FOR INTERORGANIZATIONAL COORDINATION

Both Bolivia and Honduras underwent structural adjustment in the 1980s and early 1990s. With advice and funding from the World Bank and International Monetary Fund, these countries pursued macroeconomic reforms, plus a sequence of financial sector restructuring, public sector downsizing, and privatization. Reform implementation called for close coordination among those government actors with key roles in economic management, but few arenas existed to bring these actors together to make critical decisions in a coordinated way.

In Bolivia a collaborative task force called the Macro-Group, composed of the planning minister, the finance minister, and the central bank president, was formed to oversee and monitor the implementation of economic reforms. In Honduras the president convened an ad hoc Economic Cabinet composed of four key ministries and the head of the central bank. Even though the cabinet did not have statutory authority, it served as the arena for decision-making regarding the design, implementation, and oversight of economic reforms.

Over the course of approximately ten to twelve years, these two ad hoc arenas successfully integrated national macroeconomic management across multiple agencies. While these entities had no statutory authority to make decisions or to implement policy, they had legitimacy and the collective authority of the participating ministers and senior officials to take action based on the agreements made among the actors. They were able to unblock the inertia caused by recalcitrant bureaucrats in their respective ministries, resolve "turf" issues, and provide support to the formation and realignment of national coalitions favoring policy change. These arenas were instrumental in reestablishing national and international trust and credibility regarding the Bolivian and Honduran governments' ability to manage economic reform. This was important for maintaining the support of the World Bank and the IMF, and for generating additional resources to support new policy initiatives once the adjustment cycle was completed. The donors came to consider the ad hoc organizations as the prime points of contact for policy dialogue and negotiation. Ad hoc groups such as these appear to work best as bridging mechanisms to provide the collective political will to move the policy change process forward. Because of the high degree of interaction and interdependence of economic policy reform decisions, it was extremely important to successful implementation that critical stakeholders be involved in decisions regarding policy formulation and implementation that affected their agencies.

In both Bolivia and Honduras these arenas served as coordinating structures that spanned a policy transition period when traditional decision-making processes and implementing agencies could not or would not take a leadership role. Eventually, however, mainstream government institutions began to adjust their mandates, organizational structures, and operating processes to fit the responsibilities for managing the new economic policies that emerged from the structural adjustment process. In the case of Bolivia, the Macro-Group was disbanded after a ten-year life span. In Honduras, on the other hand, the Economic Cabinet was eventually given statutory authority and continued to manage reforms even as the policy content of those reforms moved away from macroeconomic issues and into sectoral policy areas.

ZAMBIA'S CABINET OFFICE: AGENCY REDESIGN TO IMPROVE INTER-MINISTERIAL COORDINATION

When the Chiluba government came to power in October 1991, its new leaders took over the helm of a largely unfamiliar and unresponsive state bureaucracy. The president's cabinet ministers and advisors, who came from the private sector, soon discovered that business experience counted little in managing public agencies and in marshaling the support of their fragmented political coalition. It quickly became apparent that unless the top officials in the executive branch could do a better job of coordinating policy development and implementation, the Chiluba government's ability to deliver on its campaign promises of economic growth and improved service delivery would be seriously compromised. Discussions with USAID led to an organizational redesign effort to improve inter-ministerial coordination by the Cabinet Office, which took place over a five-year period from 1992 to 1997 (Garnett et al. 1997).

Redesign began with the creation of a Policy Analysis and Coordination Division (PACD) in the cabinet office. A structure was designed, staff profiles drafted, training needs identified, and recruitment undertaken. At the same time, an analysis of the existing policy management process was conducted to identify constraints and problems and to make some initial recommendations for change. As part of the PACD's start-up, a workshop convened the division's staff and other cabinet personnel to reach consensus on the mission and objectives of the new unit and to map out a plan for making the PACD operational. The division's responsibilities were to (1) analyze sectoral ministries' policy proposals submitted to the cabinet for consistency with government policies, (2) collaborate with ministries to improve the quality of their policy submissions, (3) serve as the secretariat for the cabinet (preparing minutes and transmitting policy decisions to implementors), (4) coordinate implementation of cabinet decisions across agency boundaries, (5) monitor implementation of cabinet decisions, and (6) facilitate solutions to inter-ministerial implementation problems.

The PACD then had to clarify its working relationships with entities outside of the cabinet office. This process involved facing the obstacles to coordination discussed above. Sectoral ministries resisted what they saw as the PACD's encroachment on their "turf," and actors argued over the specifics of coordination versus control. The PACD staff sought to build constituencies within the sectoral ministries for the division's mandate and to convince their collaborators that their facilitation of policy formulation and implementation represented value-added.

Gradually, over the next couple of years, the PACD developed reasonably good relationships with its sectoral partners. As a result of the experience gained in fulfilling its coordinating role, PACD staff saw the need to restructure the policy process and developed a set of recommended changes. In a workshop in early 1995 the PACD presented its recommendations to the president, cabinet ministers, and other senior officials. These were approved, with minor modifications, and were officially enacted in the form of a cabinet circular, which was sent to all permanent secretaries in the civil service. Several of the new practices related to coordination; these included the establishment of inter-ministerial committees to formulate policy proposals with membership drawn not just from government technocrats but including NGOs and community organizations. Another innovation was the creation of a new position in each ministry, a cabinet liaison officer, to serve as a point of contact to assure inter-agency collaboration.[5]

By the end of the agency redesign effort (September 1997), several positive results had emerged. First, the government defined a much more coherent national policy framework due to the increase in inter-ministerial cooperation. Second, the quality of policy proposals presented to and debated by the cabinet improved, leading to better policies with higher potential for successful implementation and impact. Third, the PACD succeeded in facilitating the policy process in ways that enhanced agreement on objectives and attention to achieving impacts. Fourth, cabinet meetings became much more efficient, focused, and shorter.

THE "COURT" OF PUBLIC OPINION:
THE PUBLIC AFFAIRS CENTRE IN BANGALORE, INDIA

Civil society watchdog organizations can usefully serve as "courts" in the sense that through the "court" of public opinion the information they share with policy stakeholders is used to enforce compliance and make adjustments in policies and programs. In this situation coordination is achieved because the overarching set of norms and rules embodied in democratic governance (especially those related to accountability and responsiveness) can lead public agencies to change their behaviors in response to the information shared.[6]

The Public Affairs Centre (PAC), a civil society organization established in 1994 in Bangalore, has developed and applied a "report card" methodology to monitoring citizen satisfaction with public services and policies based on perceptions of quality, efficiency, adequacy, and extent of corruption.[7] In 1999 PAC conducted a report card study in the city of Bangalore as a follow-up to its initial study, undertaken in 1994 (Paul and Sekhar 2000). After conducting the study, PAC first presented report cards to four of the key service providers (telecommunications, water, electricity, and the municipal government) to solicit initial reactions. The agencies did not dispute the findings, which were relatively negative, but defended themselves by citing a variety of constraints. After these initial meetings PAC circulated its report to all public agencies and senior state government officials, and held a press conference for the media, which gave the results wide coverage.

PAC then organized a two-phased workshop for senior policymakers, officials from the agencies involved, and members of the public. The first workshop was limited to public sector policy and implementation actors, and facilitated exchange and learning among them to review what some of the more responsive agencies were doing to address the criticisms. For example, the worst-rated agency—the Bangalore Development Authority (BDA)—reviewed its internal systems for service delivery, introduced training for junior staff, and along with the Bangalore Municipal Corporation, created a joint forum of NGOs and public agencies to consult on solving high-priority problems such as waste management. The Karnataka Electricity Board formalized periodic dialogues with resident associations to garner feedback from users.

The second workshop clearly reflected the "court" function of the report cards in that it consisted of an exercise in accountability in which the heads of the various agencies answered questions from NGOs and citizens' groups on what steps were being proposed to improve the quality, efficiency and adequacy of their services. One outcome was that the new chief minister of Karnataka formed the Bangalore Agenda Task Force, consisting of prominent city residents, to come up with suggestions to improve the city's quality of services and infrastructure. This was the first time a chief minister responded to persistent citizen demands, expressed through the report cards, the media, and NGOs, to push service providers to perform better and in a more accountable manner. A couple of results followed relatively quickly. First, agencies went through an exercise of developing citizen charters to provide a framework for accountability. A second result was the introduction of a system to self-assess property taxes, which brought transparency, speed, and simplicity to an otherwise corrupt and arbitrary process.

COORDINATION AND DEMOCRATIC GOVERNANCE

Systems of democratic governance and public sector management reform highlight the importance of interorganizational coordination. Participation by policy stakeholders in all phases of the policy process, not implementation alone, means that policymakers and implementors must pay attention to many groups and interests (Chapter 3). Democratic systems open the process up and create pressures and expectations for accountability, transparency, and responsiveness, as well as results. These forces bring the political aspects of coordination to the fore and intertwine them with coordination's managerial dimensions, sometimes pulling policy managers in opposite directions and imposing high transactions costs.

The coordination discussion in this chapter and the related review of partnerships in the previous one have sought to provide some guidance and lessons regarding how to cope with the demands of coordinated policy implementation. We have stressed the necessity of trying to orchestrate the efforts of these multi-actor endeavors to achieve policy results through management strategies that are cooperative rather than hierarchical, participatory rather than closed, and strategic rather than reactive. The lure of top-down, hierarchical solutions can be strong, and while hierarchy can be an appropriate solution in some situations, too often it is the only option that policy managers consider. Sometimes it seems that inclusive and participatory policy management is more about making noise than making progress. However, noise can contribute to progress. Creating legitimacy and building constituencies to move implementation forward are tasks that are inherently noisy. Coordination builds on noise. Working through the noise can be an upfront investment at the start of policy implementation that can smooth the path toward results later on down the road. Multiple actors working together in policy implementation networks and partnerships may produce overlap, duplication, and argument over who does what, but the clamor signifies vitality to be capitalized on, not eliminated (see Landau 1991). How coordination is designed and managed, and the incentives for cooperation or conflict that emerge, are key determinants of whether policy implementation actors experience the linkages among each other as lifelines or shackles.

NOTES

1. Portions of this chapter draw on Brinkerhoff (1996a).

2. The rankings in the table represent generalizations from the Implementing Policy Change Project's experience and the coordination and interorganizational literature (see, for example, Alexander 1995, Alter and Hage 1993, Bardach 1998). For particular situations, of course, exceptions are possible.

3. Some of these rules are set by the institutional context within which policy managers operate. See Ostrom (1990) and Ostrom et al. (1993).

4. We concentrate on what Bryson and Crosby (1992, 92) call place-specific forums. They also identify non–place-specific forums, such as newspapers, journals, television, and radio. As many have noted, free and open media are important for democratic governance.

5. Technical assistance activities that helped the PACD to develop improved practices, new skills, and greater capacity included the following: a study of cabinet office experience from other countries, study tours to Canada and Australia for several staff, and training in policy analysis and the preparation of cabinet memoranda. Besides Garnett et al. (1997), see Rielly (1994), and Bratton et al. (1998).

6. Achieving coordination through information exchange illustrates how implementation networks function in ways analogous to how markets operate: information on price, availability, and quality is used by consumers and producers in their transactions. In the literature on policy coordination and multi-actor networks the market metaphor is contrasted with hierarchy as an alternative approach to organizing multi-actor coordination (see, for example, Thompson et al. 1991, Lowndes and Skelcher 1998).

7. See the Public Affairs Centre's website at <www. pacindia.org>. Bangalore is the capital of the state of Karnataka, with an approximate population of 5 million, and a major industrial and high-technology center.

II

A TOOL KIT
FOR POLICY REFORMERS
AND STRATEGIC MANAGERS

6

Stakeholder Analysis

The recognition of the key role played by stakeholders in the determination of a policy, its implementation, and outcomes has made stakeholder analysis a vital tool for policy managers. Stakeholder analysis is designed to assist policy managers in identifying those interests that should be taken into account when making a decision. To that end, stakeholder analysis is directed at assessing the nature of a policy's constituents, their interests, their expectations, the strength or intensity of their interest in the issue, and the resources that they can bring to bear on the outcomes of a policy change. Stakeholder analysis is useful both when policies are being formulated and when they are being implemented. At the formulation stage it helps to ensure that policies are shaped in ways that improve their prospects for adoption and implementation. And during the implementation stage the tool helps build an appreciation of the relative importance of different groups and the role each might play in the implementation process. This chapter presents a simple methodology to assess the array of stakeholders that may be encountered in any policy implementation effort.

WHAT IS A STAKEHOLDER?

A stakeholder is defined as an individual or group that makes a difference, or that can affect or be affected by the achievement of the organization's objectives (see Freeman 1984, Mitroff 1983, Mitchell et al. 1997). Clearly these are broad criteria, capable of including nearly any group touched in even the most minor way. Certain approaches to stakeholder analysis argue that all those affected by a policy, even potentially, should be included in a stakeholder analysis. While perhaps desirable, such inclusive approaches are not very practical. To be useful, stakeholder analysis must indicate why interests should be taken into account. How do we know when an actor's interests should be given serious consideration?

There are at least three criteria that can be used to determine the relative importance of a stakeholder. First, if an actor or group is in a position to damage or weaken the authority or political support for decision-makers or their organizations, it needs to be considered. For instance, industrial producers in many developing countries are frequently opposed to reforms to facilitate a more export-driven economy. Since these stakeholders are often the most powerful economically, they are generally in a position to weaken political authority should they actively oppose the policy reform (see, for example, Haggard and Webb 1994, Alesina and Drazen 1991).

Second, if the group's presence and/or support provides a net benefit, strengthens implementing agencies, and enhances decision-makers' authority (and capacity to secure compliance with decisions), then it should be given close consideration. For example, if a group can bring new resources or provide entry into a new market, such as associations of nontraditional exporters, it should be taken into account.

Third, if a group is capable of influencing the direction or mix of implementing organizations' activities, it needs to be counted as a stakeholder. Service users and consumers are important stakeholders of organizations charged with the delivery of public services. In industrialized nations, consumer interests are protected by laws, and these stakeholders can be mobilized through advocacy and consumer protection groups. Failure to take into account their interests can put policy managers in a precarious position.

Generally, stakeholder analysis focuses on two key elements. Groups or actors are analyzed in terms of (1) the interest they have in a particular issue, and (2) the quantity and types of resources they can mobilize to affect outcomes regarding that issue. The degree to which each of these elements is analyzed and weighted varies considerably depending upon the level of detail in the analysis. As a rule of thumb, only those groups with resources that they can mobilize and apply directly for or against an issue should be included. They are the groups with the potential to affect decisions or implementation outcomes. However, for poverty-focused reforms, gender policies, and policies such as those related to HIV/AIDS, it is important to recognize that critical stakeholders may be those without voice or resources to make their views and desires heard, for example, the poor, women, children, ethnic minorities, and so forth. Sometimes policy managers will need to make extra efforts to assure that their interests are accounted for.

WHEN TO CARRY OUT A STAKEHOLDER ANALYSIS

When should policy managers undertake stakeholder analysis? There are two points at which stakeholder analysis is critical. First, when the policy is being formulated—at the point when decisions are made that will influence who will be a winner and who will be a loser. The second point is in the formulation of a strategy for implementation. It is at this point that decisions become critical in terms of assuring alliances and support. A solid analysis of stakeholder expectations and a keen appreciation of the relative importance of different stakeholder groups can be key input for the design of strategies to handle certain groups, knowing what elements of the policy should be emphasized, what kinds of policy communication will work with which audiences, and how best to craft policy messages to assure future support.

Finally, managers need to pay attention to the balance between the level of effort devoted to the analysis and the utility the information. It can be tempting to devote too much time or too much credence to the analysis. Stakeholder analysis is only a tool, one that helps to understand better the field upon which policy change and the implementation of those changes will be played. It is not an end in itself.

CONDUCTING A STAKEHOLDER ANALYSIS

The approach to stakeholder analysis presented here employs a simple matrix in which information for each group is arrayed according to the group's interests, the type and level of resources it possesses, its capacity for mobilization or resources, and the group's position on the issue in question. The matrix provides a means for estimating the importance or potential impact of the various stakeholders' interest in a given issue or policy and thereby assists decision-makers or policy managers in their determination of which of those groups ought to be taken into account in the decision-making calculus (see Table 6.1).

As with other approaches, Table 6.1 summarizes stakeholders' interests and their positions on the issues (see Honadle and Cooper 1989, Brinkerhoff 1991). The first column (Group) of Table 6.1 presents a list of relevant stakeholders. Although a full listing of stakeholders would include any person or group affected by, or able to affect, a given policy, for purposes of this analysis stakeholders are considered relevant if and only if the group or actor has significant resources that can be applied for or against the implementation of the policy. Another way to set priorities among stakeholders is in terms of their power (ability to command compliance), legitimacy (extent to which the stakeholder's claims are seen as appropriate and proper), and urgency (the degree to which the stakeholder's claims call for immediate action) (Mitchell et al. 1997). The best way to develop a first draft of this list is usually in a brainstorming session with six to ten knowledgeable practitioners. It is not unusual for such brainstorming sessions to identify twenty or thirty significant stakeholders.

This preliminary list is then evaluated and used as a point of departure for the analysis.

Table 6.1 Stakeholder Analysis Matrix

Group	Group's interest in issue	Resources available	Resource mobilization capacity	Position on issue
Name of group	Estimate of the level of interest of the group in the issue (e.g., high to low). It is also useful to indicate exactly what those interests are.	Summary of resources held by group or to which it has access. (These may include financial, information, status, legitimacy, coercion.) Include specifics.	Estimate of which and how easily group can mobilize resources in pursuit of objectives. (May be defined as high to low or may use more quantitative indicators such as +5 to -5.)	Estimate of the group's position on the issue. (E.g., pro or con, or positive to negative, or nominal quantitative measures such as +3 to -3.)

The second column (Group's interest in the issue) lists, for each stakeholder, those interests that will be affected by the policy or decision to be taken. What are the group's specific interests in the policy? The analyst should be careful to select only those two or three interests and/or expectations that are most important. The relative level or intensity of interest in each issue should also be noted to signal the relative priority of the issue for the group. Relative importance or priority has implications for what the group is willing to invest with respect to support or opposition to the issue. Although sophisticated means of specifying intensity of interest may be used, a simple indication of high, medium, or low intensity will usually suffice.

In the third column (Resources available) are noted those resources that the group possesses that could be brought to bear in the policy implementation process. Generally, the greater the level of resources a particular stakeholder can mobilize, the greater its relative influence will be on policy processes and outcomes. Close and systematic attention to the estimation of resources and the capacity of the group to bring those resources to bear on a particular policy or issue will allow policy managers to separate the important from the less critical stakeholders.

Resources may be classed into five types: financial or material resources, access to or control over vital or important information, status or social position, legitimacy, and coercion. In trying to determine economic or material resources, managers might ask if the group has the financial resources to mount a lobbying or advocacy program in favor of or against the policy. Does the group have influence over some prominent sector of the economy, and would its efforts either in favor of, or opposed to, the policy make a difference in implementation progress? Can the group offer some special knowledge or information? Does it have information critical to the formulation or implementation of policy decisions? Expertise in a new policy area can be a highly valuable commodity.

The prestige or status that a particular stakeholder can offer may be critical to assure that the policy or decision receives adequate support. Would a stakeholder's status and presence on one side of the policy issue be key to its implementation? For instance, the position of physicians on health sector reform is critical because of the high status and respect accorded them in most countries. At the same time, low social status can offset the value of other resources. For example, many poverty-focused policies are supported by the poor, but their marginalized and politically weak status means that they may not be able to serve as effective advocates for change within a country's political system (see Robb 1999). Legitimacy is a stakeholder resource that can provide policy implementors with important support to move ahead with reform (see Chapter 2 and the discussion of the implementation task framework). Conversely, lack of legitimacy can be harmful. In a parliamentary democracy, for example, if the prime minister loses the legitimacy accorded by his party (through a no-confidence vote), the government will be obliged to resign.

Finally, coercive action is a resource that, if controlled and directed, can be an important asset to a stakeholder. A labor union will typically use the threat of a strike to achieve its demands, coercing the employer by shutting down operations of the organization. Marginalized urban dwellers can use similar tactics by blocking streets and disrupting services to achieve certain demands. Urban transport owners may halt their services to force authorization of a fare hike or to protest increases in gasoline prices. However, when violence is spontaneous or cannot be controlled and directed, it is not a resource.

In the fourth column (Resource mobilization capacity), analysts should note the ease and speed with which the group can mobilize and deploy its resources. Just having resources is not enough. It is important to be able to mobilize or use those resources opportunely. Resources that can be mobilized quickly are advantageous if the issue has immediacy, but less so if the impact is further in the future. If the group cannot mobilize or make effective use of its resources, then they are not resources in any meaningful sense. If a group cannot produce a study that will sway decision-makers to its point of view, its informational resource is thereby limited. For example, if a business association is unable to raise funds for a media campaign to promote its interests, the fact that the association represents some of the country's most powerful economic interests means little. Analysts should note the group's capacity to mobilize, but also note limitations on the use of the resources at the group's disposal.

Finally, in column 5 (Position on issue), the group's position on the issue should be examined and noted. Judgment should be more discrete than a simple for or against. It should give an indication of the relative strength of the group's support or opposition to the issue. If a group is barely in favor of an issue, a convincing argument by an opposition viewpoint could be enough to change its position. A simple nominal scale of –3 to +3 can often suffice to show relative support or opposition.

While stakeholder analysis is certainly helpful to gain a better understanding of the interests and resources of the important players in policy decision-making and implementation, it is even more valuable when used in conjunction with other analytic tools such as political mapping or force-field analysis (see Chapter 8). With political mapping, stakeholder analysis helps to define the degree and relative position of support as well as comparative importance or salience of a political group on a particular issue. In the case of force-field analysis, it helps clarify a group's position on the policy at hand.

DATA GATHERING FOR STAKEHOLDER ANALYSIS

Depending on policy managers' needs and the importance of the issue, simple to very sophisticated (and expensive) strategies can be employed for collecting information on stakeholders. As with any analytic tool, the value of a stakeholder analysis lies in the quality of the data that feed into its preparation. The place to start is with written sources on the country's political, economic, and institutional situation. These sources can provide a significant amount of background information that will help to guide the search for key informants and will orient analysts to the basic sociopolitical dynamics. This information can be complemented by experts at local universities and think tanks or embassy staff. Initial data gathering should allow analysts to formulate some tentative hypotheses regarding the array of stakeholders and their relative importance for the policy issue in question.

Once in the field analysts should seek out key informants from as wide a range as feasible, since many informants will have particular agendas they wish to promote. Key informants can include journalists and other members of the media, church leaders, business groups, legislators, staff of executive agencies, members of political parties, donor agency staff, labor leaders, academics, consultants, NGOs and civil society groups, labor leaders, military officials, and so on. The wide range of informants will allow analysts to cross-check data and identify common perceptions, which increase confidence in the accuracy of the information collected.

Although personal interviews are the standard method of obtaining information, other techniques can be used. We have used informal focus groups and workshops both to collect information and to use as sounding boards for testing hypotheses. Assembling stakeholder analysis teams that pair outside experts with knowledgeable locals can work well.

Another critical data gathering issue concerns framing the interview questions. Unless the policy issue is presented in sufficiently precise terms to allow informants to identify where their interests lie, the analysis risks being too general and therefore less useful for designing and implementing policy reforms. In common with all forms of social research, how the questions are formed has an impact on the answers received (see, for example, Miles and Huberman 1994).

STAKEHOLDER ANALYSIS
FOR CENTRAL BANK REFORM IN HONDURAS

To illustrate how the process works, the following section presents an example of a stakeholder analysis carried out by an IPC team in Honduras in 1992 to assess the environment for increased financial and political independence for the central bank (BCH). The purpose of the exercise was to gauge the level and strength of support and opposition to proposed reforms in the financial system to develop a strategy for their initiation and implementation.

Greater independence and autonomy for the BCH was considered quite sensitive, because it had the potential to shift the balance of influence and power in economic policymaking. Compared to most central banks in Latin America, the BCH had little autonomy and independence. Directors of the BCH were appointed and removed at the disposition of the president. Private sector members of the BCH board of directors represented interests of the commercial banking sector and therefore presented potential for conflicts of interest. A principal concern was the removal of "politics" from the BCH through overlapping terms for board directors and the bank's president.

Banking sector opinion was divided on increased autonomy. Larger or distressed commercial banks were not anxious to alter the status quo, given the strong influence they exercised on the BCH board of directors.

Conversely, new entrants (mostly foreign banks) were interested in changing the "rules of the game" to give them a more competitive position—
and thus favored a more independent BCH. Medium-sized and smaller
banks lacking the influence of the larger banks also stood to gain from a
more independent BCH. Actors not allied with the larger banking groups
had the potential to benefit from a more level playing field and independence of the central bank. Stakeholders such as finance and credit card
companies operating at the margin of the formal banking sector had little
to gain by a stronger and more independent BCH.

Apart from the private banking sector there were several actors with a
positive interest in a more independent central bank. The president of
the bank favored more autonomy, since it would energize the modernization process. The superintendent of banks also favored greater independence to strengthen his own authority. Since the BCH's board would be
restructured and less subject to political influence, the opinions of its
members were mixed. Public sector members were more supportive than
private sector members. Some BCH staff viewed any change with reluctance, believing that change would alter the current balance of resources
and benefits. However, there were those in management and staff who
saw opportunities to be provided by more political and financial independence. The finance ministry was opposed, since it viewed the BCH as too
powerful and uncontrollable. There were apprehensions that greater independence might mean less access to resources and less interest on the
part of the bank in maintaining a constructive role in solving the
government's financial problems. Consumers generally favored a stronger and more independent BCH that could provide a more level playing
field in the banking system and thereby assure greater access to credit.
They also felt that a more independent BCH would be better positioned
to break concentrations of credit access and limit the problem of restricted
circulation of money. Private sector organizations, such as chambers of
commerce and industry and the banking association, supported greater
independence, but the strength of this support was tempered by the mixed
interests represented in each organization. These saw greater independence as a means of limiting the influences on the BCH and of providing
a more level playing field. Opposition to the reform was centered mainly
in those favored by the status quo.

The stakeholder matrix (Table 6.2) presents a summary of the stakeholders just described. Although support and opposition were divided, a
brief review of the table shows that the forces for more independence for
the BCH had a numerical majority. In politics, however, mere numerical
strength is often insufficient. What counts is the quality of support: What
does the stakeholder have to offer the policymaker? Does the stakeholder
have certain resources that will make the group a valuable ally or more

powerful opponent? By looking at the data in Table 6.2, it can be seen clearly that factors other than the stakeholder's position (interests, resources, capacity to mobilize resources) can be more determinant.

Table 6.2 indicates that opposition actors, though numerically fewer, were more powerful and influential in terms of resources and the capacity to mobilize those resources than those supporting greater independence. The quality of support, for the most part, was not high. The president of the BCH, while supportive, was reluctant to play an active role in advancing the issue of greater independence. Management of the bank, while supportive, was only lukewarm. The finance minister was opposed to increasing BCH independence. The table also reveals that other groups, particularly those in support, were ill-equipped to influence policy outcomes effectively. Faced with a well-mobilized opposition such as the large banks, the level of support for the measure in question dropped away quickly. The table shows that one of the most powerful actors (large banks and the most resource-endowed actors outside government) were solidly opposed to expansion of independence of the BCH, since it enjoyed considerable influence under the status quo. At the same time, several other prominent actors (the BCH board, the finance minister, and the congress) were either opposed or indifferent. Since they figured prominently in policy regarding the BCH, their support was vital. Its absence condemned the initiative to failure.

CONCLUSION

Stakeholder analysis should not be viewed as a "one-shot" tool to be applied at the outset of policy implementation and then not used again. As noted throughout this book, policy implementation is a long-term process. Even in a relatively stable society, stakeholder coalitions will shift over time; support and opposition will wax and wane as a function of changing interests, relative shifts in power among social groups, increases in capacity, perception of policy success, and so on. It would be imprudent for policy managers to check the financial health of their agencies only every three or four years. It would be equally unwise to check on the views of key supporters and opponents of policy change on a similar schedule. In much the same way that accounting tools are designed to allow managers to track financial status, the iterative application of stakeholder analysis will help managers to track shifting stakeholder interests and coalitions and adapt their policy implementation strategies to increase the chances of building support for reform.

Table 6.2 Stakeholder Analysis: Financial and Political Independence for the Honduras Central Bank

Group	Interest in issue	Resources available	Capacity to mobilize resources	Position on issue (+3 to -3)
Large banks	Maintain influence in central bank board decisions.	Economic power, high political influence. Intelligence, access.	Very high	-3
Foreign banks	Level playing field. Objective central bank decisions.	Linkages with outside banks. Donor access.	Very low	+2
Other banks	Avoid greater control by central bank. Loose compliance.	Moderate economic strength. Low political influence.	Low	+1
Finance companies	Flexibility in system. Maintain status quo to keep market niche.	Those associated with large banks have political influence, others few resources.	Very low	-2
Bank associations	Level playing field. Focus on central bank functions.	Weak organization, studies/information capacity. Internal conflict.	Low	+1
Pension funds	Maximum assurance of level playing field. Competition.	Major economic resources. Political influence. Growing awareness of power.	High	+3
Credit cards	"Flexibility" in system. Status quo.	Economic resources information?	Very low	-1
President central bank	More authority and independence, focus on central bank tasks. Losing interest in issues.	High status, political influence. Economic policy coordinator.	Medium to low	+3

Stakeholder	Objectives	Characteristics	Influence	Score
Management central bank	More authority and power to enforce. Maintain influence.	Knowledge of financial system, bureaucratic strength.	Low	+2
Board central bank	Maintain political influence, power.	Political influence limited by mixed organization. Final authority on central bank policy.	Medium	-1
Superintendent of Banks	More independence and power to enforce banking rules.	Dependent on central bank, subject to board decision-making.	Low	+3
Minister of Finance	Maintain access to cheap funding for fiscal deficit.	Strong political influence with president and donors. Analysis unit.	High	-1
Congress	Maintain political control in defining rules.	Legislative authority. Weakening government party discipline.	High	0
Chamber of Commerce	Level playing field but political influence on board.	Moderate influence studies capacity. Problem of management internal conflict.	Low	+2
Chamber of Industry	Level playing field but maintain influence on board of central bank.	Major consumer of credit. Moderate political influence.	Low	+2
Donors	Level playing field. Greater independence for central bank to implement policy changes.	Resources "carrot," disbursement "stick."	Low	+3

Source: Crosby and Gonzalez 1992.

7

Policy Characteristics Analysis

Policy reformers need to understand the nature of the policies they are implementing. Understanding the context of the new policy and how it alters the status quo is an important step in managing policy implementation strategically. Policy characteristics analysis is a useful tool to help reformers to better understand the dimensions and dynamics of the policy, where it came from, and where support and opposition are likely to be strongest.

Policy characteristics analysis may be used as a first step in developing an implementation strategy by dissecting the policy and the environment in which it operates. The purpose of policy characteristics analysis is to provide a systematic understanding of the policy that can carry over into more detailed appraisal, such as stakeholder analysis (see Chapter 6) or political mapping (Chapter 8), to identify mechanisms for mobilizing support or countering opposition. It is designed to help reform teams systematically think through these issues: what the policy is designed to do, the context in which the policy will be implemented, how the reactions of the public are likely to be manifest, and how consequential the changes for the bureaucracy are likely to be.

POLICY REFORM AND POLITICS

As we have stressed throughout this book, the process of policy change is profoundly political, and the characteristics of the policy shape the politics and interest group dynamics that reformers will need to deal with (Lowi 1979). The key focus of policy characteristics analysis is to examine the distribution and time frame for benefits and costs. Here we build

The original version of this chapter was authored by Daniel Gustafson and Marcus Ingle and appeared in IPC's Technical Notes Series, No. 3 (1992).

on the thinking of numerous U.S. political scientists who have been concerned with what Rivlin (1971) calls "systematic thinking" on issues of power, politics, and policies (see Bardach 1977, Dahl 1961 and 1971, Lasswell 1958, Bachrach and Baratz 1970, Lindblom 1968, Lowi 1979, Pressman and Wildavsky 1973). These issues have also been the topic of a significant amount of political economic analysis in developing and transitioning countries (see, for example, Bates 1981, Bates and Collier 1992, Bardhan 1991, Meier 1991, DeJanvry et al. 1993, Robb 1999).

All policy reforms require paying attention both to the consequences they have on the public and to bureaucratic implementation constraints. Features of the policy influence the relative importance of each and the dynamics of the implementation process. Some policies, such as the elimination of subsidies, entail little administrative complexity, can be implemented quickly, and may generate considerable and immediately visible public reaction. Other policies, such as decentralization or privatization of state-owned enterprises, require a great deal of administrative time and effort, do not have an immediate impact on the public at large, and so produce different types of public and bureaucratic response. Poverty policies, for example, often involve mobilizing marginalized stakeholders to have a voice in the policy process, which can be a management-intensive effort.

A POLICY TYPOLOGY

Lowi's (1972) classification of public policy into four types helps in being more specific about allocation of policy benefits and costs:

- *Distributive:* These are policies that use public resources to produce goods and services that accrue to some subset of the population, often based on geography. Benefits are concentrated, but costs are broadly distributed. Examples are land policies, decisions on siting of infrastructure investment, subsidies, and tariffs.
- *Regulatory:* These are policies through which government shapes, monitors, and controls the actions and behaviors of private firms, nongovernmental entities, and/or individual citizens. In this category both benefits and costs are narrowly concentrated. Examples are pollution policies or banking regulations.
- *Redistributive:* These policies specify the use of public resources for various purposes, and benefits and costs are broadly distributed. This category of policies includes many that are the topic of intense public debate. Examples are tax policies, social safety nets, education policy, and so on.

- *Constitutive:* These are procedural and rule-making policies concerning the staffing and operations of government agencies, electoral procedures, and so on. Benefits tend to be broadly distributed and costs narrowly concentrated. Examples are civil service policies, rules governing political parties and elections, zoning regulations, and laws mandating public participation.

Grindle and Thomas (1991) add to this policy typology by including the following elements along with the distribution of costs and benefits: the policy's technological complexity, its administrative intensity, its short- or long-term impact, and the degree to which it encourages participation. The decade of experience of the Implementing Policy Change Project confirmed the importance of these policy implementation features.

Based on these characteristics, Thomas and Grindle present two broad scenarios of reaction to policy change. The first scenario is that of the "public arena," where the outcome of the reform is largely determined by societal reaction to efforts to change existing conditions among groups most affected by the reforms. The other scenario is that of the "bureaucratic arena," where the outcome of the reform is largely determined by how implementing agencies (public, private, nongovernmental), public officials, and administrative routines respond to the policy change.

Our version of policy characteristics analysis employs this framework and poses a series of questions that relate to the essence of the policy, who it will affect, and the nature of the changes introduced. Before turning to the specific questions, it is useful to examine an illustration of how policy characteristics affect implementation.

THE LESOTHO AGRICULTURAL POLICY SUPPORT PROGRAM

The Lesotho Agricultural Policy Support Program (LAPSP) provides a good example of how policy characteristics affect implementation. This USAID-supported program targeted policy reforms in the early 1990s in two areas: the implementation of a national grazing fee (and related livestock and range management issues), and increased involvement of the private sector in agricultural input distribution (principally through the divestiture of a government parastatal).

The idea of a national livestock grazing fee originated with a national livestock task force and was included in a national livestock plan. It had the support of the technical leadership of the Ministry of Agriculture, the agency primarily responsible for its implementation. The policy was designed to (a) reduce herd size and overgrazing as livestock owners begin to pay for the use of a common resource, (b) contribute to improved animal and range management practices, and (c) provide locally generated resources to be used by communities for their own development programs. The policy had far-reaching implications for the way natural pastures and livestock were managed and for the role of the local village development councils.

The grazing fee represented a new tax to be paid by everyone owning livestock—a very significant proportion of the population—although the highest cost was to be paid by those with the largest herds and hence the most political clout. The cost or the "pain" of the policy would be felt over the short term and would be highly visible to the public. The benefits of improved natural resource management would accrue over the long term and would be dispersed throughout society. Significant resistance was almost inevitable.

The agricultural input policy called for (a) elimination of a subsidy on fertilizer sold in government stores, (b) opening the distribution of agricultural inputs to the private sector, and (c) divestiture of the parastatal agricultural input distributor. With the completed removal of the subsidy and the opening of the input market to the private sector, attention was focused on the divestiture of Co-op Lesotho retail outlets. Although government had discussed these reforms for a long time, there was no "national agricultural input distribution plan" or unit identified with this policy, as there was in the livestock sector, and no preexisting group providing technical leadership. Without the external pressure from the IMF's structural adjustment program, the government would probably not have proposed divestiture at that time or at the pace envisioned.

The end of the government monopoly in the distribution of agricultural inputs had an immediate, visible impact. The benefits of the next steps of this policy, through the divestiture of Co-op Lesotho assets, were less pronounced. They depended on a series of factors relating to the economics of agricultural input use and to private sector decisions to invest in new retail outlets. Reduction of the government's budget deficit was an immediate benefit of this policy but did not stir intense public reaction. Although a small number of business people or member cooperatives gained from taking over the retail outlets, the short-term benefits of divestiture to the general public were not highly visible. Similarly, the cost of the reforms were, on the whole, not felt by society at large. Some farmers were disadvantaged by the loss of nearby agricultural inputs but no more so than in any normal business change. The losers in this reform were Co-op Lesotho employees and members of the bureaucracy.

Clearly, the nature of these two reforms was quite different; and the origins, visibility, and distribution of costs and benefits of the policies generated distinct dynamics of support and opposition. These differences can be clarified by examining each policy in terms of the policy characteristics questions listed below.

POLICY CHARACTERISTICS QUESTIONS

1. *What does the policy do?* For example, in the Lesotho case it institutes a national livestock grazing fee; it eliminates subsidies and divests state-owned agricultural input distribution functions and assets. In Lowi's typology the policy has both redistributive and regulatory features.

2. *What is the desired impact of the policy reform; what is it expected to accomplish or facilitate?* For example, the grazing fee alters the economics of stocking decisions and leads to reduced herd size and ultimately to improved natural pasture and livestock management as well as increased local control over local resources. The divestiture enhances private sector participation in the agricultural input market and thereby increases availability of inputs to farmers. It also eliminates a drain on scarce government resources.

3. *Where did the impetus for the policy come from? Why was it initiated?* In the Lesotho example the National Livestock Task Force was the force behind the policy, with additional impetus from the World Bank/IMF's structural adjustment package.

4. Related to this is the question, *Who decided to pursue the policy, how, and why?* Was the policy decision simply the adoption of donor recommendations or conditionality based on economic rationality criteria? Was it part of a bargaining process, and if so, who were the negotiators, and what were their positions? Was it decided on because of personal interest of influential individuals, and if so, are they still influential and involved in the process? Examining these questions helps gauge the political will behind adoption of the policy.

5. *What is the nature of the policy benefits, and to whom do they accrue?* There are likely to be gainers in both the public and bureaucratic arenas. Specific questions should examine characteristics of benefits for both these groups. Variables include:

   - visibility of the benefits,
   - their immediacy or time between implementation and impact,
   - extent of the improvement over the status quo,

- their degree of concentration,
- extent to which the benefits appear "zero-sum."

In the case of both the livestock grazing fee and the divestiture of Co-op Lesotho assets, many of the benefits appear to accrue over the long term, are not highly visible, and are dispersed in society. An example of the reverse situation would be higher milk support prices in the United States, which lead to important and noticeable income increases for the relatively small number of dairy farmers.

6. *What is the nature of the costs of the policy reform, and who bears them?* Since there are also likely to be losers in both the public and the bureaucracy, questions similar to those regarding benefits should examine the characteristics of the costs for both these groups, such as:

- visibility of the costs,
- their immediacy or time between implementation and impact,
- extent of the deterioration over the status quo—the degree of "pain,"
- their degree of concentration,
- extent to which costs are financial, political, or status-related.

Continuing the examples mentioned above, the cost to the public of the grazing fee is immediate and very visible. The costs of the divestiture, on the other hand, do not affect the public to any appreciable extent, but are concentrated in the Co-op Lesotho staff who lost their employment.

7. *What is the degree and complexity of the changes brought about by the new policy?* This question applies both to the implementing agencies involved and to the public (winners, losers, and those not affected one way or the other). Some policies may represent a great deal of change on the part of the public but little on the part of the bureaucracy (for example, payment of a new tax in the form of the grazing fee that remains within the community). Others illustrate just the reverse (for example, those instances in which producers continue to purchase supplies from agricultural input stores that have changed hands from the public sector to a private entrepreneur). Still others may represent considerable change in both the public and the bureaucratic spheres (for example, removing the obligation to sell agricultural produce to the government parastatal will alter the role of several government agencies and the commercial practices of agricultural producers). Degree and complexity of

change can be further assessed in either the public or bureaucratic spheres. Important variables include:

- variety of changes introduced,
- departure they represent from current practices, roles, and behaviors,
- degree of technical sophistication in the changes,
- their geographic scale,
- degree of conflict about their nature or value.

8. *What is the duration of the policy change process?* Some reforms can happen from one day to the next, such as currency devaluation. Others, like the Lesotho agricultural policy reforms, require several years to reach full implementation. This relates to the "stroke-of-the-pen" versus long-haul policy dichotomy (Nelson 1989).

9. *What institutions are involved in implementing the policy?* For example, in Lesotho the following had a role: the ministries of agriculture, finance, interior; parastatals; private firms; local associations or cooperatives; judicial entities; the legislature; NGOs; and local government agencies.

10. *How administratively intense or technically complex is the new policy* (in and of itself, not including the changes that it brings about)? For example, the agricultural policy reform contained a number of complex operations: the steps leading up to the collection of the grazing fee (national livestock inventory), the fee collection process (creating the legal authority for the village development councils to do so), and the allocation of the funds collected (where, by whom, for what). The divestiture of Co-op Lesotho assets also entailed a relatively complex sequence of identifying and valuing the assets, establishing rules and regulations for their sale, and the actual transfer process.

Building on the analysis of the costs and benefits of the policies to the public and the bureaucracy, managers should examine the incentives for policy change for both. Specific variables here include:

- perceived importance of the policy issue,
- degree of political support for change,
- extent to which central-level participation is required in implementation,
- extent to which local-level participation is required,
- perceived value of the benefits,

Table 7.1 Policy Characteristics Checklist

		A Simplifying factor	B (neutral)	C Complicating factor	
	✓		✓		✓
Where did the impetus for the policy come from?		Inside the country		Outside the country	
		Inside government		Outside government	
Who decided the policy and how?		With democratic legislative process		Without democratic legislative process	
		With widespread participation		Without widespread participation	
What is the nature of the benefits and to whom do they accrue?		Visible		Invisible	
		Immediate		Long term	
		Dramatic		Marginal	
What is the nature of the costs and who bears them?		Invisible		Visible	
		Long term		Immediate	
		Marginal		Dramatic	
How complex are the changes?		Few changes		Many changes	
		Few decision-makers		Many decision-makers	
		Small departure from current practices, roles, and behaviors		Large departure from current practices, roles, and behaviors	
		Limited discretion		Large discretion	
		Low technical sophistication		High technical sophistication	
		Low administrative complexity		High administrative complexity	
		Geographically concentrated		Geographically dispersed	
		Normal pace		Urgent/emergency pace	
		Single event		Permanent changes	
		Low level of conflict about nature and value of the changes		High level of conflict about nature and value of the changes	
Total number of checks:					

- perceived costs of noncompliance,
- extent to which benefits can be restricted to those who contribute resources,
- extent to which the policy reform is a condition for additional donor resources.

A POLICY CHARACTERISTICS CHECKLIST

The questions posed above can be organized into a checklist (see Table 7.1), which serves as a rough and ready test of the "implementability" of the policy. Every check mark placed in Column A indicates a simplifying factor, and every check in Column C represents a complicating factor. A check placed in column B indicates an intermediate or neutral situation with regard to a particular policy characteristic. By counting the number of checks in Column A and subtracting the number of checks in Column C, policy managers can obtain an approximate measure of a policy's implementability. The higher the number, the easier it will normally be to implement the policy. The checklist also points toward actions that can be taken to simplify implementation; in this sense, it can help to inform implementation strategy design. Every time reformers can take actions that result in the removal of a check mark from Column C (and, if possible, modify it sufficiently to replace it with a check mark in Column A), policy implementation has probably been made easier. For example, an intervention that makes the benefits of implementing a given policy apparent to large numbers of interested parties and decision-makers almost certainly makes that policy easier to implement.

CONCLUSION

Systematically going through this set of questions and using the checklist will allow policy reformers to obtain a clear understanding of what the policy is all about and to begin to devise a plan to enhance the prospects for successful implementation. In the Lesotho case one of the outcomes of examining these issues was the realization that the original implementation timetable was overly optimistic and that additional planning was required to accommodate the necessary sequence of activities. Similarly, new ways in which pressure could be brought to bear to advance implementation were identified for each policy area, influenced by the location and concentration of their benefits and costs.

Policy characteristics analysis will be most useful when combined with several of the other tools that help to map the implementation terrain that managers function within. It is a broad-brush tool that can be used for a quick initial scan of the implementability of the policy. The features of the policy identified will point toward critical stakeholders (Chapter 6), the array of interests for and against the policy (Chapter 8), where sources of conflict may lie (Chapter 11), who it may be important to lobby for support (Chapter 10), and what policy milestones should be monitored (Chapter 12).

8

Political
and Institutional Mapping

As pointed out in Chapter 2, policies must have both ample support and resources if they are to be successfully implemented. To obtain these, policy managers must be able to convince stakeholders of the value of their policy goals, obtain the resources required to move forward, and in some cases compete successfully with other agencies. To acquire the support needed and to assure resources to implement a new policy, reformers must lobby, negotiate, develop alliances, and form coalitions (see Asilis and Milesi-Feretti 1994, Lo 1991, Nelson 1989).

As we discussed in the introduction to the previous chapter, policy change and politics are intimately related. Politics determines, as Lasswell (1958) says, "who gets what, when, and how." In a democracy or a democratizing political system, public officials need to operate in ways that respond to citizens' needs and desires, balance special interests against equity and distributional considerations, and generate political backing. To be successful they need the capacity to assess the political environment for decision-making and the ability to develop strategies that will improve their chances for success. In a context in which the need to obtain additional resources for new policies may threaten already-established programs and agencies, the need for sound political assessment and strategy development is all the more vital.

This chapter reviews political and environmental mapping and analytical techniques aimed at developing policy managers' skills for political assessment and the design of politically sensitive strategies for policy implementation. The first part of the chapter covers macro–political mapping and political resource analysis. The second part examines micro–political mapping, policy network analysis, and force-field analysis. Together these techniques help in assessing the level of competition policy managers face, the channels of access to critical decisions, and the possibilities for increasing support through alliances and coalitions to achieve objectives. These tools build on stakeholder analysis (Chapter 6) and policy characteristics analysis (Chapter 7).

POLITICAL MAPPING

In any political system there are hundreds of different actors with varying interests and interactions that shift and evolve over time. The complexity of politics, particularly when its various levels (national, regional, local, and so on) are factored in, can be overwhelming. With the quantity of information available, political analysis and determination of what is important are daunting tasks. The difficulty stems largely from problems of processing the information; that is, how to organize the information and make it useful (see Lindenberg and Crosby 1981). The purpose of political mapping is to organize information about politics in a way that makes it useful for managers facing decisions. The map identifies the most important political actors and spatially illustrates their relationships to one another. Political mapping can serve several purposes:

- It can provide a graphic representation of the political health of a regime or government.
- It can offer clues about the vulnerabilities of the regime.
- It can detect the existence of opposing alliances and potential support coalitions.
- It can give an indication of the level of authority possessed by the regime.
- It can help indicate implementation capacity of various actors.
- It can detect new directions in policy.

ORGANIZATION OF THE POLITICAL MAP

In the real world the many interactions in the political context create a constantly moving picture. For purposes of making sense of that complexity, a political map (Figure 8.1) simplifies the real world in two dimensions: horizontal and vertical. Since the government is the primary focus of decision-making regarding how the benefits of society will be distributed, it is always placed at the center of the map. Political activity is centered on and directed toward influencing the government and its policy decisions. Along the vertical axis the different types of political actors are organized into four sectors: external sectors, social sectors, political parties, and pressure groups. The purpose of the horizontal axis is to assess the degree to which each group supports the government.

Support for the government varies from core or central support to ideological or mild support while opposition is differentiated as either legal opposition or anti-system opposition. Support or opposition also can be labeled "left" or "right," although in today's world these traditional political terms are less useful analytically than they used to be.

One problem with political mapping is lack of dynamism. Changes in political landscapes can occur often and sometimes rapidly. A single political map may be likened to a snapshot. It is a loyal interpretation of the political system at a particular point in time, but not at another. While it is certainly true that a particular map represents a specific point in time, by combining a series of maps over time, reformers can begin to appreciate the dynamics of politics—just as time-lapse photography (through a series of individual photos) can reveal the opening of a flower. Actors begin to take on movement, managers can see how support for the government waxes and wanes, and we can see coalitions take shape and later fall apart.

Figure 8.1 Political Map

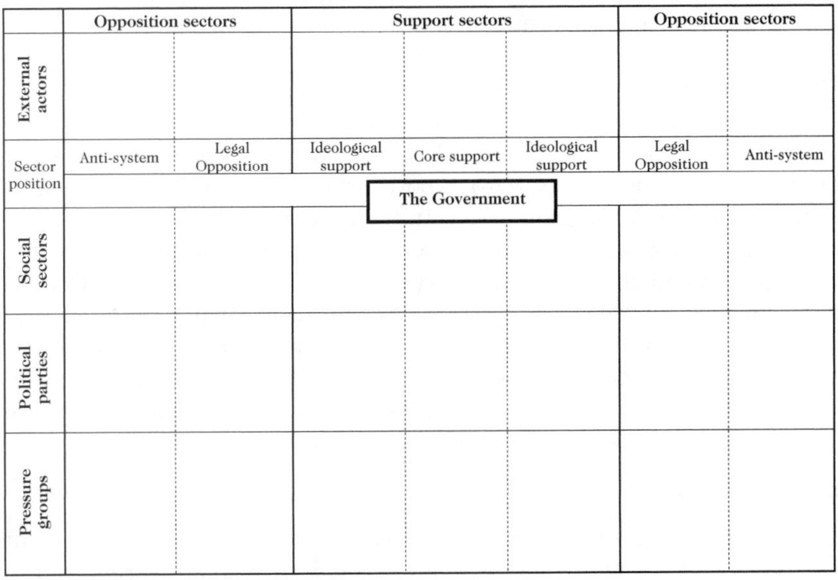

	Opposition sectors		Support sectors			Opposition sectors	
External actors							
Sector position	Anti-system	Legal Opposition	Ideological support	Core support	Ideological support	Legal Opposition	Anti-system
				The Government			
Social sectors							
Political parties							
Pressure groups							

Political Actors

The Government

The government is the single most important political actor. It is ultimately responsible for deciding among different and/or conflicting alternatives and demands, and it is the source to which other actors turn when they cannot resolve disputes among themselves. A government need not be elected, nor need it be legitimate in the legal sense; rather, it is the actor that has the role of final arbiter. The head of government may be a president, a general, a dictator, a junta, a "national directorate," or whoever is designated the role of final decision-maker. When mapping is applied to the sub-national level, the regional or local government becomes the entity that serves as the final decision-maker. If mapping is applied to a single ministry, the "government" then becomes the minister; in a municipality, "government" is the mayor or the local council.

In addition to the government there are four other sets of political actors: external actors, social sectors, political parties, and pressure groups. While each is important, the relevance and degree to which each type of actor is mobilized varies.

External Actors

These groups are similar to pressure groups in that they represent particular interests, though their origins are from outside the country. External actors include multinational corporations, foreign embassies, international NGOs, and bilateral and multilateral donor agencies.

Social Sectors

These are large groups that share some general characteristic or affinity, such as urban workers, the urban middle class, small farmers, large landholders, industrialists, agro-export farmers, urban professionals, or minority groups. Such groups vary in the extent to which they are organized and/or mobilized. Their common interests are generally manifested through mass mechanisms such as elections. They are most highly mobilized during electoral periods, and most electoral campaign messages and rhetoric are directed at these groups. Political parties and candidates often single out certain groups for special attention. Once the electoral period is over, however, social sector groups can lose relevance if they are unorganized and are unable to mobilize effectively.

Political Parties

These are groups, often composed of several social sectors, whose main objective is to influence public policy through the direct exercise of the instruments of power. Political parties exercise their greatest influence at or around the electoral process, selecting candidates for office and appointing loyalists to government jobs once elected. After the election the political party's influence and relevance wane as the organization disbands or reduces operations until the next electoral cycle. In parliamentary democracies, parties continue to exercise influence through their parliamentary delegations.

Pressure Groups

These are groups that share a relatively narrow set of concerns and seek to defend or advance their interests by influencing the direction of public policy. Unlike political parties, pressure groups do not seek the direct exercise of power. Virtually any group, as long as it seeks to influence policy and not exercise power, can be considered a pressure group. Labor unions, business associations, church organizations, NGOs, or professional associations can all function as pressure groups. Though public sector actors are part of the government, they act as pressure groups when they try to influence public policy and resource allocation. Pressure groups serve a vital role in articulating and channeling demands and in the design and determination of public policy (see Chapter 10 on lobbying and advocacy).

Opposition and Support: Locating the Actors

Once actors have been categorized, attention may then be turned to analyzing their support or opposition to the government. Support for the government is broken into two categories: central or core support, and moderate or ideological support. Opposition is also divided into two types: legal or so-called loyal opposition, and anti-system opposition.

Core Support

Groups in this category are vital to maintaining the government in power and to assuring its decisional authority. It includes actors such as the ruling political party, senior officials in the state bureaucracy, the military, and key constituency groups. They are usually unequivocal in their support for the regime and closely identify with the government's objectives and policies. Because such groups invest heavily in the government (in terms of support) and risk the most, they also benefit most and are the most influential in the policy process. Loss of core support can have a grave effect on the government's ability to implement decisions or, in extreme cases, on its survival. While core support actors provide political solvency to the government, this comes at a price. In exchange they seek and expect benefits and influence. When the government has relatively few benefits to provide to competing groups, the political dynamics become zero-sum, and a decision favoring one group may cause the exit of another.

Moderate or Ideological Support

Groups here agree with the government on most issues, but their support is weaker and less committed than core support. Included are minor coalition partners, large constituency groups such as farmers or labor, and supportive pressure groups of minor consequence to the government. Their support entails little investment of resources or commitment and little risk. They receive relatively few benefits in return and are largely unable to exert much influence on policy. Importantly, moderate support groups are candidates to become core support should others withdraw. The government must take care not to alienate or ignore moderate support groups. Their demands must be attended to or satisfied with some regularity, or they will eventually withdraw support and seek satisfaction elsewhere. Since the satisfaction of such groups does not require significant resources, the government can comfortably afford to maintain several groups in the moderate support sector.

Legal Opposition

These groups disagree with the policy decisions of the current government, but they firmly support the rules of the political system. In systems characterized by alternation, the legal opposition has the opportunity to become the next government. In a democracy the legal opposition presents an alternative and at the same time exercises an accountability function. Depending upon the configuration of the political system (for example, "winner take all" versus proportional representation), the government in power needs to be attentive, if not always compliant, to the views of the opposition. Among legal opposition groups might be found principal opposition political parties and important or powerful pressure groups.

Anti-System Opposition

These groups not only oppose government policy, they are opposed to the system as a whole. They oppose not only who makes the decisions but also how the decisions are made. Satisfaction of these groups requires drastic change in the rules of the political game and allocation of resources. Because they do not follow the norms of the existing system, they are often repressed and frequently resort to illegal and/or violent means of expressing their demands. In the anti-system one might find guerrilla groups or radicalized pressure groups.

Locating Actors on the Map

The location of a group or actor on the map depends on a number of variables, not simply the degree to which the group supports the government. In locating a group on the map there are two dimensions to be considered. First, the location of the group in terms of its support or opposition to the government; and second, the position of the group to the left or the right of the regime in power.

The placement of a group to the left or the right of the regime is often a subjective decision. The reason for dichotomizing the map is to separate visually those with little in common or who differ substantially on general policy orientation, ideology, or values. Such actors will rarely form coalitions or work together. When there are two powerful but opposite actors in opposition to a particular policy, they tend to cancel out each other's influence and only present a very diminished threat to the government.

The placement of a group to the left or the right of the government will depend on whether the analyst believes that the group is more "progressive" or more "conservative" than the government, whether the group is more "interventionist" or less "interventionist" than the state, and whether the group is more "leftist" or more "rightist" than the regime. As can be seen, such judgments will be situational and will depend on the context in which one is making the judgment. Regardless of which criteria are chosen for making such decisions, they ought to be clear and consistent. In certain cases the distribution of right and left can change overnight, as is the case when a socialist government is defeated by a party with neoliberal leanings.

Reading the Map

Reading the political map involves answering a series of questions. Beginning at the center and moving out toward the extremes, the first set of questions looks at the degree of support for the regime. How much support exists, and how intense or committed is that support? Are critical actors in the center or are several off to one side or the other, indicating only lukewarm support? Is support balanced, or is it too reliant on a particular type of group, such as labor unions or the military? In general, a political map should be read with an eye to identifying the broad picture of support and opposition rather than concentrating on particular details.

A look at Figure 8.2 shows that the government represented has fairly substantial support in the core sector, but it is concentrated among a few powerful business and economic interests (typical in countries undergoing structural adjustment). International donors, whose economic resources make them powerful interests, provide further support. While the government is not overly reliant on a particular group, "winners" in this scenario are few, while those in opposition are many.

The next set of questions deals with cohesiveness of support. Occasionally, one might have support from the senior leadership of a group, but the rank and file may be opposed. Under these circumstances, can the leaders exercise sufficient control over their members to assure continued

Figure 8.2 An Illustrative Political Map

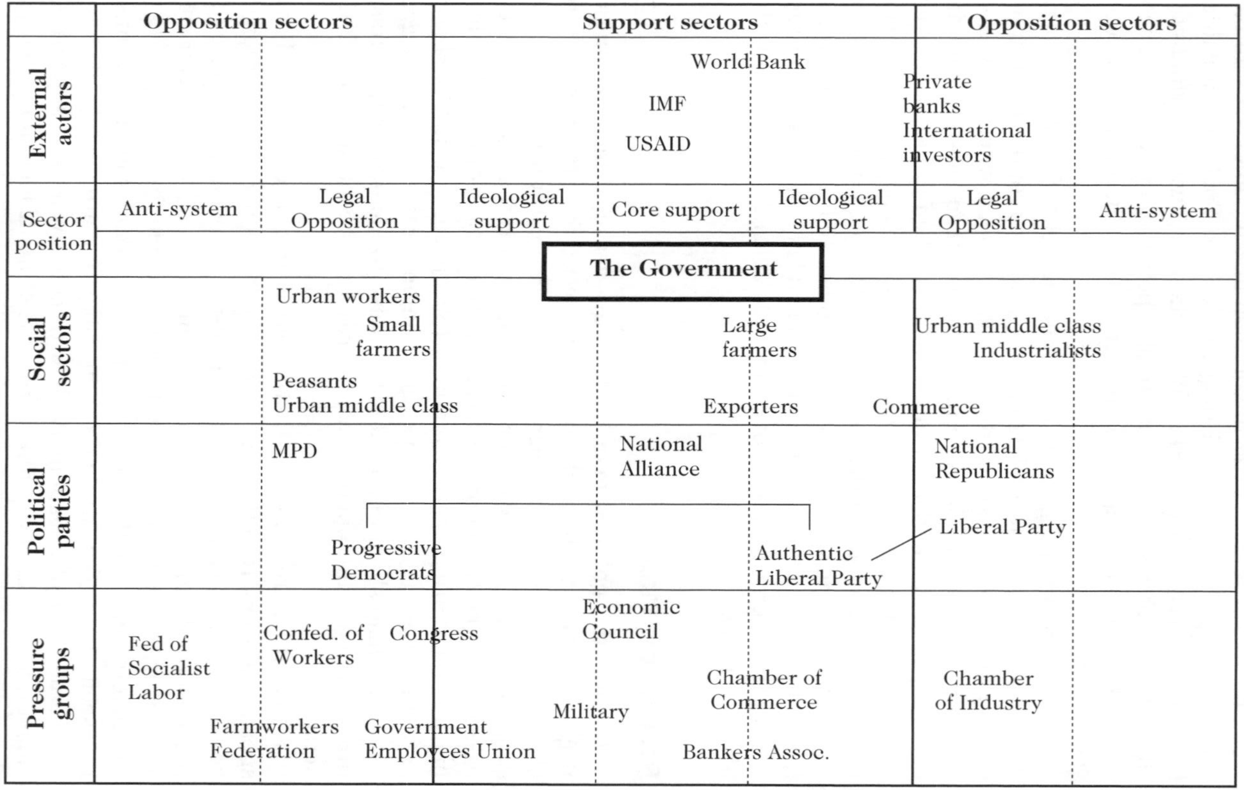

	Opposition sectors		Support sectors			Opposition sectors	
Sector position	Anti-system	Legal Opposition	Ideological support	Core support	Ideological support	Legal Opposition	Anti-system
External actors				World Bank, IMF, USAID		Private banks, International investors	
Social sectors		Urban workers, Small farmers, Peasants, Urban middle class		Large farmers, Exporters		Urban middle class, Industrialists, Commerce	
Political parties		MPD, Progressive Democrats		National Alliance, Authentic Liberal Party		National Republicans, Liberal Party	
Pressure groups		Fed of Socialist Labor, Farmworkers Federation, Confed. of Workers, Government Employees Union, Congress		Economic Council, Military, Chamber of Commerce, Bankers Assoc.		Chamber of Industry	

The Government

and reliable support? Figure 8.2 shows a serious problem with cohesion within the government's coalition National Alliance, where there are two major factions. Progressive Democrats sit on the border between opposition and support, while the Liberal Party is split from the Authentic Liberal Party. With polarized partners, coalition management will be difficult, and failure here could result in an opposition congress and loss of key cabinet ministers.

Finally, does the map reveal particular concentrations of support? If heavily concentrated in the core support area, there may be significant maintenance costs over the long haul. Are there important groups concentrated in the ideological support area? If so, what would it cost the government to mobilize them? The government may need to build up or maintain an adequate reserve of such support precisely so that it can be mobilized later.

Next, how many groups are in the opposition? It should not be surprising to find more opposition than active support. In developing countries resources to satisfy demands are in scarce supply, so only a few groups can be satisfied, leaving many others discontent and ripe for opposition. If these potentially dissatisfied stakeholders grow in number, or begin to form coalitions, there will likely be cause for worry. Social sector groups are often in the opposition because they are the most amorphous, least identifiable, and least committed, and hence the most difficult and costly to satisfy. If an election is approaching, however, some of those groups ought to be returning to the support sectors. If not, the governing party will certainly suffer on election day.

How intense and committed is the opposition? If relatively uncommitted, prospects of mobilization against the government will diminish. However, a committed opposition will be much more aggressive in countering government positions and policies. Figure 8.2 shows a good deal of opposition, but it does not appear to be particularly intense, as can be noted by those groups straddling the line between opposition and support. The lack of clear linkage between groups, which can concentrate opposition, also attests to their relative weakness.

Are there important alliances in formation? Is the opposition balanced? When there are roughly the same numbers of opposition actors on one side as the other, there will be a neutralizing effect. Figure 8.2 does not reveal any alliances or coalitions in formation. The lack of ties among either business or labor groups allows the government the possibility of playing one group off against another. In this case the lack of ties between opposition on the left means the government can concentrate on keeping the business community happy and not worry too much about labor, at least until the next election. The government in Figure 8.2 faces two challenges. First, it must maintain the support of the business community by maintaining an adequate flow of resources and benefits to it. Second, it needs to shore up its coalition. The repercussions of shifts into the opposition of key players would be quite serious in terms of capacity to make and implement policy.

A word of caution. Although a political map can be a useful instrument for clarification, it is neither a crystal ball nor a substitute for good analysis or judgment. The map is merely a tool, and like other tools, its usefulness will depend on who prepares it, the quality of data that goes into the construction of the map, and the seriousness and quality of interpretation given the data on the map.

POLICY-MAPPING TECHNIQUES

The variety and complexity of political, social, and bureaucratic processes found in policymaking and implementation call for a wide variety of tools for mapping, diagnosis, and analysis. In this section we turn to an examination of three policy-mapping techniques highly useful for fine-tuning managers' understanding of the environmental in which they work: micro–political mapping, policy network mapping, and force-field analysis.

Micro–Political Mapping

Although a macro–political map (Figure 8.2) shows overall support for the government, it does not necessarily reveal support on specific issues. Though a government may have solid overall support, on specific issues there may be massive or particularly intense opposition. A micro–political map can clarify the distribution of support for specific issues, indicate how certain sectors will react to particular policies, and clarify the positions of different organizations within the same sector. If a particular minister wishes to promote a policy altering the nature of relationships within the sector, a map can reveal the extent of support for the policy, where support is located, where opposition lies, and possibilities for alliances or coalitions—should they be necessary. A serious lack of support would certainly be an indication to either drop or substantially modify the idea, rather than wasting precious resources. Suppose that the agriculture minister of a country, call it Boliguay, wished to evaluate support for reducing price controls on grains in order to stimulate production. The forces around the issue might be arrayed as illustrated in Figure 8.3.

In general, the government of Boliguay enjoys widespread support with little threat from serious opposition. The micro–political map, however, indicates less support than one might assume from simply looking a macro–political map. The reason is that the particular issue of price controls on

Figure 8.3 Micro–Political Map of Boliguay: Agricultural Sector
(Reduction of Price Controls)

Opposition	Ideological support	Core support	Ideological support	Opposition
Urban middle class	MINISTER OF AGRICULTURE			
CONGRESS		ECONOMIC COUNCIL		
PRD		IMF		Chamber of Commerce
		International donors		
Urban workers unions				
Small farmers MILITARY		Chamber of Agriculture Grain farmers		

grains is of interest to a limited number of actors, and in this instance most are opposed to controls. But judging from the array of actors present and the controversy that socially charged issues like price controls provoke, in order to pursue the issue, the minister would need to increase support. The ambiguity of support from powerful actors such as the congress, the military, and a significant part of the governing PRD political party poses a very uncertain environment for pursuing the elimination of price controls.

If at least two of these powerful actors could be brought on board, however, their support would probably be enough to cancel the strong but amorphous and difficult-to-mobilize opposition of the middle class, urban workers, unions, and small farmers. The combination of forces arrayed both for and against price controls on the micro–political map suggests that in order to go ahead the minister would need to modify the policy to decrease opposition. Tactics and strategy apart, it is quite clear that although there may be a strong general level of support for the government, the micro–political map indicates that this particular policy may face implementation difficulties and may generate some political opposition.

Should the minister give up? Not necessarily. The micro–political map can help indicate who needs to be satisfied in order for the policy to progress. Can a coalition (perhaps consisting of small farmers, grain farmers, and the chamber of agriculture) be put together that will be strong enough to prevail over the opposition? Although there is significant opposition, much of it is concentrated on the left, presenting opportunities for an opposition coalition. However, the minister might think about how he might bargain with congress and the PRD to attract their support, thus significantly weakening the opposition on the left. If that is not possible or desirable, is there a way to neutralize key opposition actors? What changes would have to be made in the policy and what kinds of concessions would have to be made to those key actors? All these questions can be addressed through a stakeholder assessment (see Chapter 6) of the interests, level of resources, and mobilization capacity possessed by each of the key actors identified on the map.

Policy Network Maps

There are instances when officials would like to concentrate on a particular policy idea and would like to target the most important stakeholders. The construction of a policy network map can be extremely helpful in such circumstances. There are several steps to developing a policy network map. First, each decision point through which a policy passes to become approved and implemented should be noted and described. Second, the actor(s) in charge of each step should be listed, and some indication of how to gain access to these actors should be noted. If there are other actors, though not officially part of the process, that have substantial influence over those who decide, they too should be noted and described. Finally, contacts, access, or relationships that might be influential in the decision process also should be noted. Figure 8.4 presents a simplified illustration of a policy network map for health sector reform (cf. Nelson 1999). It shows actors that might potentially have access to important decision-makers (for example, the president, cabinet ministers, congress) are arrayed or grouped around those decision-makers. Solid lines, showing direct access or contacts, and dotted lines indicating indirect access illustrate the type of relationships among actors.

Let us assume that in Boliguay the health minister wishes to reallocate the health budget away from centralized curative care facilities (the apex hospitals in the capital) to strengthen primary care services in the rural areas for under-served populations. The key actors in the policy decision process are the health minister, the finance minister, the president, and the congress. Within that process several others also influence decisions. The finance ministry's staff is charged with preparation of the budget and shapes most of the process, including many decisions about which programs will be maintained and which will be curtailed. Who, then, are the members of this staff, and might there be some way to gain access to and to influence them?

Figure 8.4 Policy Network Map: Health Sector Reform in Boliguay

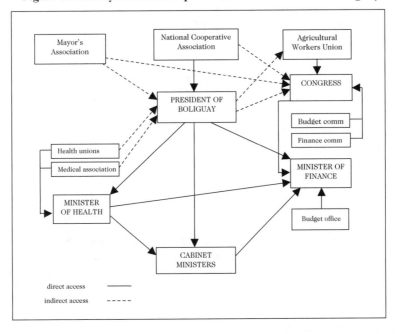

Among the more important constituents of the president's political party are the health workers' union and the medical association. They are likely to be opposed to the budget reallocation, so the minister will need to take steps to accommodate their interests and to counter the pressures on the president that they may be able to mobilize. Within the congress the committees on budget and finance are in charge of approving the budget submitted by the president. Might there be some way to influence directly the committee or their members charged with the preparation of legislative authorization bills for the budget? Which members of the committee have an interest in the problems of rural health? Which have connections to the powerful health workers' union or the medical association? Perhaps the minister could bolster those members' interest with pertinent and timely information that could be used to defend the policy in committee debates or hearings.

Finally, the pressure of diverse groups such as the Mayors' Association, the National Cooperative Association, and the Agricultural Workers Union might also be brought to bear. While these groups are not direct players in the policy process, in contrast to members of congress or the minister, their support for the policy can have an influence on elected officials.

While all these stakeholders may have interests in the health policy, to be useful they must be mobilized. This will require initiative, time, and

Figure 8.5 Force-field Analysis for Reduction of Price Controls

(-) Oppose	(0) Neutral	(+) Favor
Urban middle class		Economic Council
PRD		IMF
CONGRESS		International donors
MILITARY		Grain farmers
Urban workers unions	Chamber of Agriculture	
Small farmers		
Chamber of Commerce		

energy on the part of the minister and the minister's team. Some of them may be interested if the minister casts the policy issue around decentralization and freeing up of resources for regions and municipalities, not simply as a health issue.

Force-field Analysis

Force-field analysis is a simple method to illustrate support and opposition to a particular policy, particularly when there is not sufficient time to develop a full-blown micro–political map. The technique for applying the analysis is simple and straightforward. Using the data gathered on stakeholder positions on the issue at hand, groups are placed on a continuum from "oppose" to "favor." The middle of the continuum is a neutral position.

The product is a graphic illustration of who supports and who opposes a particular policy. It is particularly useful as a first cut at sorting out positions of different stakeholders and for giving reformers a quick impression of sources of major opposition and support. An example of force-field analysis application to the Boliguay price control example is shown in Figure 8.5. The analysis shows a great deal of opposition to the proposed reduction of price controls simply in terms of the number of groups opposed or supportive. But it does not indicate why such groups are opposed. It is not clear if some groups go along with the idea simply because they are part of the government's coalition. Nor does it say if groups are opposed for the same reason. Finally, nothing is said about either the quality or resources of the opposition or support. In this particular situation the oppositional configuration of the force-field analysis ought to signal the reformers to analyze these questions more closely before making any strategy choices.

Force-field analysis has certain limitations. Unlike the techniques for political mapping described earlier, force-field analysis does not examine questions of political support for the government on the policy or the value of a group's support on the issue, the degree to which the group supports a particular policy, or how much influence the group might have in determining the configuration or final outcome of the policy. Force-field analysis merely states whether the group is for or against the policy. Since the design of strategies for policy implementation generally requires more information, reformers likely will find the tool most useful for initial analysis.

9

Workshops for Managing Policy Reform

Workshops have proven to be highly effective in establishing and supporting strategic management processes and also in providing opportunities for participation in policy change by affected parties. Effective workshops contribute to economic efficiency gains by improving coordination across implementing agencies and sectors, elaborating jointly understood operational roles and rules, and disseminating information to clients and user groups. Workshops generate political benefits in the form of establishing common ground and areas of agreement, increasing support for policy issues and solutions, and building constituencies and ownership for reform. This chapter provides some background information on workshops, describes the ways workshops can be useful for participatory policy implementation, elaborates how to use them, and provides an example of a strategic management workshop conducted in The Gambia as part of institutional strengthening for the finance ministry.

WORKSHOPS
AS A MANAGEMENT TOOL

A workshop can be defined as an organized meeting, usually from one-half to four days in length, with the following features: (a) a custom-tailored set of objectives, tasks, and outcomes; (b) a blend of learning a new tool or approach with applying it to an immediate task; (c) a participatory orientation that engages attendees actively in both learning and application; and (d) a limitation on attendance to those with some direct link to the workshop's objectives and tasks. These features differentiate workshops from other meetings of limited duration, such as seminars, in which the emphasis is on more general instruction and learning with attendance open to anyone interested in the subject at hand; conferences, whose orientation is similar to seminars but usually includes exchanges of experience in the subject area between invited speakers and attendees;

and briefings, where the focus is on one-way information transmittal to a recipient audience.

In the management context, workshops integrate the technical with the process side of managing change. They serve as tools that help groups of people work more effectively together on common tasks. Workshops serve as mechanisms for team building and decision-making, often as part of an organizational development (OD) program intended to improve an organization's performance by helping it use its resources more effectively. These workshops usually have external consultants, who design and conduct the workshops jointly with a team from the organization. The organization's staff members (and sometimes its clients) participate in the workshop and carry its outcomes and learnings back into the work place for application. Much of the OD literature deals with workshops for team and consensus building and for performance improvement (see, for example, Dyer 1987, Miles 1981). OD started in the private sector but quickly spread to public agencies (including the military), and to non-profit organizations as well. Workshops are widely used in all three sectors.

In the international development arena, workshops as a management tool evolved in the context of donor agency and developing country concerns with project implementation and management. Evaluations of project experience found that failure to undertake detailed implementation planning with the staff of the agencies responsible for project implementation (either as part of project design or start-up) accounted for a significant portion of the management weaknesses that projects suffered from. Further analysis revealed that the process side of implementation was frequently neglected as well, that is, clarifying objectives, agreeing on roles and responsibilities, and building ownership and commitment for objectives and plans. Such oversight resulted in misunderstandings, disputes, and conflicts among project staff, donor agency personnel, and beneficiaries. This finding suggested the applicability of the OD approach to development project implementation teams.

As a means to improve project implementation, USAID began to support the development of workshop methodologies that addressed implementation planning and team building in tandem, particularly targeted at the transition in the project cycle between design and implementation. Initially employed on an experimental basis, the methodology was refined and now has become standard procedure in several donor agencies. In USAID such workshops are called project start-up workshops or team planning meetings (TPMs); in the World Bank they are referred to as project launch or action planning workshops (see Eckert and Kettering 1984, Edwards and Pettit 1987, Silverman et al. 1986; see also Liebler 1994).

After their original international development application to project start-up, workshops were integrated into institutional strengthening projects as a management technology that could be used at any phase of the project cycle: problem identification, design, implementation, and/or evaluation. Further, the technology can be transferred to developing country managers for use in their own operations, whether linked to a donor-funded project or not. The workshop methodology, referred to as action training, has become a cornerstone of management training efforts (EDI 1989, Kerrigan and Luke 1987) and of institutional capacity building (for example, Cassels and Janovsky 1991, Foster et al. 1990, Jones 1990, Schmidt 1991). More recently, workshop-based methodologies have been used in World Bank–funded projects for collaborative decision-making around an environmental assessment framework called appreciation influence control (AIC) (see World Bank 1996, 183).

THE PLACE OF WORKSHOPS
IN THE STRATEGIC MANAGEMENT OF POLICY REFORM

Workshops are useful to bring together the various stakeholders involved in the policy reform process for a range of purposes. Because they combine learning and application, workshops are appropriate mechanisms for introducing analytic and management tools. They can help to keep policy reforms on track and to manage the change process strategically. At each step of the strategic management model introduced in Chapter 2, workshops can be used to bring together the appropriate people who need to be involved, undertake the tasks required at the particular step, gain understanding of the outputs to be produced, and agree upon what needs to be done next. Participation of a variety of groups increases the quality of the outputs and the likelihood that those outputs will be "owned" and supported by those involved. Workshops are ideal settings for achieving these outcomes.

Because policy implementation cuts across the nominal authority and statutory responsibility of any individual agency, management of the implementation process calls for mechanisms that bring together the relevant parties in ways that reduce the potential for conflict and increase the possibilities for effective coordination. Workshops can serve effectively as one of these mechanisms. They are non-hierarchical and participatory, their objectives explicitly target building consensus and agreement, and their emphasis on practicality can assure that participants address issues concretely in terms of what is to be done and who is responsible for which actions.

The use of workshops throughout the life of a policy creates periodic venues for taking stock of progress, comparing targets with accomplishments, revising plans, addressing conflicts, reinforcing or renegotiating agreements, and sustaining new behaviors among participants. These outcomes serve to provide the information necessary for policy monitoring and reporting, to move policy reform forward in an adaptive way, and to operationalize basic principles of democratic governance such as participation, transparency, and responsiveness.

GUIDELINES FOR DESIGNING AND CONDUCTING WORKSHOPS

A common misperception regarding workshops is that the major expenditure of effort takes place once the workshop starts. Effective workshops, on the contrary, call for significant attention to design and preparation to lay the groundwork for success. These guidelines are divided into suggestions for the preparation phase and for actual conduct of the workshop.

Workshop Preparation

Clarify workshop objectives. The first step in workshop preparation is to determine the purpose to be achieved. Why hold a workshop, and what is to be accomplished? This step establishes the foundation for all subsequent decisions. A good way to answer these questions is to begin by interviewing some key stakeholders. Reasons policy managers might want to hold workshops include team building, consensus building, analyzing a problem, developing an action strategy and plan, identifying and agreeing on roles and responsibilities, and others. These can be used as starting points for discussions with relevant personnel. Once this first step has been initiated, the following guidelines are applicable. Although presented here in a linear sequence, in practice these actions tend to take place simultaneously and/or cyclically until final decisions on workshop preparation and design are taken.

Build ownership for the workshop. The interview process to clarify the workshop's purpose and define objectives can also serve to plant the seeds of ownership among senior officials, potential workshop participants, agency clients, and other relevant actors. The workshop should have formal sponsorship from one or more of the agencies responsible for the policy's implementation. Even if top-level officials do not participate in the workshop, their recognition of its importance and attention to its outcomes are critical for the application of the workshop's products. Incentives for participants to take the workshop seriously are enhanced when they know that their superiors have an interest in the activity. To reinforce this message a senior official can be invited to preside over the workshop's opening and/or closing session(s), and participants can present a summary of results to the official as part of the final session.

Select participants. Without the right people at the workshop, the desired outcomes will not be possible. To some extent selection takes place as part of the discussions around the workshop's purpose. As a general rule, broader participation from multiple levels increases the probability that (a) relevant information and perspectives will not be overlooked, (b) potentially debilitating conflicts can be averted, (c) better understandings can be reached, and (d) key actors will not feel left out and therefore will be less prone to engage in obstructionist or subversive behaviors later. Selection can become a sensitive issue, however, if there are too many trade-offs between those who need to attend for technical reasons and those whose presence is dictated by political considerations. One solution is to hold separate sessions, or even separate workshops, for different categories of participants; for example, organizing a formal "supporting" forum for politically important attendees, thereby fulfilling their participation needs and desires.

At a certain point, though, logistical considerations enter in. Workshops with more than forty to fifty people become difficult to manage, and the ability to reach operationally concrete outcomes is hampered. Again, size is partially dependent upon purpose. If the workshop has a major focus on building understanding of what needs to be done to implement a particular policy and create consensus, then a larger size might be appropriate. If the aim is to do detailed operational planning for a specific set of activities, then a smaller group is likely to be more efficient and effective.

Determine workshop length and timing. Most of the people who are involved in policy implementation are busy. Those at the higher levels of government tend to be especially overloaded. For management workshops, shorter is better. Getting the right people to attend means adjusting workshop length to their availability. Three days is usually the maximum that can be realistically programmed. One solution in cases in which availability is a problem is to include within the workshop a shorter session geared to high-level personnel attendance, with the majority of participants attending for a longer period.

Timing is determined by the particular policy situation. If the workshop is to prepare a team for an assignment, obviously it must be held prior to the start-up of team activities in the field (and generally will last one day or less). If workshops are being programmed as part of a long-term policy implementation effort, it may be possible to establish dates and times in advance, for example, quarterly. This kind of advance planning will increase the likelihood that participants can build attendance into their schedules.

Identify location and facilities. In some situations the sponsoring agency will want to hold the workshop at its own facilities, which may or may not offer the best physical setup for the sessions. Budgetary considerations often enter in as well, putting limits on what is possible. The ideal is a location that minimizes interruptions to workshop activities, one where participants cannot easily be drawn away to attend to routine business. Because of the action-oriented nature of the workshop and the fact that outputs from previous sessions usually are inputs to subsequent ones, having participants drop in and out of sessions is highly detrimental to achievement of intended objectives. Sometimes a local training institute can be a suitable location for a workshop. If participants are coming from other cities or countries, hotels are the preferred option, funds permitting.

Facilities need to include, at a minimum, a meeting room large enough to accommodate all the participants comfortably and several smaller rooms nearby where task groups can work (break-out rooms). The setup in the large room should be arranged to facilitate interchange and discussion. Classroom and lecture-hall formats with rows of tables and chairs all facing a central podium are inappropriate. Avoid any facility where chairs and desks are bolted to the floor. The ideal is a U-shaped layout with space at the open end of the U for the session leader or facilitator to present material or guide discussion and to move into the U. There should be adequate space in the plenary room for side tables for trainer/facilitator materials, overhead projectors (if needed), and coffee/tea and snacks.

Other desirable features in facilities include whiteboards and/or flip-chart stands, walls that will not be damaged by taping flip-chart paper to them, air conditioning and adequate ventilation (particularly if smoking is permitted), sufficient lighting, and availability of telephones and access to computers. Obviously, workshop organizers will need to be flexible about the physical layout, since in most situations the choice of facilities requires some trade-offs in amenities available.

Prepare workshop design. Content details for individual workshop sessions clearly depend upon the particular situation. However, policy management workshops share a common design framework. The underlying structure for workshop design is a flow that begins with developing mutual understanding of the issues to be addressed, the objectives to be achieved, and what needs to be done to make progress; moves to reaching agreements on tasks and responsibilities; and culminates in preparing action/monitoring plans and determining next steps. Within this general structure, workshop design reflects several basic principles.

The first principle is *simplicity.* Designs should concentrate on achieving a few critical objectives, based on a realistic assessment of what can be done in the time available, given the backgrounds and capacities of the participants. Pressing people to do too much is counterproductive; marathon sessions quickly reach the point of diminishing returns. Overly complex and ambitious designs lead to frustration and disappointment, as well as a feeling that policy implementation is an excessively daunting endeavor.

The second principle is *flexibility*. Just as in implementation planning itself, not all actions can be completely specified in advance. The design should allow for changes in sessions, reallocation of time if some activities take longer than anticipated, and slots where new activities can be inserted if necessary. Designs can usually accommodate these changes by being generous in estimating session times, which builds in slack that can be used when called for.

The third principle is *action*. In practice this means a design that mixes presentations and discussions with small-group exercises, preparation of work products, and decision-making. Do not program extended periods of time in which participants sit passively for speeches, lectures, or other kinds of exposition. If background information is important, the design includes distribution of material to participants beforehand with a clear expectation that reading is to be done prior to attending the workshop. Workshops as a rule avoid prolonged plenary discussions where "air time" is limited to a single speaker at a time. The preference is to design small-group discussions, in which more interchange among greater numbers of participants is possible, followed by plenary sessions that highlight the key points of the small groups' thinking and synthesize conclusions for all participants.

Workshop Conduct

Conducting the workshop successfully blends attention to content with concern for process. As mentioned earlier, the substantive content of the workshop will be determined by the key issues the policy addresses, the objectives and plans established, and the particular policy implementation situation, thus it is difficult to provide general suggestions. Guidelines here focus on the process side of conducting the workshop.

View the design as a road map as well as a destination. As noted in the guidance for workshop preparation, the design should be flexible. The workshop, agenda is not a blueprint. The aim is to achieve the purpose of the workshop, not to pursue the planned sessions as scheduled. The organizers should use the design to monitor progress. If it appears during the workshop that more or less time is needed for particular sessions, the agenda should be modified. For example, workshops that combine participants who did not previously know each other, or who have not worked together before, require a certain amount of "breaking in" before the group can become fully functional. This factor calls for flexibility in determining session schedules.

Treat the participants as adults. Because so much of people's experience with learning takes place in schools, workshop organizers and participants alike have a subconscious tendency to transfer the attitudes associated with early educational experiences to the workshop. If organizers act like parents and teachers, then participants readily take on the role of children. Policy management workshops, however, consider participants as self-directing adults who share responsibility with the organizers for workshop success and outputs. This perspective is made operational, for example, by clarifying expectations for the workshop at the opening session and by involving the participants in decisions about modifying the agenda. A useful technique is to begin each day's sessions with a summary review (by a preselected participant) of the previous day's activities, with commentary from the group, followed by a presentation of the agenda for the day, with an opportunity for questions or changes.

Focus on learning in combination with operational relevance. This recommendation relates to treating participants as adults in that adults learn more readily by confronting and consolidating new knowledge with their own experience. Workshops should give participants the opportunity to apply directly new techniques, tools, and approaches to the immediate tasks of managing policy change. Throughout the workshop, session leaders should stress the links between new material and operational applications. Part of this linkage is assured by the design, which follows presentations with small-group exercises to apply what has just been presented. In addition, organizers can reinforce the connections during discussions and question-and-answer periods.

Emphasize participation. Since a key feature of policy management workshops is to bring together the major actors associated with a particular policy reform, it is important that everyone's knowledge and perspectives be brought out. Organizers should be attuned to the patterns of communication in both plenary and small-group sessions. If some participants remain silent or appear reticent to share their views, they should be gently encouraged to express themselves. The work products generated during the workshop will be more useful to the extent that they include everyone's expertise and reflect all participants' points of view. Also, people will be more apt to accept the results if they feel that they contributed to them. Sessions should include opportunities to ask the group explicitly if everyone understands what is under discussion and if there is agreement on implications, intended outcomes, next steps, and so on.

Use facilitators. Workshops frequently employ a co-trainer approach that pairs someone with expertise in the technical content of the policy being implemented with a specialist in training and workshop process, known as a facilitator. Facilitators manage the process of the workshop to assure that objectives are met in a way that builds participants' abilities to work together effectively and produce the intended outputs, but they do not take positions on the policy or workshop content. The advantages of using a facilitator include these: (a) the important process dimensions of the workshop are effectively handled, (b) the workshop sponsors are freed to participate on the content side, because the facilitator is managing the process, and (c) the workshop results are better accepted because a neutral facilitator can defuse the potential suspicion that outcomes were engineered in advance by the organizers.

AN EXAMPLE FROM THE GAMBIA

USAID/Banjul turned to IPC to assist the Ministry of Finance and Economic Affairs (MFEA) to improve its capacity to plan and manage The Gambia's economic policy framework in support of the fiscal, financial, and market reforms being undertaken by the government. The capacity building intervention consisted of three steps: (1) analysis, (2) planning and action training, and (3) implementation of the plan and follow-up support. The first step was a management audit of the MFEA. Three consultants spent two weeks helping the MFEA, through interviews and discussions, to analyze its organizational objectives, structure, strategy, human resource base, and operating environment and to lay the groundwork for launching a strategic planning process using the workshop methodology.

The second step centered around a strategic management retreat for the MFEA. During this stage the MFEA established a steering committee to oversee the policy reform. A three-person team worked with the steering committee and ministry leadership to customize the draft workshop design and facilitate the three-day event for the staff (see Box 9.1). The workshop addressed four objectives: (1) introduce the basic concepts of strategic planning and management, (2) lay the foundation for strategic planning at the MFEA, (3) clarify the ministry's objectives and mission, and (4) analyze the organizational strengths of the MFEA and the challenges it faces. Meetings were held following the retreat for the MFEA task force to identify strategic options and to develop an action plan for a performance improvement strategy.

The task force that emerged out of the retreat was charged with implementing the action plans developed in the post-retreat meetings. This was the third step of the capacity building effort. Ownership of and responsibility for the plan rested with the MFEA task force members. The IPC team conducted periodic follow-up, providing short-term process facilitation and technical support to the members of the various task forces, helping them to identify indicators, track progress, and revise strategies as needed. The ministry leadership credited the initiation of a strategic planning and management process with greatly enhancing the MFEA's confidence and ability to deal with its ambitious mandate.

Box 9.1 MFEA Policy Management Retreat

Friday, 28 January

4:00 – 4:15	Opening remarks by the minister and permanent secretary, MFEA
4:15 – 4:30	Introduction to the workshop
	• *Review of objectives of workshop, schedule, and format*
4:30 – 5:00	Concepts of strategic management
	• *Presentation on strategic management: What is it, why do we care about it, what is its relevance to the MFEA?*
5:00 – 5:15	MFEA mission statement and objectives
	• *Presentation on mission statements and their links to an "objective tree"*
5:15 – 6:00	Small-group sessions on MFEA mission and objectives
6:00 – 6:30	Small-group presentations
6:30 – 7:00	Discussion, summary, and plenary-group consensus
7:00 – 8:00	Cocktail reception

Saturday, 29 January

9:00 – 9:30	Strategy and the SWOT framework
	• *Presentation on the identification of strengths, weaknesses, opportunities, and threats for the MFEA*
9:30 – 10:00	Overview of the external operating environment
	• *Presentation of categories of external factors, key factors affecting the MFEA, and explanation of the small-group exercise*
10:00 – 10:45	Small-group sessions
	• *Identification of key external factors for the MFEA, setting priorities among factors, identification of implications for MFEA*
10:45 – 11:00	Coffee break
11:00 – 12:00	Small-group presentations and plenary discussion
	• *Discussion of small-group results and points with most/least consensus; plenary discussion to reach consensus across groups*
12:00 – 2:00	Lunch break
2:00 – 2:15	Introduction to internal assessment of the MFEA
2:15 – 2:45	Small-group sessions
	• *Identification and analysis of the MFEA's internal strengths and weaknesses*

2:45 – 3:00	Coffee break
3:00 – 3:30	Small-group sessions (continued)
3:30 – 4:30	Small-group presentations and plenary discussion

- *Discussion of small-group results and points with most/least consensus; plenary discussion to reach consensus across groups*

4:30 – 5:30	SWOT synthesis and plenary discussion

Sunday, 30 January

10:00 – 10:30	Interministerial round table: MFEA stakeholders

- *Identification of the MFEA's key stakeholders; presentation of a stakeholder analysis matrix*

10:30 – 11:30	Small-group sessions

- *Discussion and analysis of the performance criteria shared by the MFEA and its key stakeholders*

11:30 – 12:00	Small-group presentations and plenary discussion

- *Discussion of small-group results and points of agreement and disagreement; plenary discussion to reach consensus across groups*

12:00 – 1:30	Lunch break
1:30 – 1:45	Identification of strategic issues and performance gaps

- *Presentation on classifying strategic issues and identifying performance problems*

1:45 – 2:30	Small-group sessions
2:30 – 2:45	Coffee break
2:45 – 4:00	Small-group presentations and plenary discussion

- *Discussion of small-group results and plenary consensus on strategic issues and performance gaps*

4:00 – 4:30	Closing remarks

- *Wrap-up and commentary on the retreat by the minister and deputy permanent secretary; discussion of the next week's agenda and mini-workshops for task force members, and links to the retreat.*

10

Advocacy for Policy Reform

In many developing and transitioning countries, the forces opposed to reform in various sectors remain strong. Nelson (1999), for example, points to the power of employee unions in the health and education sectors to counter change and maintain the status quo. If significant policy change is to occur, reformers and their allies need to work together to mobilize constituencies, influence key stakeholders, and build and sustain momentum to move forward. With the trends toward democratization (Diamond and Plattner 1995, 1996) and the rise of civil society, both nationally and internationally (Burbidge 1997, Florini 2000), governments in many countries are more open to policy input from citizens, and citizens are better organized to provide such input. One important tool for influencing outcomes in democratic polities is advocacy, also called lobbying. Policy advocacy can be defined as the effort of individuals or groups to influence policymakers and to have an impact on public policy decisions and the actions of government.

This chapter examines the nature of advocacy, what is required to do it effectively, and when and how it can best be used to influence policy decisions. This chapter's viewpoint differs from that of the others in this book in that the focus is not primarily on the public sector policy manager but rather on the external actors seeking to participate in the policy reform process and assure that their views are incorporated into policy and implementation decisions. This does not necessarily mean operating completely independent of government, though that is one option. As several of the examples in Chapter 4 illustrate, advocacy activities can be engaged in through partnerships with state actors or with other NGOs. Throughout this book our discussion has shown that policy reform frequently requires action on the part of large numbers of actors, both inside

---

This chapter draws on the IPC Technical Note on lobbying, co-authored by Benjamin L. Crosby and Deborah M. Orsini. It appeared as Technical Note No. 7 (1996).

and outside of government, all with a stake in policy outcomes and potentially a role to play in influencing the direction of implementation. For
policy managers, advocacy can be particularly important for the implementation tasks of constituency building and resource mobilization (see
Chapter 2).

SOME CAVEATS REGARDING ADVOCACY IN DEVELOPING AND TRANSITIONING COUNTRIES

Before proceeding it is worthwhile noting several issues and caveats
surrounding the application of advocacy techniques in developing and
transitioning countries. The idealized notion of pluralist democracy sees
interest aggregation of constituencies and the communication of demands
to policymakers as central to citizens' exercise of voice through the ballot
box and other channels, and the provision of incentives for government
to respond.[1] However, several caveats arise. The first relates to the conditions under which advocacy techniques will lead to advancing policy pluralism. Without functioning systems of accountability and transparency,
interest-group lobbying risks reinforcing existing patronage arrangements
and corruption. In many developing and transitioning countries these
systems are weak.[2]

The second caveat has to do with the difference between the idealized
version of interest groups and what happens in practice. While there are,
as we have noted, expanded openings for democratic practices in many
developing and transitioning countries, the reality is that governments
rely strongly on support from powerful economic and social interests.[3] In
systems dominated by interlocking elites and reinforced by patronage,
building advocacy capacity among disenfranchised or marginalized groups
is unlikely to be sufficient to modify these dynamics significantly, absent
other changes.

These caveats suggest that we should be cautious concerning expectations for the transfer of advocacy techniques to developing and transitioning
countries. The idealized version of pluralist democracy is the one that international donors have tended to export abroad, along with interest-group
advocacy (see Carothers 1999). For example, much of the support that
USAID has provided to civil society groups has aimed to develop advocacy skills and capacities (see Hansen 1996, Ottaway and Carothers 2000).
Further, in the eyes of many observers, advocacy and lobbying techniques
are Western, and particularly North American, political tools, and thus
their applicability in other cultural settings may be questionable. Despite
these cautions, there are documented cases of successful grassroots lobbying for policy change, often with assistance from international civil
society groups and donors. The mobilization and influence of women's

groups on gender issues are a good example of such success.[4] With these caveats in mind, we turn to take a closer look at advocacy.

THE NATURE OF ADVOCACY AND LOBBYING

Advocacy involves influencing decision-makers and thus is a political activity. As part of that influencing process, advocacy also entails identifying and championing issues to get them on policy agendas, educating officials and citizens regarding the issues, mobilizing support, and creating coalitions. While these activities may be carried out by individuals or private firms interested in influencing the direction or outcome of a particular policy, they are generally undertaken by organizations holding shared views on policy issues; these organizations are known as interest groups. In developing/transitioning countries numerous civil society groups are organized around advocacy, either as individual entities or in advocacy networks (see, for example, Cardenas and Richiedei 2000). In advanced democratic political systems, lobbying tends to be highly competitive, with multiple groups focused on the same issue (though from different perspectives) vying for the attention and support of decision-makers and citizens. In developing and transitioning countries the degree of competition tends to be lower, a more pressing concern being gaining access to the policy process.

Effective lobbying is achieved through the presentation of persuasive arguments to policymakers (and other stakeholders). To produce persuasive arguments usually means the development of solid expertise concerning the issue under consideration and the ability to communicate with policymakers using information and arguments that resonate with their concerns. Information should be presented to highlight a group's interests, targeting the most important and relevant issues from the group's point of view. Such packaging is vital to persuasive advocacy.

Besides packaging the policy message, timing can be crucial for successful lobbying. Policy "windows" open and close, and in democratic systems policymakers come and go as a result of elections. If advocacy groups are to have impact, they must get to know the relevant policymakers and the system within which they operate.[5] Delays in action could result in missed opportunities, or conversely, lobbying for a policy issue before it has become salient may cause the message to fall on deaf ears.

In sum, the nature of advocacy comprises (a) articulating priorities, (b) identifying and understanding who needs to be influenced, (c) crafting the message to be communicated, and (d) devising a set of activities to carry out the strategy. The guidelines presented below elaborate on how to do these tasks. Given the importance of the political environment in developing and transitioning countries, we move next to a discussion of matching advocacy strategies to the degree of openness in the political system.

ADVOCACY STRATEGIES

As many observers have detailed, the degree to which governments are open to advocacy on the part of NGOs, citizens or business associations, and other civil society groups varies (see, for example, Clark 1991 and 1995, Fisher 1998, Fiszbein and Lowden 1998, Fowler 1991 and 1997, and Korten 1990). When governments are suspicious of efforts to organize and discourage or repress dissent, advocacy groups may have to think about interacting with public officials in a non-threatening way in order to build credibility and access. By biding their time, building trust, developing a comparative advantage, and consolidating access to policymakers, groups can potentially move toward taking more initiative and toward scaling up (see Edwards and Hulme 1992). On the other hand, when governments are more open and democratic, advocacy groups can establish linkages with a variety of decision-makers and begin their efforts with an aggressive or even confrontational stance.

IPC's experience, for example, with the West African Enterprise Network (presented in Chapter 4) indicates that advocacy groups need to match their lobbying strategies to the political environment. We illustrate the options for different strategies in Figure 10.1, which shows these as a continuum from issue-specific collaboration to continuous advocacy. As the figure shows, the choice of a particular lobbying strategy depends on the degree to which the political system and its policy process are centralized or open. The "open-closed" dimension can be thought of as a shorthand for the degree of democratic governance. The more open and democratic the system, the more alternative decision-making centers are available, and the more possibilities for lobbying exist. At the same time, the more open the system, the greater the opportunity for use of independent or confrontational advocacy strategies.

The figure also indicates that advocacy NGOs will need different levels of resources and skills to carry out each of the strategies. Issue-specific collaboration is the least demanding and requires the fewest skills and resources, while a permanent advocacy capacity calls for considerable skill, commitment, and resources. What is important to note is that groups must choose a strategy that matches the opportunity for access to decision-makers with their own skills and resources. A centralized political system probably will allow little space for effective action by a permanent advocacy group. In that setting it would likely be more effective to pursue a less confrontational, more collaborative approach—one that consolidates access by working in partnership with government (see Chapter 4).

Figure 10.1 Strategies for Lobbying: From Collaboration to Advocacy

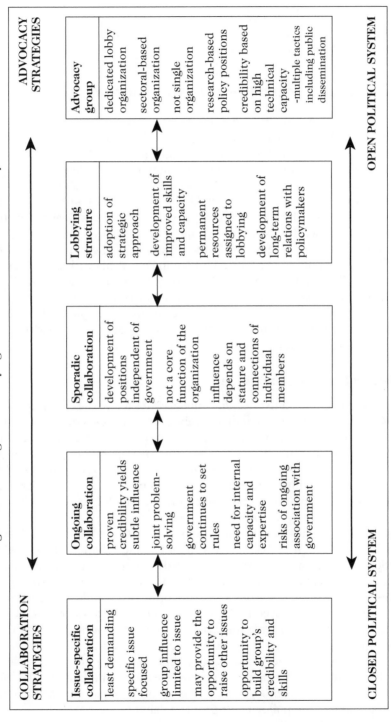

Issue-specific collaboration	Ongoing collaboration	Sporadic collaboration	Lobbying structure	Advocacy group
least demanding	proven credibility yields subtle influence	development of positions independent of government	adoption of strategic approach	dedicated lobby organization
specific issue focused	joint problem-solving	not a core function of the organization	development of improved skills and capacity	sectoral-based organization
group influence limited to issue	government continues to set rules	influence depends on stature and connections of individual members	permanent resources assigned to lobbying	not single organization
may provide the opportunity to raise other issues	need for internal capacity and expertise		development of long-term relations with policymakers	research-based policy positions
opportunity to build group's credibility and skills	risks of ongoing association with government			credibility based on high technical capacity
				-multiple tactics including public dissemination

COLLABORATION STRATEGIES

ADVOCACY STRATEGIES

CLOSED POLITICAL SYSTEM

OPEN POLITICAL SYSTEM

Source: Scribner and Crosby 1997.

If over time the political system moves toward the more democratic end of the continuum, however, groups will need to increase their skills and resources and acquire new capacities.

GUIDELINES FOR ADVOCACY

The following guidelines support the development of a set of key capacities for groups pursuing advocacy strategies. These capacities include (1) an understanding of the issues, (2) a grasp of how the policy decision-making process works, (3) a comprehension of the political environment for policymaking, (4) knowledge of who the policy decision-makers are and how they fit into the policymaking process, (5) identification of potential allies and their potential support, and (6) identification of their strengths and weaknesses. These capacities fall within the looking out, looking in, and looking ahead framework of strategic management presented in Chapter 2 (see Box 2.1). Looking out deals with issue identification and understanding the policy environment and the various stakeholders. Looking in involves the assessment of the group's resources, strengths, weaknesses, and comparative advantage. Looking ahead combines these elements into the pursuit of advocacy actions along with tracking outcomes and impacts over time.

Identify Priorities and Issues

Lobbying groups must decide which themes and issues are important, and then decide which are indispensable. Most interest groups have more interests and needs than can possibly be dealt with under resource limitations. Therefore, the need to set priorities is imperative. The more narrowly focused a group's interests, the easier it is to set priorities. However, groups encompassing a broad range of interests, such as chambers of commerce, will find the task much more difficult because interests of one subgroup may conflict with another.[6]

Setting priorities begins with an assessment of what policy changes would be in a group's interest. These might include changes such as elimination of government restrictions on market entry or access, the establishment or creation of fiscal incentives, or the reduction of certain regulations on business operations. Setting priorities should be determined by degree of impact or concern that an issue presents to groups' key interests, the issue's urgency in terms of short-term versus long-term effects, the immediacy of the issue with respect to a possible timetable for treatment or adoption by the government, how hospitable the political environment is with respect to groups' positions, the likelihood of success by competing claims, and whether or not groups can feasibly affect the outcome of the policymaking and decision process.

Determining priorities may be achieved by a variety of methods. Small working groups in specific areas of key interest may be established. These may be formally established, as in the case of South Africa's Chamber of Business (SACOB), which created permanent working groups that met regularly both to set priorities and to monitor issues in various areas (for example, export and trade policy, fiscal and taxation policy). Another example from the same country is the Sunnyside Group (a small-business advocacy coalition), which formed informal working groups on an ad hoc basis as issues arose. When the issue was dealt with, the task group dissolved.

Once groups have set priorities for their issues, they need to assure consistency of presentation by developing a position statement. This may be a formal position paper or simply an outline on a set of transparencies. Regardless of the form, it should be concise, clear, factual, and moderate in tone. This document can be used with politicians, policymakers, the press, potential allies and members of the interest group, and donor agencies. Where helpful, graphs, charts, and diagrams can be used to illustrate concepts visually. Position papers also can be used as the basis for testimony at public hearings or for other public communication.

Understand the Policy Issue

If groups are to influence policy outcomes, then they need a solid understanding of the issue under consideration. Tools such as policy characteristics analysis (see Chapter 7) can be very helpful in developing a systematic analysis. Groups should understand and be able to comment on alternative or conflicting positions on the issue, as well as grasping their own perspective. By providing information to government policymakers to use in formulating policy, groups can gain indirect influence on the policy agenda-setting process. Developing expertise, especially in the more technical aspects of the issue, will serve to increase credibility and can leverage access. Sometimes a reputation for expertise means that policymakers will request assistance in preparing speeches on the issues or in developing legislation.

Expertise can be developed in-house or obtained on a contract basis. In-house capacity can be developed in several ways. A low-cost approach is to encourage members of the group with particular issue expertise to develop their capacities more fully. Groups might also create in-house teams with experts in particular areas, which could be temporary or permanent. If greater expertise is needed, groups might create a formal policy analysis unit whose principal task is research on issues and the development of alternative positions. This option requires considerable resources and is not recommended for groups with sporadic needs for expert information or analysis.

When analytic capacity is needed only periodically, groups can contract for such expertise when needed and can develop outside sources of information. These might include local or international experts on certain issues, government officials responsible for policy planning and implementation, and published information on the issues, such as journals, newsletters, or government documents. Much useful information is available on the Internet. Working with universities or coalitions with other groups can also be explored. Developing mechanisms to reinforce the group's expert status with stakeholders can be very helpful. This might be done through publication of studies, opinion editorials, position papers, issue analysis reports, political impact reports, and the like. The important thing is to make the group's expertise visible.

Understand the Policy Decision-making Process

Without a clear understanding of how policy decision-making works, lobbying risks ineffectiveness. However, in many countries it is often not at all clear how the decision-making process actually works. In centralized political systems characterized by closed policy circles, there can be hidden and/or unofficial channels of access. Although most countries have written statements and procedures about how policy initiatives are transformed into laws or regulations, frequently informal processes are as important as official channels, if not more so. Further, policy development follows different paths through the decision-making process depending upon the issue. The effort expended in comprehending the process will allow lobby groups to pinpoint their efforts. Once they know how the process works and who is involved, influence options become clearer. Questions for exploration include the following: If the initiative must be passed by the legislative body, who submits the initiative and through what procedure? Does the bill go to a committee? which one(s)? how many "readings" or debates are there? Are hearings held, and are the hearings public? What other processes are involved, and who is involved in those processes? If one is interested in changing a regulation, how is that accomplished? How are changes proposed, and who can do so? Are legal opinions sought?

Interest groups should avoid the trap of assuming that the processes prescribed by the country's law and constitution are those that actually prevail. Generally, an informal decision-making process parallels (or in some countries supplants) the formal one.[7] The better groups understand the informal processes, the more effective they will be. Since issues vary widely in content, no single process fits all cases.

Identify Decision-makers and Stakeholders

In addition to understanding the policy decision-making process, it is also critical to know who makes decisions. When political and decision-making systems are highly centralized, a good evaluation of decision-makers and their advisors can often lead to concealed channels of access. Even where the system is open, knowledge about decision-makers can help lobbyists to influence a policy issue more effectively. Relevant questions include: Who are the different actors involved in the decision? What can be learned about them and their respective interests or level of information? In which part of the decision-making apparatus or at what stage of the process are they located? Are they at points in the process where key decisions will be made? What sort of influence do they have on or over the process or its outcomes? Key stakeholders may be spread among several agencies. For example, if a group is concerned with trade policy, it will find that several ministries might have an influence on that policy. These might include ministries of commerce, finance, industry, and the central bank. Each, however, will likely have different sorts of stakes in the policy. The commerce ministry, for example, might want to eliminate tariff barriers, while the finance ministry might want to maintain them in order to minimize a potential budget deficit. If the legislature intervenes as well, then there may be one or more committees that the group will need to be concerned about. The group must therefore learn what specific interests each has and how it can influence those interests.

Groups also need to understand why key actors are interested in a particular issue and what their record has been on that issue. Groups should become sufficiently familiar with these actors to understand what appeals to the decision-makers and how to make the issue attractive to them. Groups should know what motivates decision-makers. They should be able to assess decision-makers' needs regarding the issue and how they might help. They should also determine who decision-makers' key advisers are and how can they be reached. Do these key actors have allies that are accessible and can be influenced? A stakeholder analysis can be particularly useful to systematize such information (see Chapter 6). Once the key decision-makers are identified, groups may engage in direct face-to-face lobbying with them.

Comprehend the Political Environment

There are always at least two sides to any issue. Groups will likely compete with other interests for favorable outcomes for policies under consideration. In any political system there are multiple forces trying to capture limited resources. If groups are to be effective, they need to develop a solid comprehension of the political environment and those forces with which they will have to compete to achieve their policy influence and advocacy goals. The questions to ask are these: What does the balance of forces in the environment look like? Does that balance favor the sorts of interests represented by the group? Beyond the executive branch agencies and the legislature, who are the major players in the system?

Are these political parties, other organized interest groups, civil society organizations, think tanks, or citizens' associations? How do these actors' concerns line up with respect to the group's interests?

In both established and emerging democracies the balance of forces can be more or less unstable and may shift rapidly. If groups have continuing interests in a particular issue or a variety of issues, they will need to monitor the political environment periodically. There are several tools available to assist in this process. For instance, political mapping or force-field analysis can provide an assessment of such forces (see Chapter 8).

Understand the Group's Strengths and Limitations

If groups are to be effective, they must have or be able to offer something that will appeal to the decision-maker targeted for lobbying. What do they have that would make policymakers listen to their views? That something might be their status or credibility, their ability to mobilize human and/or material resources, the size or quality of their membership, their commitment to the issue, their access to other decision-makers, or their special knowledge of the issue. Are the groups recognized as having superior knowledge about some issues, and can that be put into digestible, persuasive form for decision-makers? Do the groups have some special social status in society that assures their opinions will be heard? Can they easily mobilize financial resources to pay for advertising campaigns? Can they mobilize large numbers of constituents for demonstrations or for letter-writing campaigns?

Lobbying organizations' leaders bear a significant responsibility for promoting the interests of their members and for developing personal contacts with key decision-makers. Leaders need to have both a good understanding of their group's strengths and limitations and a good sense of how to employ their resources effectively. Leaders should also recognize that while they may understand the issues better than anyone else in the group, they may not always be the best individuals to transmit the group's message. Spokespersons should be credible and possess both strong communication skills and the ability to listen. Such a person may not be the group's leader but rather a representative who can best articulate or present the group's interests and views. Indeed, given the choice between a brilliant analyst and one considerably less brilliant but with superior interpersonal skills, Smucker (1991) argues that one should opt for the latter.

Develop a Comparative Advantage

As Chapter 3 points out, decision-makers face a large number of potential participants in policymaking and implementation, and they have limits on how many stakeholders they can listen to. Successful advocacy groups need to differentiate themselves from other groups making similar demands; the problem is how to do so. One strategy is to develop some sort of comparative advantage that sets the group apart from others. How can groups characterize interests that will make them different from others? Do they have distinctive capabilities, and how can those capabilities best be put to use? Even if there are several groups that have very similar interests, a group can set itself apart from the others by articulating its message in a distinctive way.

To be effective, groups seeking to use their comparative advantage must fine-tune it to decision-makers' needs. For instance, if the group determines that the decision-maker has fairly constant needs for a certain kind of information, it can specialize in the production of high-quality analysis in that area. For example, in the United States, the Worldwatch Institute specializes in identifying environmental trends and reporting on their policy implications. In India, a civil society organization in the state of Gujarat, Developing Initiatives for Social and Human Action (DISHA), built in-depth knowledge of the state budget through its advocacy work for tribal groups and the poor (Buhl 1997). DISHA's analytic competence became so strong that state legislators regularly asked the organization for assistance in understanding their own budget.

Besides information, groups can exploit a comparative advantage in delivering political support and votes. In democratic systems politicians are sensitive to the views of vocal, well-organized, and active local groups, especially if an election is approaching. Grassroots advocacy and constituency mobilization can be important assets in the eyes of politicians. If groups are adept at mobilizing constituents behind certain issues, then policymakers may find them useful. This is a classic comparative advantage of labor unions, which can publicly endorse candidates running for office, or organize demonstrations backing or opposing the positions of certain decision-makers (Nelson 1999, Lindenberg and Crosby 1981). Another comparative advantage can be the mobilization of funds for campaign financing, by which groups can in essence "buy" influence over elected officials through financial contributions to their campaigns (however, there is controversy concerning whether such practices help or harm democracy and the policy process).

Identify Allies and the Support They Can Provide

Frequently, groups discover that they do not have sufficient resources or clout to promote a particular issue on their own. In this case they need allies to influence and persuade decision-makers. Groups may find coalitions helpful in advancing their interests. Joining with other associations in permanent or temporary alliances can be effective in leveraging support and convincing government officials that the interests defended are not just those of a narrow special-interest group (see Sabatier and Jenkins-Smith 1993). Often it is necessary for lobbying groups to work with a coalition of other organizations to have long-term effectiveness. While coalitions reduce the risk for their individual members, there are costs. For example, potential allies may exact a price for their support that is higher than lobbying groups are willing or able to pay. In this case negotiation may be necessary, involving time and effort to determine the importance of the requested support, what the allies have to offer, and what incentives could induce them to cooperate. Further, expanding coalitions can dilute a group's focus. As Chapter 4 pointed out, this was a problem that the West Africa Enterprise Network faced; it solved the difficulty by creating sub-networks to represent specialized interests.

When evaluating the need to work with other groups, lobbyists should be cautious, regardless of the initial appeal of others. Overall objectives should be congruent. Allies should bring something concrete to the deal at a price that is within reason. Groups should also be certain that common priorities exist or can be developed. Should it turn out that the presumed allies are actually pursuing objectives or priorities that are at cross-purposes, a coalition or alliance can do more harm than good.

Develop Communication Strategies and Capacities

Effective communication of messages to policymakers and constituencies is perhaps the single most crucial factor in the success of interest groups. No single strategy will be effective for all issues and audiences. Tailored communication strategies will need to be developed. While a detailed report on the cost-benefit nuances of proposed legislation may be useful for dealing with policy specialists, it will probably be much less effective with the general public. Groups need to understand the concerns of their different audiences and what sorts of messages they will find appealing and convincing.

Groups also need to access different communication channels, for example, position papers, radio and television interviews, flyers for distribution to the public, posters, newsletters, articles in newspapers and magazines, as well as paid ads in the media. As the literature on lobbying attests, communication techniques, especially use of the press, can be highly effective in issue promotion (Laothamatas 1988, Garrity and Picard 1991, Lo 1991). Forums, such as public-private dialogues, debates, town hall meetings, and round tables or public hearings offer the opportunity for interested parties to discuss and debate policy issues and to build consensus and constituencies (see the discussion of forums in Chapter 5). Finally, new information technologies are a burgeoning advocacy channel, encompassing electronic mail (e-mail), Internet, teleconferencing, cell phones, and so on (see McNutt and Boland 1999).[8]

For example, the West Africa Enterprise Network used a number of communication options. Its national network members organized dinner meetings to foster exchange between private entrepreneurs and government officials, and in some countries they prepared white papers on particular issues for distribution to technocrats and policymakers. At the regional level, the network organized annual conferences that received high visibility in both the print and broadcast media, and it produced a newsletter mailed to all its constituents and supporters.

NOTES

1. According to this model, lobbying performs functions that are fundamental to democratic systems of government. If multiple interest groups can express their positions in open debate, there is more openness and equity in the policy process and chances for conflict are diminished. By attempting to arrive at decisions that emerge from a consensus among the interested parties, the government achieves greater legitimacy and serves its citizens better.

2. See the informative discussion of accountability issues in emerging democracies in Schedler et al. (1999).

3. As we have indicated in previous chapters, interest-group politics (within which advocacy plays a large role) in Western democracies is viewed by some observers as undermining rather than advancing the public interest (see, for example, Lowi 1979, Schneider and Ingram 1997).

4. See, for example, the *International Journal of Organization Theory and Behavior* 2/1&2 (1999), "Special issue on grassroots organizations and influencing public policy processes: Lessons from around the world." The overview can be found in Coston (1999). Regarding gender, see the articles on women's organizations in Turkey (Kardam and Erturk 1999), and on women's involvement in civic education in Mongolia (Coston and Butz 1999).

5. This highlights the importance of stakeholder analysis (Chapter 6) and political and institutional mapping (Chapter 8).

6. The free-rider problem might emerge as well (Olson 1965).

7. This is the case, for example, in Africa (see Gulhati 1990); in the United States, see Bardach (1977).

8. Some dramatic examples of the use of information technology by civil society groups include the contribution of fax machines to organizing protest in China in the late 1980s and 1990s and, more recently, the use of cell phones in the Philippines to organize "instant protests" calling for the resignation of President Estrada (Chandrasekaran 2000).

11

Conflict Resolution

There are many opportunities for disagreements and disputes to arise among stakeholders when a country's policies are being changed or reforms are being implemented. Conflicts can arise between winners and losers when resources are redistributed. Some groups are empowered at the expense of others; latent political, economic, social, and cultural problems rise to the surface. New grievances are aired, and government imposes new regulations and procedures. In many developing countries access to and control over natural resources are prime areas that generate conflict, which in some cases escalates to violent levels (see Klare 2001).

While the potential for conflict as part of the policy process is ever present, as we have noted throughout this book, policy implementation calls for shared and coordinated action by numerous stakeholders. Desired outcomes can be achieved only if they find a way to cooperate and act interdependently, despite their differences (see Chapter 5). Thus, implementing policy change provides a simultaneous and sometimes contradictory stimulus both to seek resolution to conflict and to build a new consensus. Happily, most techniques that are labeled "conflict resolution mechanisms" are equally useful in helping parties recognize their commonly shared problems and find mutually acceptable ways to cooperate.

Understanding and activating the agreement motive in policy implementation situations can be a powerful tool for policy managers to tackle barriers to cooperation and move implementation forward. Conflict resolution techniques stimulate stakeholder participation, encourage policy ownership, and build institutional capacity. Typically, they are implemented through group facilitation approaches. They are designed to be sensitive to their context and thus are adaptable to changes in the situation. Ultimately, these techniques are forward-looking mechanisms, seeking to bolster a transformation of the situation from the negative to the positive. This chapter

---

Bertram I. Spector is the author of the original version of this chapter, which appeared in IPC's Technical Notes Series No. 9 (1997).

offers guidance on the application of conflict resolution methods to policy reform. An understanding of these techniques can help deal with the conflicts that often threaten to disrupt progress in implementing reforms.

CONFLICT IN THE INTERNATIONAL DEVELOPMENT CONTEXT

Societies emerging from civil war, ethnic strife, democratizing, or pursuing extensive policy reform often encounter conflict among stakeholders (see, for example, Kumar 1997). Recognition and successful diagnosis

Table 11.1 Conflict Situations and Potential Responses

Conflict situation	Possible conflict resolution response
Post-conflict transitions involving refugee repatriation and resettlement, the continuation of religious and ethnic cleavages, and necessitating the rebuilding of the economy, extensive land reform, and reconstruction of housing and infrastructure	Joint interactive problem-solving workshops and third-party mediation
Resource maldistribution	Traditional host country conflict resolution mechanisms, such as forms of arbitration or mediation
Demobilizing and disarming combatant units	Unilateral confidence building measures
Long-standing grievances	Dispute management systems, such as grievance commissions
Complex emergencies involving natural and manmade disasters, terrorist/insurgency attacks, collapsed state institutions and authority, and the distribution of humanitarian assistance	Facilitation workshops, negotiation, joint collaborative projects
Conflicts of interest that arise between state-owned enterprises and private businesses that compete with each other in the same industry	Arbitration and mediation
Tensions among entrepreneurs and government officials concerning corrupt practices and organized crime	Problem-solving workshops
Environmental degradation and shared resources	Mediation and negotiation

require an understanding and awareness of the different situations that are prone to conflict. Table 11.1 identifies some of the conditions that can trigger conflict, along with some possible conflict resolution responses.

DIAGNOSIS: IF AND WHEN
TO APPLY CONFLICT RESOLUTION APPROACHES

What are the key factors that policy reformers need to be aware of prior to and during policy implementation that can alert them to the potential for disruptive conflicts? What are the conditions that should prompt them to decide to employ conflict resolution techniques? The problem is to anticipate conflict or cooperation needs and then do something about it, thereby preventing or averting possible negative effects on the main task of implementing policy change.[1]

Operationally, this entails continuous fact-finding and diagnostic activities. Information must be gathered from all perspectives on the problem, emerging threats, warnings, differences of opinion, and outright disputes. To do this, ongoing monitoring of the particular situation and its broader context is required. Maintaining a constant informal dialogue with the various stakeholders and observers of the situation is essential.

Table 11.2 provides specific guidance on the information needed to make assessments. Rapid diagnoses must be conducted to assess the presence of cooperation needs and future conflicts. This information can be categorized into several early warning indicators. Practitioners and consultants need to answer these questions about the issues, actors, processes, strategies, and situation on a continual basis, since the situation is ever changing. If the answers to any of these questions suggest potential conflict, dissension, or the need for interdependent action, they should be viewed as early warnings of possible disruption to the policy implementation process and responses should be taken to institute conflict resolution approaches.

WHAT TO DO: IDENTIFYING APPROPRIATE CONFLICT
RESOLUTION TECHNIQUES

Four basic conflict resolution mechanisms are available. There are multiple variations of these mechanisms that can be designed and tailored to each particular circumstance.

Confidence Building

This method is used to develop trust and confidence among parties that may be in conflict or that need to enhance their cooperative bonds. Confidence building is usually a step-by-step process in which graduated unilateral concessions are made by one party and in-kind reciprocation

Table 11.2 Diagnostic Questions
to Assess Conflict and Cooperation
in Policy Implementation

	Conflict questions	Cooperation questions
Issues	• What are the contentious issues? • Do these issues deal with basic needs or concrete interests? • What priority do these issues have with the parties? • What is the extent of differences between stakeholders on these issues? • For how long have these issues been in contention?	• What factors keep the parties apart? • Are there issues on which stakeholders must cooperate to achieve their goals? What are they? • How much and what type of cooperation is needed?
Actors	• Do the major stakeholders perceive that they are participating effectively in policy implementation activities? • Do these stakeholders hold extreme goals or positions on the major issues? • How flexible are the positions of these stakeholders? Are they intent on "winning" or open to compromise? • Do these stakeholders have historical enmities? • Are there major differences in power or resources available to the stakeholders? • Have there been changes in the leadership among any of the stakeholders that may produce a change in position or flexibility?	• Do the stakeholders perceive a common issue/problem on which they must jointly cooperate in order to achieve their objectives? • Do the stakeholders appear willing to cooperate?
Process	• Are the policy formulation and implementation processes under way perceived as fair and just by all participants? • Are the dialogue and debate among stakeholders carried out in an open and free manner? Are all parties given equal access to the debate?	• Is there a ready forum to commence dialogue on an interdependence agreement?
Strategies	• Are the strategies and tactics being used by any of the stakeholders overly aggressive, threatening, or provocative? • Are any of the stakeholders being evasive, deceptive, or failing to participate openly in the policy implementation process?	• Are there alternatives to interdependence among the stakeholders to handle the problem/issue? • What are the costs and benefits of cooperation?

	Conflict questions	Cooperation questions
Situation	• Are external parties or events influencing the situation or any of the stakeholders in a way that might destabilize the implementation process? • Is there heightened public awareness of the issues that could influence or clash with any of the stakeholder's positions?	• Are there existing institutions or procedures that can facilitate cooperation? • Are there factors that could prevent or hinder the development of cooperation? • How does public opinion view the need for cooperation? • Are there external parties (for example, donors) who are interested in establishing cooperation on the issue?

is sought from the other parties. By indicating good will and an honest desire to cooperate, confidence building mechanisms often lay the foundation for additional conflict resolution methods.

Joint Problem-Solving

Problem-solving involves the joint search for ways to deal with a dispute that divides the parties or a problem that they both need to resolve to mutual satisfaction. Interactive joint problem-solving is usually conducted in workshops (see Chapter 9) that are facilitated by third parties who set the terms of reference and agenda for the sessions. In these workshops the parties can share differing perspectives, think and problem-solve together, find opportunities for creative idea generation, and overcome deeply rooted conflicts through dialogue. Success in problem-solving often leads to the commencement of negotiations.

Mediation

Mediation involves third parties who facilitate a process of dialogue among the principal protagonists. Mediation is a viable alternative if the actors in conflict are willing to find a solution but require the services of a third party to help them reach it. Third parties can be governmental officials who carry the weight, power, and influence of their governments into a mediation effort, or they can be nongovernmental, unofficial mediators, practicing what has become known as track two diplomacy. Mediation can be a catalyst to begin negotiations or can be used to overcome an impasse within a negotiation (see, for example, Martin and Hamacher 1997).

Negotiation

Negotiation is a process of joint decision-making in which the principal parties seek to accommodate their conflicts of interest and develop a mutually acceptable solution. Negotiation typically seeks to achieve integrative solutions, in which an outcome is found that satisfies and reconciles the conflicting interests of all sides, but neither side views itself or the other as a clear winner or loser. All parties usually benefit in such integrative agreements (see, for example, Faure 1998).

APPLYING CONFLICT RESOLUTION TECHNIQUES TO POLICY MANAGEMENT

As Chapter 2 discusses, strategic management of the policy implementation process extends over a sequence of stages, each facing the potential for emergent conflict and changing needs for cooperation. Disputes over policy change can develop at any time, and the appropriate response may differ at each stage. Therefore, the questions in Table 11.3 can act as a guide for policy reformers in selecting among alternative conflict resolution approaches.

In the early strategic management stages of policy change (steps 1–3), the use of confidence building, joint problem-solving, and mediation techniques are generally beneficial. They can help to develop a sense of trust among the stakeholders, ensure a shared perception of the problem, and envision a common outcome and solution in principle, if not in detail. In the middle stages (steps 4–7), mediation and negotiation tend to be useful to search for common ground on the conflict issues, as compromises, trade-offs, or innovative integrative solutions are often required to bridge the gap between parties. In the latter stages (steps 8 and 9), joint problem-solving techniques again become appropriate to resolve differences that arise in the management of implementing change. In these stages, problem-solving should prove sufficient to iron out the details of already mediated or negotiated agreements.

Table 11.3 Conflict Resolution for Strategic Management of Policy Change

Step 1. Agreement on the process
Sources of potential dispute or the need for cooperative action:
Are any major stakeholders being excluded from the strategic management process?
Have there been delays in initiating the process or has it been accelerated too quickly?
Is there recognition, acceptance, and agreement on the joint problems facing the stakeholders?
Is there mutual trust or distrust of other stakeholders?
Prominent conflict resolution mechanisms:
Confidence building
Joint problem-solving
Mediation

Step 2. Identification and clarification of the organization's mission, objectives, and current strategies

Sources of potential dispute or the need for cooperative action:

Does the organization have conflicting objectives? Does achievement of particular objectives negate the seeking of others? Does that put certain subgroups within the organization at a disadvantage?

Do the objectives of the organization clash with the needs of clients, stakeholders, and constituents?

Does the organization employ strategies to achieve its objectives that may produce conflict internally or with its clients?

Is the problem facing the stakeholders high on their agendas?

Are their interests in the problem closely aligned? Are there clear formulas by which the problems can be solved to the satisfaction of all?

Step 3. Identification of the organization's internal strengths and weaknesses

Sources of potential dispute or the need for cooperative action:

Are the organization's resources distributed inequitably?

Does the organization fail in performing any of its major functions?

Are there major cleavages among the organization's clients, stakeholders, or constituents?

Are the organization and its members adaptable and prepared for change or rigid and inflexible?

Does the organization have available procedures and/or institutions to deal with solving problems jointly with other organizations?

Step 4. Assessment of threats and opportunities in the external environment

Sources of potential dispute or the need for cooperative action:

Are there political, economic, social, or technological changes that will influence or cause disruption in the direction or shape of the organization's policies and objectives?

Prominent conflict resolution mechanisms:

Mediation

Negotiation

Step 5. Identification of key stakeholders and their expectations and resources

Sources of potential dispute or the need for cooperative action:

Do the key stakeholders have conflicting goals or use conflicting means to achieve their goals?

Are the interests of various stakeholder groups shifting?

Step 6. Identification of key strategic issues

Sources of potential dispute or the need for cooperative action:

Do stakeholders define key issues differently?

Do stakeholders have differing visions of how problems can be solved?

Step 7. Design of an implementation strategy

Sources of potential dispute or the need for cooperative action:

Is the strategy controversial among the stakeholders?

Are there likely to be negative side effects from certain strategies, making particular stakeholders into losers and others into winners?

Will implementation of the strategy strain the resources of the organization?

Is the strategy incompatible with the organization's objectives and the legal/bureaucratic environment?

Step 8. Implementation of the strategy

Sources of potential dispute or the need for cooperative action:

Are the stakeholders willing to accept the changes involved in implementing the strategy?

Prominent conflict resolution mechanisms:

Joint problem-solving

Step 9. Monitoring and review of performance

Sources of potential dispute or the need for cooperative action:

Are the stakeholders willing to adapt the strategy over time as demanded by changes in the environment?

MAKING AN IMPACT: APPLYING CONFLICT RESOLUTION TECHNIQUES EFFECTIVELY

What can policy reformers do to improve the likelihood that the techniques they use will succeed? Research shows that the presence of certain situational factors are likely to advance the resolution process while others are likely to throw up roadblocks. The questions presented in Table 11.4, based on research findings, provide insights into possible opportunities and barriers in applying conflict resolution approaches effectively.

While policy reformers are often thrust into conflict situations, they can sometimes find ways to "engineer" them, thus improving the chances of the conflict resolution process. Answers to the questions in Table 11.4 can provide useful guidance for this situational engineering. For example, prior to negotiations, consultants can encourage opposing stakeholders to study the issues jointly rather than apart, thereby enhancing the success of the process. Many informal meetings can be conducted to seek enhanced cooperation among the conflicting parties. As well, establishing deadlines can produce concessions by all parties just before the scheduled conclusion of negotiations. Suggested adjustments to—or engineering of—situational factors such as these, with the advice and consent of the stakeholders, can make the difference between success and failure of conflict resolution efforts.

INSTITUTIONALIZING CONFLICT RESOLUTION: DISPUTE MANAGEMENT SYSTEMS

Dispute management systems (DMS) are long-term, prearranged, and institutionalized dispute resolution mechanisms that aim to either prevent or contain conflict, foster constructive social relationships over time among potential disputants, and provide opportunities to build local capacity and ownership over the process of dispute resolution. Examples include formal structures associated with democratic governance, such as ombudsman's offices or grievance commissions where conflicting parties can voice their differences and seek an impartial hearing. They also include more informal procedures, such as negotiation sessions that are triggered automatically when opposing stakeholder groups seek to express their opinions about newly proposed administrative regulations, mediation mechanisms that offer disputants the support of neutral third parties who can search for common ground when the parties refuse to speak to one another directly, and cooling-off periods to enable disputing parties to regain their composure and reevaluate their positions and interests.

DMSs are usually created before there is a conflict, in anticipation that implementation situations may engender disputes in the future (Ury, Brett, and Goldberg 1991). While the stakes are still low, a DMS mechanism can be designed that is perceived as fair and acceptable to all stakeholders and that spells out an orderly and rational process by which future disputes can be recognized, dealt with, and managed.

An example from West Africa illustrates the operation of a dispute management system. The West African livestock policy partnership, described in Chapter 4, established National Coordinating Committees (NCC) in Mali, Burkina Faso, and Ivory Coast to promote cooperation among these countries for cross-border livestock trade. Membership in the committees included the major stakeholder groups—governmental ministries

Table 11.4 Situational Factors Influencing Conflict Resolution Success

	Situational questions	Effects on conflict resolution process
Issues	• Are stakeholder positions based on narrow interests or broad ideology?	• The more explicit the link between positions and ideologies, the less likely parties will be willing to compromise.
	• Do the stakeholders' goals seek comprehensive or partial agreements?	• Breaking an issue into parts or separating packages of issues facilitates achieving agreements.
	• Are there any salient solutions to the conflict that are perceived by the stakeholders or observers?	• Salient outcomes are coordination points that facilitate compromising.
Background factors	• Do the stakeholders prepare for conflict resolution separately or jointly?	• Unilateral strategy formation reduces flexibility. Joint study of the issues increases flexibility.
	• Are the stakeholders familiar with their opponents and their positions?	• Familiarity increases the willingness to debate, to reverse roles, and to appreciate the complexity of issues and positions.
	• Do any of the stakeholders have a better alternative than reaching a peaceful resolution to the dispute?	• Attractive alternatives to a peaceful resolution reduce the willingness to concede, to expedite the agreement process, or to be flexible.
Context	• Do the stakeholders have a friendly or antagonistic relationship?	• Amiable relationships enhance cooperation and facilitate resolving of large issues.
	• Is there a choice over where the conflict resolution activities will take place?	• Conflict resolution activities conducted in peripheral locations (for example, in the countryside rather than in the capital) reduce public commitments to rigid positions and enhance cooperation.
	• Is it possible to influence the extent of publicity or media coverage that the conflict resolution activity will have?	• Public or well-covered conflict resolution activities tend to harden positions and increase the importance of saving face.

cont.

Table 11.4 Situational Factors Influencing Conflict Resolution Success, cont.

	Situational questions	Effects on conflict resolution process
Structure	• Are the stakeholder representatives that are participating in the conflict resolution activity serving as primary decision-makers or delegates?	• If the representatives have the sole responsibility for the outcome, they are less likely to be willing to compromise. Delegates, on the other hand, are more willing to find accommodations.
	• Do some stakeholders appear to have a power advantage over others?	• Stakeholders with a power advantage are likely to be less flexible and less prone to compromise.
	• Are meetings between stakeholders frequent and informal?	• Frequent and informal meetings enhance cooperation.
	• Have any of the disputing parties made large or frequent concessions?	• Increases in concession rates by one party tends to stimulate reciprocation from the other side.
Immediate situation	• Is stakeholder leadership seen as creative or innovative?	• Creative leadership is likely to result in the discovery of formulas or principles around which agreements can be formed.
	• Are there natural or imposed deadlines for resolving the dispute?	• The existence of a deadline often results in large concessions as an "end effect."
	• Is there a trusted and active third-party mediator involved in the dispute?	• Active third parties can increase the flexibility of stakeholders to reach agreement by introducing new ideas and helping them save face.

Adapted from Druckman (1993).

and agencies, livestock producers and traders, butcher syndicates, private transporters, professional organizations, and consumers—each with its own interests to maximize. Through the dispute resolution mechanisms of the NCCs, these groups negotiated and built consensus on such contentious issues as taxes, fees, services, and corruption. The NCCs managed disputes and rivalries between livestock transporters and brokers over new fees for customs services and the excesses of uniformed security services. They also lobbied and negotiated successfully with their respective governments over the threatened imposition of higher taxes and fees for customs clearances. The NCCs provided a venue for policy dialogue on livestock trade issues and the mechanisms for resolving disputes before they escalate into hardened positions, deadlock, and even violence.

Table 11.5 presents different categories of dispute management systems; the particulars of any system usually are determined by the circumstances, the norms of the society, and the creativity of the designer. A unique aspect of DMSs is that they are preestablished. They are developed in the belief

Table 11.5 Types of Dispute Management Systems

Type	Description
Preventive DMS	
• Early warning network	Continuous information gathering and diagnosis from all stakeholder groups
• Notification and consultation	Procedures to offer prior announcement and conduct discussion among stakeholders before an action is taken
• Post-dispute analysis and feedback	Procedures to evaluate and learn from previous disputes
• Establishing a forum	Regular meetings among stakeholders to discuss issues that may eventually cause disputes
• Ombudsman office	Impartial trusted person is available to hear grievances and intervene before dispute emerges
Containment DMS	
• Information base/ analytical model	Establishment of an information bank or analytical model that all sides can use, test their assumptions, and design new proposals
• Joint problem-solving	Established procedures that call on disputants to conduct joint problem-solving with the support of third-party facilitators
Negotiation • Early handling • Multi-step/multi-entry • Mandatory	Early handling of disputes through preestablished negotiation procedures Negotiations can occur through different points of entry and automatically progresses to higher levels until resolved Mandatory requirement for negotiations to occur under certain circumstances
Mediation • Peer mediation • Expert mediation	Third-party intervention by peers of the disputants Third-party intervention by experts from the outside
• Cooling off period	Agreed-on separation of the parties allowing them to reconsider the situation and identify new proposals
• Arbitration	Entrust neutral third party with authority to hear all sides to a dispute and adjudicate a binding decision

that it is easier to deal with future conflicts and crises in a particular issue area if an agreed-upon procedure is in place. In many international agreements and treaties a special dispute settlement clause is now included when the accord is first negotiated spelling out the manner in which the parties agree to manage future controversy and disagreement related to the accord. DMSs can also be anticipated in policy legislation and directives to deal with potential disruptions to the domestic implementation of policy. Foresight in establishing DMSs early in the policy management process can facilitate effective implementation later on.

CONCLUSION

Policy reformers need to ask the right questions to cut through to the essential issues and provide meaningful advice or guidance to their clients. The questions offered in this chapter can focus their inquiries and information-gathering activities specifically on the important factors that need to be diagnosed to yield insight into effective conflict resolution applications. As with all strategic management tools, the value of these questions depends upon the skill and sensitivity with which they are used, the meaningfulness of assessments made, and the perceptiveness of implications drawn from the information gathered.

NOTE

1. The fields of conflict prevention and diplomacy contribute to understanding of what can be done on a practical level to anticipate disputes. For more, see Boudreau (1991), Evans (1993), Malan (1997), Spector (1994), the United Nations (1992), and Zartman (1998).

12

Policy Monitoring

As Chapter 2 elaborates, monitoring is the sixth task in the six-step policy implementation model.[1] Monitoring policy reform implementation is critical to keeping activities and progress on track, reporting on results, identifying when changes are needed, and assessing the effectiveness of reform strategies. In addition, for each of the six implementation tasks, monitoring figures as one of the components of managing them strategically. Successful strategic managers routinely seek feedback on performance and progress, and undertake adjustments in strategy as a function of results achieved and changing circumstances.

A fundamental element of policy monitoring and evaluation (M&E) has to do with collecting, analyzing, and reporting on the technical content of policy. These activities are often formalized in program or project information systems, which are integral to supporting and strengthening evidence-based policymaking. Such information systems allow policy-makers and reformers to track reform progress, to assess impacts on outcomes, and to make adjustments. While the technical side of M&E may appear at first glance to be relatively simple, policy and program decisions are made within highly fragmented political and administrative systems. The kinds of information wanted and needed at different points and levels within these systems varies considerably. These differing needs and desires reinforce the political dynamics of policy monitoring and point to why M&E can generate controversy and conflicts.[2]

As has been stressed throughout this book, policy reform combines technical, political, and process dimensions. Information from a well-designed monitoring system can be instrumental in dealing with the politics of policy implementation. It can promote dialogue and discussion among stakeholders to build legitimacy, develop supportive constituencies, and create momentum for ongoing progress. It is also a necessary ingredient for the transparency and accountability that are hallmarks of democratic governance.

Within the public sector a variety of agencies exercise monitoring and oversight functions besides the agency charged with overall responsibility for implementation (see Schedler et al. 1999). In the United States, for instance, the Government Accounting Office undertakes periodic program and policy reviews of various government agencies and publishes the results. In some developing countries the Office of the Inspector General serves a similar review function. Legislative bodies, for example, through parliamentary oversight committees, have program and policy monitoring responsibilities and convene hearings to review agency performance and results. International donor agencies are, of course, another important set of actors in policy monitoring.

Beyond the state, civil society organizations (CSOs) can play a role in M&E. Related to the technical side of policy monitoring, they can track service delivery impacts and quality. Service delivery surveys, for example, are one monitoring tool that CSOs are employing, often with assistance from donors (see Paul and Sekhar 2000, Uruena 1996). In countries where governments are shifting to private provision of public services, there is experimentation with delegating service quality monitoring to associations. For example, in Kazakhstan, among the functions of Family Group Practice Associations is the monitoring of primary health care services provided by newly privatized health care providers (see Chapter 4). Involving the associations has led to a closer link between identification of quality problems and their resolution. Thus, policy monitoring is an interactive and cross-sectoral process with multiple actors and stakeholders.

There is an extensive literature on monitoring and evaluation methodologies and tools, and in this chapter we make no pretense of offering a comprehensive review.[3] Rather, we examine some of the basic issues in policy monitoring, with an emphasis on process; provide a brief introduction to different methodological approaches to monitoring, along with some examples; and conclude with some guidance for policy managers. We begin with some additional discussion of the context for policy monitoring.

CONTEXTUAL FEATURES OF POLICY MONITORING IN DEVELOPING AND TRANSITIONING COUNTRIES

Several features of the context for policy monitoring are important to highlight. First, to a large degree (although not always) M&E for policy reform take place as a function of international donor assistance loans and grants, which almost invariably mandate some form of M&E (see, for example, OED 1998, USAID 1996). This feature has two important implications: (1) demand for policy M&E tends to be externally driven; and (2) approaches to, and objectives for M&E respond first and foremost to the needs of the funders. Thus, one element of the policy-monitoring task is transferring ownership to policymakers in the country, and adapting systems to their needs. This transfer and adaptation are hampered in some cases by the political economy of the policymaking process. As a variety of observers have noted, particularly at senior levels, policy decisions tend to be politically driven rather than evidence-based. It is mainly below the political level, among mid-level managers and sectoral specialists, that M&E tools and techniques find a receptive home.

A second feature is that M&E in many countries take place within a changed institutional framework. As we have discussed in earlier chapters, public sector downsizing, reduced availability of resources, and new roles for the state affect policy implementation, including M&E. As states become more democratic, new monitoring burdens fall on government, with citizens' increased expectations for accountability, responsiveness, and participation. Similarly, as states shift from being direct service providers to financing service provision by the private sector or NGOs, their need for additional monitoring increases. For example, ministries of health have traditionally focused on disease surveillance and service supply and utilization. Health sector reforms have changed the role of health ministries by separating service provision from funding, transforming ministries into what the World Health Organization calls "stewards" of health systems and "strategic purchasers" of services (WHO 2000). This role shift means that ministries need to monitor experience with new financing mechanisms, changes in health care costs, and impacts on service quality and consumer satisfaction, as well as their traditional set of indicators.

One implication of this changed institutional framework is limited capacity to undertake M&E, the question of willingness and commitment aside. For example, this is a critical problem in poor countries for agencies with financial oversight and accountability functions, and limits the ability of M&E to contribute to assuring efficient use of public resources, combating corruption, and reinforcing democratic governance (see Schedler et al. 1999).[4]

A third feature of the context in developing and transitioning countries is the relative absence of M&E expertise that is independent of the state and that can serve as a countervailing force to government views on policy issues and policy outcomes. Despite the rise of civil society, the increase in advocacy NGOs, and some well-publicized success stories, in most poor countries this expertise is highly circumscribed. Donor-funded participatory appraisals and poverty assessments have helped to make some inroads, but power and resource inequalities remain major constraints (see Leurs 1998, Eurodad 2000, Robb 1999). Transnational civil society organizations are an increasingly important actor in addressing these constraints, along with international donors.

These constraints do not mean that an expanded role is not possible or desirable. As we noted above, CSOs conduct service delivery surveys in some countries, which usually track what services are delivered, their distribution and quality, and how clients respond to the services. For example, the Public Affairs Centre in Bangalore, India, has produced service delivery report cards since its founding in 1994 that have served to improve service delivery agencies' performance and to modify government policies (see Chapter 5). Think tanks can also serve as independent policy monitors and feed the results of their analyses into policy dialogue, as the Bulgaria small and medium enterprise policy case described in Chapter 4 illustrates.

CSOs can also engage in monitoring that relates to democratic governance. Some countries have initiated court watch programs, in which CSOs monitor and report on the actions of the judiciary, tracking basic indicators of due process and judicial efficiency. In Argentina, for example, a CSO called Poder Cuidadano undertakes election monitoring and reporting on the financial assets of elected officials (Smulovitz and Peruzzotti 2000). These watchdog CSOs can, to a certain extent, constitute a source of countervailing power to that of the state by enforcing accountability.

COMPONENTS AND CHARACTERISTICS OF AN EFFECTIVE POLICY-MONITORING SYSTEM

Given these contextual features, what kind of policy-monitoring system makes sense? The basic components of a good M&E system include (1) a management information system based on targeted indicators, (2) stakeholder monitoring to track the responses of winners and losers to the policy reform measures, (3) diagnostic studies to devise practical solutions to implementation problems, and (4) process and impact evaluations to support learning over time.[5] These four components can serve the needs of a range of decision-makers at various levels. Best practices suggest that the design of each component should be based on the principles of adaptation to user needs and availability of resources, user participation, parsimony (the least amount of information and cost required to do the job), and simplicity. Thus, an effective M&E system that adequately tracks, and thus effectively supports, the policy reform process usually includes the following characteristics:

- Provides a user-friendly means of understanding the current status of the policy, both for reformers tracking progress and for other stakeholders to whom the information is disseminated.

- Follows the reform process through to completion of policy implementation.
- Is cost-effective for the operating agency (or unit), matching the system with institutional capacity and relying upon a parsimonious (not exhaustive) set of targets and indicators.
- Describes the stages or events used for rating progress (when this method is used).
- Describes the methodology or process employed for rating.
- Defines the key terms used (for example, "operational," "fully functioning," or "fully implemented").
- Provides a rationale for how future performance targets are set.
- Includes policy reform stakeholders as participants in reviewing implementation progress, in setting future performance targets, and in some cases in conducting M&E.
- Feeds information on progress into implementation diagnosis and problem-solving.

WHAT TO MONITOR?

Our perspective on policy implementation, as we argue in Chapter 1, recognizes that policy has both a content side and a process side. Policy monitoring needs to focus on both. The starting point for answering the question of what to monitor is the content of the policy reform itself. Whether embodied in national legislation, standard operating procedures of government ministries, and/or in a donor-funded loan or grant agreement, the policy package specifies some combination of targets, expected milestones, intended outcomes and results, new organizations or units to be established, schedules, and so on. In the case of donor-funded reforms, phased release of funds is usually included, each tranche of funding contingent upon achievement of agreed-upon events and milestones. For example, USAID supported IPC to work with a policy reform program in the Philippines in the late 1980s and early 1990s that focused on increased effectiveness of public expenditure, fiscal reform, and increased competitiveness of the private sector. Each of these policy objectives was subdivided into targets (for example, streamline duty drawback and value-added tax [VAT] credit systems), which were elaborated into phased milestones (for example, one-stop duty drawback and VAT center created and operating effectively, procedures for prompt approval of 40 percent of VAT credit claims implemented). The IPC team helped to design an M&E system to enable the policy managers in the Department of Finance and the National Economic Development Authority to track all these targets and milestones, verify their achievement, and take corrective actions as needed (see Morton 1997).

When setting monitoring targets, it is important to characterize accurately the components of the reform to be achieved and the sequence of milestone events associated with forward movement in the policy reform process. Setting targets requires a great deal of thoughtful judgment and in-depth knowledge of both the technical and process sides of the reform. For example, a World Bank program designed to strengthen social policy in the transitioning economies of the former Soviet Union developed indicators to track legitimization and constituency building for social policy. Country teams monitored such process indicators as (a) increases in parliamentary debate on social policy issues, (b) increases in media coverage of social policy, and (c) the content and frequency of public statements relating to social policy by senior officials of relevant government agencies (EDI 1998).

This example highlights the process side of policy monitoring. The tasks in the implementation model discussed in Chapter 2 offer some guidance on what sort of process milestones could be tracked, such as indicators of legitimization, constituency building, and resource mobilization. Process indicators and events associated with these tasks can be incorporated into an M&E system that can follow where a policy is in the implementation process, highlighting problems or opportunities that may allow managers to take actions that will enhance chances for effective implementation. For example, such milestones might include:

- Development of ownership and support of the policy at various levels of government and/or within civil society.
- Development of a detailed policy implementation plan.
- Creation and/or expansion of constituencies for reform, possibly including political compromises among stakeholders who stand to lose power or resources from the implementation of the new policy.
- Allocation and disbursement of the financial resources needed to fund implementation.
- Accomplishment of organizational changes necessary for policy reform.
- Increased technical and managerial capacity required for implementing the reform.

It should be noted that many of these implementation process milestones are difficult to specify in unambiguously measurable terms; thus, determinations of their presence, absence, or degree will be subjective. This highlights the importance of attention to definition of key terms in developing indicators and of including multiple actors in the assessment of those indicators. Expanding the pool of monitors can help combat subjectivity and bias as well as contribute to consensus and ownership (see below).[6]

When considering various milestones for policy implementation, it is important to note that these events rarely occur in a single linear sequence. For example, efforts to create supportive constituencies will likely need to continue throughout the reform process. Legislation may have to be redrafted if it is found to be incomplete or ineffectual. Advocacy groups may need to continue lobbying for a given reform throughout the process to maintain pressure and demand for the new policy. M&E systems should be flexible enough to accommodate the iterative and unpredictable nature of policy reform, and a well-crafted system will provide useful input to implementors in coping with this complexity and unpredictability.

Because the process milestones associated with the implementation task model either occur repeatedly or describe ongoing processes rather than discrete events, it is important that policy reform monitoring includes periodic status checks when feasible. Managers may want to design their M&E systems to note the first time a given milestone event occurs and to track whether and to what extent it continues. For example, a system to monitor anti-corruption reforms might track the growth in constituencies for curbing corruption. The system could identify events (such as conferences, press stories, prosecutions and trials, the formation of advocacy groups, and so forth) and then conduct surveys or focus groups to measure the degree of support for anti-corruption efforts, changes in perceptions regarding levels of corruption and/or effectiveness of anti-corruption measures taken, and so on. Transparency International, the international NGO dedicated to fighting corruption, undertakes a variation of this monitoring approach on a worldwide basis and publishes the results in its annual corruption perception index.

In addition, M&E systems should ideally include attention to unintended consequences and changes in environmental conditions.[7] For sectoral reforms this can mean including some indicators that look at linkages with outcomes in other sectors. For example, health sector reformers might want to track a set of economic and social factors, and similarly economic policy reformers could add social and sectoral indicators to their economic tracking systems. In South Africa, for instance, an unanticipated outcome of the Durban conference on HIV/AIDS was a decline in foreign investment; the publicity about HIV/AIDS generated at the conference frightened away potential outside investors. In sub-Saharan Africa economic policy monitoring systems were constructed to track the impacts of structural adjustment on the poor after anecdotal evidence began to emerge suggesting that an unanticipated effect of macroeconomic policy reform was that the poor were worse off than before (see Sarris 1990). Another example is the story of gender sensitivity in development policy. Early M&E systems were essentially gender blind, but as evidence grew regarding the unintended and unnoticed impacts of various policies and programs on women, gender indicators and assessments have been gradually mainstreamed into most M&E systems (see Moser 1995).[8]

Including in the policy M&E system attention to unanticipated consequences and to challenging the design assumptions built into the policy supports a strategic orientation to policy implementation (recall the looking out and looking ahead features of strategic management's three-way orientation summarized in Box 2.1). This type of system provides policymakers and managers with a more detailed and realistic picture of the policy reform process in its technical, political, and administrative aspects, which will assist in making the adjustments necessary to achieve success.

QUANTITATIVE AND QUALITATIVE MONITORING APPROACHES

The simplest approach to policy monitoring focuses on quantifying indicators of policy progress and then counting them over the life of the reform. Two variants of quantitative monitoring approaches can be identified. The first is to break the reform into a sequence of annual targets and monitor the number of targets achieved in a given year, using a binary (yes/no) assessment. As explained below, such approaches are rarely used independent of an accompanying narrative to provide description of reform progress achieved in a given year as well as additional relevant background information.

The second quantitative approach employs the same sequence of annual targets and develops some form of score card, for example, simple indices to report on the percentage achieved of the entire set of targets to be reached over the life of the reform. In creating indices of progress on reform agendas some monitoring systems weight each reform step being pursued according to its importance for the realization of the ultimate policy objective. When this is done, it is important to provide explanatory information for the weighting rationale and the methodology used to rate the current status of the reform steps being pursued. Table 12.1 provides an illustration of a quantitative index. As a general rule, the more user friendly the index, the more useful it will be.[9]

While the simplicity of quantitative monitoring methods is appealing, much useful and relevant information is left out when complex events are encapsulated in a single numerical or yes/no rating. For this reason almost all policy monitoring systems use qualitative methods, which combine numbers with words (see Miles and Huberman 1994). Qualitative M&E approaches use data that consist of words, which can be collected using a variety of techniques (direct observation, extraction from documents, individual interviews, focus groups, and so on). In their primary form these data are unwieldy for either analysts or managers and need to be reduced (though not necessarily to a number). Data reduction can take place through summary in short narratives, application of rating scales (high, medium, low), or assignment of quantitative rankings or indices.[10]

Table 12.1 provides an example of qualitative policy monitoring where indices are combined with narrative explanatory material. It comes from a USAID-funded macroeconomic policy reform implemented in Egypt in the mid-1990s. In this example the ratings were assigned biannually by a panel of outside experts, based upon detailed definitions of the indices in the scoring scale. Such indices are frequently, but not necessarily, based on phases or stages identified as milestone events and are expressed numerically. Each phase or stage in the reform process is assigned a number or value depending upon an assessment of progress. An important consideration is the development of explicit and consistent criteria for the assessment to avoid, to the extent possible, imprecise, subjective, and inconsistent application. This also increases inter-rater reliability.

Table 12.2 provides a variant of this qualitative approach to policy monitoring from a financial sector policy reform supported by USAID/ Mozambique. It dispenses with indices and develops descriptions of key events in the policy reform and the planned results in terms that permit a relatively objective comparison of planned to actual outcomes and then monitors their achievement throughout the performance period. This approach requires sufficient descriptive information so that managers, reviewers, and interested stakeholders can understand and appreciate the current status of the reform process. However, too much detail can obscure aspects of change that are occurring and contribute to information overload. Additional narrative can be used when preparing reports to provide further explanation of particularly noteworthy events or to explain why forecasted progress has not been achieved. This can avoid cluttering the more routine management information system with excessive detail.

Another example of qualitative monitoring is a participatory "storytelling" methodology that collects and interprets "stories" from various policy stakeholders and uses them as inputs to a participatory process of tracking change and reporting to organizational superiors and funders (see, for example, Roe 1991). A highly publicized application of this methodology is the World Bank's "Voices of the Poor" study, which has had an impact on the design of poverty-focused policies and programs.[11] Dart (1999) describes an application of this monitoring approach in Australia. Instead of precise indicators, participants agree upon "domains" of change that the reform will produce, and these become the focus of the stories. The stories are prepared both by policy beneficiaries and by implementors; they are vetted by regional committees, which

Table 12.1 Monitoring Macroeconomic Policy Reform in Egypt

Policies	January results 7/1/94 – 12/31/94	July results 1/01/95 - 6/30/95	January results 7/1/95-12/31/95	Status
A. Foreign exchange market rate system	2.00	1.40	1.72	Forward at a slow pace
B. Interest rate and monetary policies	2.33	3.00	3.72	Some movement forward at a quicker rate
C. Fiscal reform				
a. overall	0.36	1.32	3.72	Quicker, especially deficit, movement forward
b. fiscal deficit	2.33	2.80	3.22	movement forward
c. taxes	0.50	0.60	0.29	
d. expenditures	0.50	0.60	0.38	Slower minor forward movement

Scoring scale: 10 represents at least one major or significant step forward; 9 to 7, important movement forward; 6 to 4, some movement forward; 3 to 1, a little movement forward; zero, no movement or no progress; –1 to –3, a little backward movement; –4 to –6, some backward movement; –7 to –9, serious backward movement; and –10 at least one major or significant backward step. The scoring is accompanied by narrative text for each reform that provides details on the nature of forward or backward movement.

Scoring method: Every six months USAID/Egypt invited the "distinguished members of the Amun Oracle Panel" to score and comment on the Egyptian government's progress in achieving major policy reforms and to estimate their impact on key economic variables.

Note: This scoring scale does not presume that movement in the policy reform process will only be forward. However, there is no score that denotes full implementation of a given policy. This means that it is difficult or impossible to determine where the reform process is in the aggregate.

Table 12.2 Policy Monitoring Through Description and Forecasting of Key Events

Policy area	FY 1995 baseline	FY 1996 planned	FY 1997 planned	FY 1998 planned	FY 1999 planned
Financial sector reform, bank privatization, and market access to foreign exchange	Actual: Commercial and central bank functions split in 1993; by 1995, several private commercial banks open; non-bank institutions legally engage in foreign exchange	Sale of BCM* to private buyers, with govt. shares < 49% Actual: Completed July 1996	Sale of BPD** to private buyers, with govt. shares < 49%; conduct assessment of legal/regulatory obstacles to rural and micro-financial services. Actual: BPD privatized; analyses and dialogue (govt., private sector, NGOs, donors) begun	Establish legal framework (including supervision regulations) for private and member-owned non-bank financial institutions to mobilize savings and make loans	At least one non-bank financial institution established

Note: The key events described for each year are specific to this particular reform. The last planned performance target in FY 1999 is a key event that gives proof of the implementation of the reforms.

*BCM: Banco Comercial de Mozambique
**BPD: Banco Popular do Desenvolvimento

select a subset of the stories (one for each change domain) for transmission to a central committee. In turn, on a quarterly basis, the central committee reviews and discusses the stories and selects from them a sample that best captures the outcomes achieved and issues encountered. These stories are summarized in an annual progress report, which is then discussed with policy and program funders, who rank the stories in terms of their satisfaction with the results achieved. This approach is highly participatory, decentralized, and relatively time-consuming to employ. However, it has the benefit of closely integrating policy monitoring with making adjustments in implementation strategy, since the story discussion and review process leads to learning on the part of implementors.

WHO PARTICIPATES IN POLICY MONITORING?

Policy-monitoring systems are more effective when they are both designed and operated with explicit attention to external stakeholders. Participation mechanisms can range from informal consultation, to the establishment of working groups, to delegation of monitoring responsibilities to independent bodies. As Chapter 3 notes, increased participation characterizes policy formulation and implementation at all levels, from local-level PRAs (participatory rural appraisals) to donor-driven policy frameworks such as PRSPs (Poverty Reduction Strategy Papers).[12] Participatory monitoring is an integral component of these efforts.

For both quantitative and qualitative approaches to monitoring, policy stakeholders can play a useful role. Involving members from a participatory monitoring group in defining the phases or stages of an index and its associated scoring scale will increase confidence and understanding in the use of the instrument and create a sense of joint ownership of the monitoring system. Another method is to engage a panel of acknowledged experts on the subject matter pertaining to the policy to review and rate the current status of the policy process, as was done in the Egypt example presented in Table 12.1. Whatever means are used, all parties involved in rating the current status of the policy process must understand and agree upon the scoring scale.

For any policy-monitoring system, the cooperation of policy stakeholders from various constituencies in the public and private sectors and in civil society will facilitate setting monitoring targets and reviewing performance. Stakeholder analysis can be used to identify who should be included (see Chapter 6). Given the political nature of reforms, stakeholder participation in this process will be vital for both identifying the stages through which a policy will have to proceed and for predicting the time required to reach each stage until implementation has been achieved.

The result will be a monitoring system that is more realistic and relevant to the set of reforms being undertaken. Convening such a group to help create the monitoring system and set targets will also help when it is time to rate progress.

The reform team's confidence in its policy-monitoring system and performance assessment will be increased through involvement of a representative group of monitors and reviewers. A well-constructed M&E system can be used on an ongoing basis to focus discussion and examine problems impeding the policy implementation process, as well as to brainstorm on strategies to address these problems. It can be used as a feedback mechanism to provide concrete information that will inform judgment on the strategies employed to introduce and implement reforms as well as on the impact of those reforms. Further, the information it produces can be helpful in crafting policy communication campaigns to inform and educate beneficiaries and other stakeholders. This information can then be used for influence and advocacy (see Chapter 10).

Besides these technical benefits of a participatory approach to policy monitoring, who participates in target setting and tracking results is important from a political economy perspective. Societal groups that are part of the monitoring process are more likely to see policies and programs reflect their interests and to have agencies respond to their needs and demands. Such participation will enhance the chances of sustained results from the policy reform effort and in addition will lay the groundwork for accountability. Further, a participatory monitoring system will contribute to increased ownership of the reform and to commitment to implementation. The presence or absence of democratic structures and procedures has an impact on the possibilities for participatory monitoring, as the discussion in Chapter 3 makes clear.

SUMMARY

Emerging from this chapter are several suggestions for monitoring policy reform.

1. *Recognize that monitoring policy reform can often contribute substantially to advancing implementation.* The benefits of monitoring policy reform are not necessarily limited to agency management and reporting. The monitoring process can be used as a catalyst to keep the reform process on track ("what gets monitored gets done") and can serve to enhance legitimacy, build constituencies, and assure accountability and sustainability. The six-step implementation task model (Chapter 2) can serve as a template for implementation process monitoring.

2. *Define a list of stages or milestone events in the reform process.* This serves to break the process of policy reform into a sequence of components that are more easily understood and tracked. Even if the monitoring approach chosen does not explicitly incorporate discrete reform stages, this step will help managers to better analyze and understand any monitoring and evaluation information that is collected.

3. *Use qualitative approaches in the monitoring system.* Tracking policy implementation and using monitoring information to inform management decisions can best be served by a monitoring system that combines numbers and narrative.

4. *Involve implementing partners and policy stakeholders in the design and operation of policy-monitoring systems/approaches to take advantage of their unique perspectives, experience, and knowledge.* Partners and stakeholders should participate in discussions and analysis aimed at setting policy reform targets, not simply be brought in later to track indicators already identified. Focus groups, workshops, and round tables are mechanisms that can be used to organize this participation.

5. *Select a monitoring approach that best reflects the needs and constraints of agencies involved in policy implementation.* For example, if the policy reform effort is donor funded, it is likely that a policy matrix specifying targets to be monitored and reported on was developed as part of the design process. This will necessarily form the core of the monitoring framework. If monitoring and evaluation capacity is limited, the monitoring approach should not impose too heavy a data collection and analysis burden. The monitoring system should support implementation, not impede it. Consider including capacity building as part of system development. While developing an approach, keep issues of cost-effectiveness in mind.

6. *Consider delegating some monitoring responsibility to external groups, such as community organizations, think tanks, or watchdog and advocacy CSOs.* This strengthens the demand side of policy reform, contributes to transparency (through public reporting of progress and results), and reinforces accountability.

NOTES

1. This chapter owes a debt of gratitude to Patricia Vondal, who contributed to IPC's thinking about policy monitoring. She further developed that thinking for USAID's Center for Development Information and Evaluation, which appeared in USAID (2000). We draw upon that document here.

2. Many of the core sources on program evaluation and policy research address the politics of monitoring and evaluation. See, for example, Lindblom and Cohen (1979), Weiss (1977), and Wholey (1979). See also the informative overview of the evolution of the policy research field in Hellstern (1986).

3. Some of the classics include Miles and Huberman (1994), Patton (1978, 1980), Rossi et al. (1999), and Weiss (1972). Two of the classic sources on evaluation in developing countries are Casley and Lury (1981) and Casley and Kumar (1987). For some interesting recent sources, see Picciotto and Rist (1995), Mosse and Sontheimer (1996), and Mark et al. (2000). A useful website is MandE NEWS at <http:www.mande.co.uk/>.

4. An IPC team that conducted an anti-corruption assessment in Madagascar in 1999 found the resource and capacity constraints on state "agencies of restraint" to be a critical problem. For example, the Inspector General's Office is charged with monitoring the accounting and financial-management practices of all public agencies, state-owned enterprises, and any entity that receives any form of state financial support. However, the office's operating budget and equipment are grossly insufficient. Staff members have no means of travel; when conducting investigations they are forced to rely on the kindness of those under investigation for lodging, transport, and food. In the main office in the capital the aged and dust-covered computers, the majority of desks with no telephones, and the stacks of moldering files in battered metal cabinets attest to the magnitude of the capacity gap.

5. These are the basic components of a project/program M&E system as proposed by Casley and Kumar (1987). In our view this framework can be expanded for application to policy implementation.

6. There are qualitative data analysis techniques that can deal with these problems (see Miles and Huberman 1994).

7. Most policy and program designs, particularly donor-funded ones, specify a policy objective and then elaborate a set of cause-and-effect links that comprise the necessary steps to achieve the objective. This, for example, is the basic methodology of USAID's Logical Framework (or logframe) and its descendant, the Results Package that USAID currently uses. M&E systems built on the logframe methodology focus on whether or not the planned activities were carried out and the intended objectives achieved. Such models fit well with needs for accountability and control. Critics argue that this kind of M&E ignores unintended consequences, promotes overconfidence in the validity of the initial policy/program design, and encourages managers to make only minor adjustments during implementation rather than contemplate the possible need for major changes in strategy, shifts in goals, and so on. This debate has been going on for decades (see, for example, Brinkerhoff and Ingle 1989, Rondinelli 1983). For an interesting recent exchange of views, see Gasper (2000), Bell (2000), and Smith (2000).

8. For example, the labor demands of new agricultural technologies on women in farming systems in which women are the primary agricultural producers were initially overlooked because project and program M&E systems did not separate data by gender. In Nigeria, for instance, the Federal Agricultural Coordinating Unit created a Women in Agriculture (WIA) program in 1988 to address gender-related gaps in agricultural extension and technology transfer policy. The WIA established a participatory problem-identification, monitoring, and learning process that brought government staff and women farmers together. The results were increased dissemination of technologies, better access to inputs and credit, and improved productivity (see World Bank 1996, 89–95).

9. Computerized monitoring and decision-support systems vastly increase the sophistication and power of quantitative M&E, particularly when these include geographic information systems (GIS). For example, USAID funded the development of a computerized monitoring system in the Philippines for the Municipal Environmental Coastal Initiative, designed to reduce industrial pollution and negative impacts on health. The World Bank funded a system to track the impacts on the poor of the Nicaraguan government's Social Development Fund. The World Resources Institute's "Forest Watch" program uses GIS data to track and analyze forest resource exploitation patterns. One governance-related outcome is that WRI has been able to document cases of corruption in which government officials have exploited protected areas for private gain.

10. As Miles and Huberman (1994) point out, the data reduction task is an integral part of data analysis. The policy implementation analytic tools presented in Part II of this book (stakeholder analysis, policy characteristics analysis, political and institutional mapping) are examples of combining data reduction and analysis. Using sophisticated analytic tools, qualitative data can be manipulated statistically to identify patterns and draw conclusions.

11. See the website at <http://www.worldbank.org/poverty/voices/index.htm>.

12. For a discussion of the use of PRA techniques for policy design and monitoring, see Leurs (1998). For an overview of participation in poverty reduction strategies, including policy monitoring, see McGee and Norton (2000).

Appendix

Field Activities
of the
Implementing Policy Change Project,
1990–2001

AFRICA

Ghana *Export policy* Aug '91–Oct '91
Support to policy dialogue among government officials and export firms on export promotion and economic policy reform.

Guinea-Bissau *Judicial reform* Jan '92–Jan '94
Support to the Judicial Reform Working Group and other reform stakeholders. Activities included development of draft legislation separating the executive and the judiciary, and a new budget law; training and study tours for magistrates, court officials, and lawyers; updating legal codes and statutes; and design and implementation of a communications and outreach strategy regarding the operations of the judiciary.

Guinea-Bissau *Trade and investment policy reform* Jan '92–Jul '94
Policy analysis to identify the major economic, political, and legal reforms needed to promote trade and investment. In cooperation with public and private sector leaders, conduct of stakeholder analysis and development of organizational mechanisms to manage the formulation and implementation of policies, laws, and regulations supportive of trade and investment in the critical growth sub-sectors.

Guinea-Bissau   *Governance reform*   Oct '97–Apr '98
Planning and conduct of a national seminar on democratic governance for government officials and civil society groups.

Kenya   *HIV/AIDS policy*   Mar '01
Design and conduct of a workshop for health ministry staff and NGOs on strategies and tools for HIV/AIDS policy implementation and management.

Lesotho   *Agricultural policy reform*   Apr '92–Sep '92
Analysis of the Lesotho Agricultural Policy Support Program to identify problems and review options for resolving them. Workshops for program staff and stakeholders to address indicators, roles, responsibilities, and procedures for implementation. Support to help stakeholders reach consensus on priorities and to develop action plans.

Madagascar   *Anti-corruption*   Apr '99–Jul '99
Assessment of anti-corruption activities and stakeholders, start-up assistance to national Transparency International chapter.

Malawi   *Performance-based budgeting*   Mar '96–Apr '96
Support to environment-sector government agencies to develop guidelines for establishing a performance-based budgeting system.

Mali   *Telecommunications policy*   Mar '96–Jul '96
Identification of policy and technical constraints in telecommunications and information policy, and development of an action plan for addressing them.

Mozambique   *Decentralization*   Sep '95–Jul '96
Organization and facilitation of national and provincial level workshops for government and civil society stakeholders on strategies, constraints, actions, roles, and responsibilities to implement decentralization.

Mozambique   *Railway privatization*   Jun '92 –Nov '92
Policy analysis and conduct of a senior-level workshop to assist decision-making regarding outplacement of workers resulting from railroad parastatal privatization.

Namibia   *HIV/AIDS policy*   *Feb '01*
Design and conduct of a workshop for health ministry staff
and NGOs on strategies and tools for HIV/AIDS policy implementation and management.

Nigeria   *Governance and*   *Apr '99–Jun '99*
                        anti-corruption reform
Design and conduct of a series of workshops for newly elected
National Assembly members focused on constituency relations;
the role of elected officials in a democracy; and accountability, transparency, and anti-corruption activities. Some workshops included civil society groups and local government officials, as well as legislators.

Rwanda   *Budget reform*   *Nov '93–May '94*
Support to the development of a collaborative action plan for
reforming the budget process in Rwanda to increase transparency and accountability.

Sierra Leone   *Conflict diamonds policy*   *Sep '99–Mar '01*
Technical assistance to the government to design and implement a community development fund capitalized by a portion
of the diamond export tax. Training for mines monitoring of-
ficers. Development of public information campaign on the fund
and on conflict diamonds policy.

South Africa   *Consultation for*   *Oct '95–Oct '96*
                        democratic governance
Facilitation of a broad-based consultative process with USAID
partners to define, implement, and evaluate USAID strategies
for consolidation of democracy at the national and provincial
levels. Major program elements included mechanisms for civil
society participation in national and provincial governance,
equitable access to the legal system, protection of human rights,
innovative approaches to conflict resolution, and capacity building for schools of public administration.

South Africa   *Public management reform*   *Aug '93–May '94*
Assistance to the South African Foundation for Public Management and Development to establish structures and procedures, develop a strategic plan for its first year, and begin efforts in curriculum development, case writing, and research.

The foundation's mission is to foster South Africa's transition to a post-apartheid civil service at all levels of government.

South Africa   *Small enterprise policy advocacy*   *Sep '93–Dec '95*
Technical support in lobbying and advocacy to the Sunnyside Group and the National Federation of African Chambers of Commerce to promote a policy and regulatory environment supportive of small business in general, and black small business in particular.

Tanzania   *Tax policy*   *Oct '97–Oct '99*
Assistance to the Tanzania Revenue Authority to establish a functioning Tax Research and Policy Unit to enhance the authority's capacity to identify and analyze the fiscal, economic, and social implications of alternative tax policies.

The Gambia   *Institutional capacity building,*   *Aug '93–Jun '94*
Ministry of Finance
Assistance to the Ministry of Finance and Economic Affairs in analyzing its organizational strategy, structure, systems, and human resource base for policy formulation and implementation. Capacity building to help the ministry to be strategic in the analysis of policy options and the management of policy implementation.

The Gambia   *Institutional capacity building,*   *Nov '92–Dec '93*
Ministries of Agriculture and Trade
Capacity building for human resource and organizational development for the Ministries of Agriculture and Trade. Constraints analysis in transferring the skills, procedures, and technology required for policy analysis and implementation.

Uganda   *Decentralization policy*   *Oct '99–Mar '01*
Capacity building for the Ministry of Local Government, local officials in eight districts, and civil society groups to implement decentralization. Improve local government performance and create partnerships between local government and civil society. Partnerships focused on service delivery and infrastructure. Provide training to elected women councilors in leadership, coalition building, and policy platform development.

Uganda   *Private sector policy reform*   *Jul '92–Dec '92*
Technical assistance to government officials and private sector actors to conduct policy dialogue. Design and facilitation
of a high-level national forum on private sector development,
chaired by the president, that resulted in the development of
action plans and the establishment of national task forces in
the areas of trade, taxation, financial sector development, and
investment promotion. Support to the task forces in policy
analysis and policy monitoring.

Zambia   *Central government*   *Apr '93–Apr '94*
                         policy coordination
Support to the creation and start-up of a Policy Analysis and
Coordination Unit in the Cabinet Office. Capacity building for
the unit to fulfill its role in supporting, monitoring, and coordinating policy formulation and implementation.

Zimbabwe   *Private sector policy*   *Jan '92–Mar '94*
Analysis, options design, legislative drafting, and technical assistance in implementation for the Ministry of Industry and
Commerce to control monopoly power and other restrictive
business practices and to promote competition and competitiveness. Institutional design to establish a Monopolies Commission.

Regional   *Strategic management training*   *Sep '93–Oct '94*
Conduct of strategic management skill-building workshops for
policy managers in The Gambia, Madagascar, and Zambia.

Regional   *Environmental policy*   *Nov '91–Jan '98*
                         implementation
Six-country study of environmental and natural resources management policy: Madagascar, Mali, Botswana, The Gambia, Zimbabwe, and Uganda. Information exchange workshops on study
results and assistance to develop action strategies to facilitate
implementation of environmental action plans.

Regional   *Private sector policy advocacy*   *Aug '92–Sep '97*
Creation of and technical support to a private sector network
of entrepreneurs in West Africa to engage in policy advocacy

for the promotion of private sector development. Facilitation and capacity building for regional and national enterprise networks, development of strategic action plans for network reform agendas in each country, and interest aggregation among private sector actors.

Regional   *Livestock trade policy*   *Sep '92–Sep '97*
Facilitation and technical support to public-private partnerships to promote policy implementation for improved efficiency of West Africa regional trade in livestock and livestock products in Mali, Burkina Faso, and Côte d'Ivoire.

Regional   *Regional economic*   *Oct '96–Oct '97*
                          policy coordination
Promotion of economic cooperation in West Africa. Facilitation of collaborative policy planning with the Economic Community of West African States and the West Africa Economic and Monetary Union.

Regional   *Natural resource management*   *Sep '96–Sep '97*
                          (NRM) policy
Assistance to African institutions to improve data-based policy planning and implementation of NRM policy, and to develop better policy-reporting systems.

Regional   *Central government*   *Sep '98–Mar '01*
                          policy coordination
Support to the establishment and operation of a network of senior officials to exchange experience with policy coordination, institutional development for cabinet offices, and relations between the executive the the legislature. Creation of an electronic discussion group (ExecNet), and facilitation of regional conferences.

Regional   *Regional telecommunications*   *Oct '94–Nov '95*
                  and transportation policy
Technical assistance to the Southern Africa Development Community (SADC) member countries to develop policy agreements and negotiate treaties in the areas of railways, roads, ports and shipping, air transport, telecommunications, postal services,

and meteorology. Facilitation of a participatory consultative process among public and private sector actors to build consensus on the content of the policies and to plan for implementation.

Regional   *Regional trade, agriculture*   Mar '97–Jun '97
                      and water sector policy dialogue
Technical assistance and facilitation support to SADC in the preparation and conduct of a series of regional policy dialogue workshops in the areas of trade, agriculture, and shared water resources.

ASIA/NEAR EAST

Egypt   *Participatory rural*   Jan '97–Jan '99
                      governance and decentralization
Assistance to the Ministry of Local Administration and the Organization for the Reconstruction and Development of the Egyptian Village to achieve incremental devolution of authority to the local level. Development of systems and procedures for increased village council participation in public investment decision-making.

Palestine   *Decentralization*   Apr '97–Jun '97
Preparation of a concept paper on decentralized local government for the Palestinian self-rule areas.

Palestine   *Policy analysis unit*   Sep '99–Dec '99
Feasibility study for establishing a policy development, analysis, and monitoring capacity within the Palestinian Authority.

Philippines   *Export promotion policy*   Aug '91–Mar '94
Improvement in the administration of the VAT credit and duty drawback systems. Assistance to Department of Finance and the National Economic Development Authority in systems design and implementation, monitoring and evaluation, strategies to anticipate and respond to implementation problems, and assessment of reform impacts on the export sector and the economy.

LATIN AMERICA AND CARIBBEAN

Bolivia   *Policy reform evaluation and*   *Apr '91–Jul '91*
                   capacity building project design   *Feb '92–Apr '92*
Evaluation of USAID's Policy Reform Project. Development of
a preliminary design for the Technical Support for Policy Reform Project.

El Salvador   *Judicial reform*   *Sep '92–Mar '93*
Training for the justice sector working group to conduct stakeholder analysis and develop a strategic management plan for
the start-up implementation of judicial reform.

Guatemala   *Education policy reform for*   *Mar '00–Mar '01*
                  cultural pluralism and gender equity
Support to the Consultative Commission for Education Reform
and civil society groups to implement bilingual education policy
for the Mayan indigenous population, especially girls. Facilitation of Mayan civil society groups' participation in policy dialogue and decision-making.

Guyana   *Private sector investment policy*   *Nov '93–Jan '94*
Analytic support to the Ministry of Finance and Ministry of
Trade, Tourism and Industry to identify institutional improvements to enhance their capacity to implement private sector
investment policy.

Haiti   *Policy and administrative reform*   *May '91–Jan '92*
Diagnostic studies, administrative reform program design, and
technical assistance to the prime minister's office, the finance
ministry, and the city of Port-au-Prince to increase government effectiveness and capacity in policy priority setting and
implementation.

Honduras   *Policy analysis*   *Jun '93–Mar '01*
                   and implementation unit
Analytic and technical support for the establishment and operation of a Policy Analysis and Implementation Unit to assist
the president's Economic Cabinet to improve the policy deci-

sion-making process and to conduct effective implementation of the government's economic reform program.

Jamaica   *Fiscal policy reform*   Mar '92–Feb '95
Design of an action plan to strengthen policy analysis and implementation capacity in the Ministry of Finance. Support for the creation of a Fiscal Policy Management Unit and technical assistance during the unit's start-up and first years of operation.

Jamaica   *Sustainable urban*   Sep '96–Jan '97
                           development policy
Assistance to USAID and Jamaican municipal agencies in the design of policies and programs to promote economic development and protect natural resources in urban areas.

Peru   *Policy reform*   Jul '94–Dec '94
                           and management evaluation
Management review of the Policy Analysis, Planning and Implementation (PAPI) Project, and recommendations to USAID and Peruvian government decision-makers on improving policy reform management effectiveness.

Regional   *Eastern Caribbean*   Aug '91–Mar '92
                           agricultural policy
Design and conduct of a workshop for agricultural policymakers and program managers in the Eastern Caribbean States region. Development of country plans to implement regional policies.

EASTERN EUROPE AND FORMER SOVIET UNION

Bulgaria   *Small and medium*   Sep '96–Mar '01
                           enterprise policy
Support to the establishment of a public-private partnership to engage in policy dialogue, and legislative development in support of small and medium enterprise. Assistance to business associations and parliament in policy advocacy and constituent relations.

Bulgaria   *Democratic local governance*   *Sep '98–Mar '01*
Technical assistance to local governments, private sector associations, and civil society groups to increase citizen participation in municipal and regional governance, develop transparent and accountable budget and finance systems, and improve local service delivery capacity. Assistance to the Ministry for Regional Development and Public Works on the legal and regulatory framework for decentralization and intergovernmental relations.

Poland   *Social policy*   *Dec '94–Feb '95*
Analytic support to Polish policymakers to assess the provision of social services and benefits, and to develop a new framework to create a social safety net. Provision of recommendations for pension, welfare, and health policy reforms.

Ukraine   *Anti-corruption*   *Jun '97–Dec '97*
Support to local business groups and municipal officials to develop and carry out anti-corruption activities.

Ukraine   *Environmentally sound*   *Aug '96–Sep '97*
                     business development
Assistance to private sector actors and regional government officials to implement an action plan for environmentally sound business development, including ecotourism, in the Carpathia region.

Ukraine   *Small and medium*   *Sep '98–Jun '99*
                     enterprise policy
Assistance to the State Committee for Entrepreneurship Development to design, plan, and conduct a survey of small and medium enterprises as part of the implementation of private sector policy reform.

Regional   *Anti-corruption*   *Sep '98–Jun '99*
Support for policy dialogue, information exchange, and constituency building for anti-corruption policies and programs. Facilitation of a regional workshop that led to the establishment of

the Anti-Corruption Network for Transition Economies, the creation of a website (www.nobribes.org), and the organization of an electronic discussion group for the network. Support to a workshop in Bulgaria on public-private partnerships against corruption.

Bibliography

Adler, Hans A. 1987. *Economic appraisal of transport projects: A manual with case studies*. Baltimore, Md.: Johns Hopkins University Press.

Alesina, Alberto. 1994. Political models of macroeconomic policy and fiscal reforms. In *Voting for reform: Democracy, political liberalization and economic adjustment*, edited by Stephan Haggard and Steven B. Webb, 37–61. New York: Oxford University Press.

Alesina, Alberto, and Allan Drazen. 1991. Why are stabilizations delayed? *American Economic Review* 81(5): 17–89.

Alexander, Ernest R. 1995. *How organizations act together: Interorganizational coordination in theory and practice*. Amsterdam: Gordon and Breach Publishers.

Alter, Catherine, and Jerald Hage. 1993. *Organizations working together*. Newbury Park, Calif.: Sage Publications.

Ames, Barry. 1987. *Political survival*. Berkeley and Los Angeles: University of California Press.

Angell, Alan. 1996. Improving the quality and equity of education in Chile: The Programa 900 Escuelas and the MECE-Basica. In *Implementing policy innovations in Latin America: Politics, economics, and techniques*, edited by Antonia Silva, 94–119. Washington, D.C.: Inter-American Development Bank, Social Agenda Policy Group.

Armijo, Leslie, Thomas Biersteker, and Abraham Lowenthal. 1994. The problems of simultaneous transitions. *Journal of Democracy* 5(4): 161–75.

Asilis, Carlos M., and Gian Maria Milesi-Feretti. 1994. *On the political sustainability of economic reform*. Washington, D.C.: International Monetary Fund, Research Department, PPAAI9413.

Bachrach, Peter, and Morton S. Baratz. 1970. *Power and poverty: Theory and practice*. New York: Oxford University Press.

Bardach, Eugene. 1998. *Getting agencies to work together*. Washington, D.C.: Brookings Institution.

———. 1977. *The implementation game*. Cambridge, Mass.: Massachusetts Institute of Technology Press.

Bardhan, Pranab. 1991. On the concept of power in economics. *Economics and Politics* 3(3): 265–77.

Bates, Robert H. 1981. *Markets and states in tropical Africa: The political basis of agricultural policies*. Berkeley and Los Angeles: University of California Press.

247

Bates, Robert H., and Paul Collier. 1992. The politics and economics of policy reform in Zambia. Oxford: Centre for the Study of African Economies (February).

Bates, Robert H., and Anne Krueger, eds. 1993. *Political and economic interactions in economic policy reform: Evidence from eight countries*. Oxford: Basil Blackwell.

Bell, Simon. 2000. Logical frameworks, Aristotle and soft systems: A note on the origins, values and uses of logical frameworks, in reply to Gasper. *Public Administration and Development* 20(1): 29–33.

Benjamin, Peter. 2001. Community development and democratisation through information technology: Building the new South Africa. In *Reinventing government in the information age*, edited by Richard B. Heeks, 194–210. London: Routledge.

Berman, Bruce J., and Wisdom J. Tettey. 2001. African states, bureaucratic culture and computer fixes. *Public Administration and Development* 21(1): 1–15.

Bhatnagar, Bhuvan, and Aubrey C. Williams, eds. 1992. *Participatory development and the World Bank: Potential directions for change*. Washington, D.C.: World Bank, Discussion Paper No. 183.

Billings, James, and John Miller. 1995. Final report: Executive summary and text, Protocol Development Project. Volume I. Washington, D.C.: U.S. Agency for International Development, Center for Democracy and Governance, Implementing Policy Change Project (November).

Blackburn, James, and Costanza de Toma. 1998. Scaling-down as the key to scaling-up? The role of participatory municipal planning in Bolivia's Law of Popular Participation. In *Who changes? Institutionalizing participation in development*, edited by James Blackburn and Jeremy Holland, 30–40. London: Intermediate Technology Publications.

Blair, Harry 2001. Institutional pluralism in public administration and politics: Applications in Bolivia and beyond. *Public Administration and Development* 21(2): 119–31.

Blair, Harry. 2000a. Civil society, empowerment, democratic pluralism, and poverty reduction: Delivering the goods at national and local levels. In *New roles and relevance: Development NGOs and the challenge of change*, edited by David Lewis and Tina Wallace, 109–21. Bloomfield, Conn.: Kumarian Press.

———. 2000b. Participation and accountability at the periphery: Democratic local governance in six countries. *World Development* 28(1): 21–39.

Bothwell, Robert. 1997. Indicators of a healthy civil society. In *Beyond prince and merchant: Citizen participation and the rise of civil society*, edited by John Burbidge, 249–62. New York: PACT Publications.

Boudreau, Thomas. 1991. *Sheathing the sword*. New York: Greenwood Press.

Bragdon, Susan H. 1992. *Kenya's legal and institutional structure for environmental protection and natural resource management: An analysis and agenda for the future*. Washington, D.C.: World Bank, Economic Development Institute, McNamara Fellowships Program Paper (May).

Bratton, Michael. 1990. Non-governmental organizations in Africa: Can they influence public policy? *Development and Change* 21: 87–118.

———. 1989a. Beyond the state: Civil society and associational life in Africa. *World Politics* 41(3): 407–30.

———. 1989b. The politics of government-NGO relations in Africa. *World Development* 17(5): 569–89.

Bratton, Michael, and Nicolas van de Walle. 1997. *Democratic experiments in Africa: Regime transitions in comparative perspective.* Cambridge, U.K.: Cambridge University Press.

Bratton, Michael, Harry Garnett, Julie Koenen-Grant, and Catherine Rielly. 1998. *Executive offices and policy management in Africa's new democracies.* Washington, D.C.: U.S. Agency for International Development, Center for Democracy and Governance, Implementing Policy Change Project, Monograph No. 7 (November).

Brautigam, Deborah. 2000. Foreign aid and the politics of participation in economic policy reform. *Public Administration and Development* 20(3): 253–65.

Brinkerhoff, Derick W. 2000. Democratic governance and sectoral policy reform: Tracing linkages and exploring synergies. *World Development* 28(4): 601–15.

———. 1999a. Exploring state-civil society collaboration: Policy partnerships in developing countries. *Nonprofit and Voluntary Sector Quarterly* 28(4, Supplement): 59–87.

———. 1999b. The implementation of environment and natural resources policy in Africa: Blending regulatory enforcement with community participation. *International Journal of Organization Theory and Behavior* 2(1 and 2): 233–59.

———. 1997a. An analytic framework for policy implementation: Assessing progress with Madagascar's National Environmental Action Plan. In *Policy analysis concepts and methods: An institutional and implementation focus*, edited by Derick W. Brinkerhoff, 203–35. Greenwich, Conn.: JAI Press, Policy Studies in Developing Nations Series. Vol. 5.

———. 1997b. Integrating institutional and implementation issues into policy decisions: An introduction and overview. In *Policy analysis concepts and methods: An institutional and implementation focus*, edited by Derick W. Brinkerhoff, 1–19. Greenwich, Conn.: JAI Press, Policy Studies in Developing Nations Series. Vol. 5.

———. 1996a. Coordination issues in policy implementation networks: An illustration from Madagascar's environmental action plan. *World Development* 24(9): 1497–1511.

———. 1996b. Process perspectives on policy change: Highlighting implementation. *World Development* 24(9): 1395–1403.

———. 1995. African state-society linkages in transition: The case of forestry policy in Mali. *Canadian Journal of Development Studies* 16: 201–28.

———. 1992. Linking applied research and technical cooperation in strategic management for policy change. Washington, D.C.: U.S. Agency for

International Development, Center for Democracy and Governance, Implementing Policy Change Project, Research Note No. 1.

———. 1991. *Improving development program performance: Guidelines for managers*. Boulder, Colo.: Lynne Rienner Publishers.

Brinkerhoff, Derick W., and Marcus D. Ingle. 1989. Between blueprint and process: A structured flexibility approach to development management. *Public Administration and Development* 9(5): 487–503.

Brinkerhoff, Derick W., with Nicolas Kulibaba. 1996. Perspectives on participation in economic policy reform in Africa. *Studies in Comparative International Development* 31(3): 123–51.

Brown, L. David, and Darcy Ashman. 1996. Participation, social capital, and intersectoral problem solving: African and Asian cases. *World Development* 24(9): 1467–81.

Brown, Michael, Jill Rizika, James Cawley, Ira Amstadter, Jeffrey Clark, and John Prendergast. 1993. *Non-governmental organizations and natural resources management: An assessment of eighteen African Countries. Executive summary*. Washington, D.C.: World Learning, Inc., CARE, World Wildlife Fund, PVO-NGO/NRMS Project.

Bryant, Coralie, and Louise G. White. 1982. *Managing development in the third world*. Boulder, Colo.: Westview Press.

Bryson, John M. 1988. *Strategic planning for public and non-profit organizations*. San Francisco: Jossey-Bass Publishers.

Bryson, John M., and Barbara C. Crosby. 1992. *Leadership for the common good: Tackling public problems in a shared-power world*. San Francisco: Jossey-Bass Publishers.

Buchanan, Paul G. 1995. *State, labor, capital: Democratizing class relations in the Southern Cone*. Pittsburgh, Pa.: University of Pittsburgh Press.

Buhl, Dana. 1997. *Ripple in still water: Reflections by activists on local- and national-level work on economic, social and cultural rights*. Washington, D.C.: Institute of International Education, International Human Rights Internship Program, Appendix D.

Burbidge, John, ed. 1997. *Beyond prince and merchant: Citizen participation and the rise of civil society*. New York: Pact Publications, for the Institute of Cultural Affairs International.

Burkey, Stan. 1993. *People first: A guide to self-reliant, participatory rural development*. London: Zed Books.

Burki, Shahid Javed, and Guillermo E. Perry. 1998. *Beyond the Washington consensus: Institutions matter*. Washington, D.C.: World Bank.

Caiden, Naomi, and Aaron Wildavsky. 1974. *Planning and budgeting in poor countries*. New York: John Wiley and Sons.

Callaghy, Thomas M. 1990. Lost between state and market: The politics of economic adjustment in Ghana, Zambia, and Nigeria. In *Economic crisis and policy choice: The politics of adjustment in the third world*, edited by Joan M. Nelson, 257–321. Princeton, N.J.: Princeton University Press.

Cammack, Paul. 1992. The new institutionalism: Predatory rule, institutional persistence, and macro-social change. *Economy and Society* 21(4): 397–429.

Cardenas, Susana, and Sue Richiedei. 2000. Participatory policy processes in Turkey: A case study on the NGO advocacy network for women (KIDOG). Washington, D.C.: U.S. Agency for International Development, Center for Population and Health, POLICY Project (April).

Carothers, Thomas. 1999. *Aiding democracy abroad: The learning curve.* Washington, D.C.: Carnegie Endowment for International Peace.

Carroll, Thomas F. 1992. *Intermediary NGOs: The supporting link in grassroots development.* West Hartford, Conn.: Kumarian Press.

Casley, Dennis J., and Krishna Kumar. 1987. *Project monitoring and evaluation in agriculture.* Baltimore, Md.: Johns Hopkins University Press.

Casley, Dennis J., and Dennis A. Lury. 1981. *Data collection in developing countries.* London: Oxford University Press.

Cassels, Andrew, and Katja Janovsky. 1991. *Strengthening health management in districts and provinces: Handbook for facilitators.* Geneva: World Health Organization, SHS/DHS/91.3.

Cernea, Michael. 1992. The building blocks of participation: Testing a social methodology. In *Participatory development and the World Bank: Potential directions for change,* edited by Buvan Bhatnagar and Aubrey C. Williams, 96–109. Washington, D.C.: World Bank, Discussion Paper No. 183.

Chandrasekaran, Rajiv. 2000. Philippine activism, at push of a button: Technology used to spur political change. *The Washington Post.* Sunday, December 10, A44.

Charlick, Robert. 2001. Popular participation and local government reform. *Public Administration and Development* 21(2): 149–59.

Chazan, Naomi, Robert Mortimer, John Ravenhill, and Donald Rothchild. 1992. *Politics and society in contemporary Africa.* Boulder, Colo.: Lynne Rienner Publishers.

Chhibber, Ajay. 1998. Institutions, policies, and development outcomes. In *Evaluation and development: The institutional dimension,* edited by Robert Picciotto and Eduardo Weisner, 34–47. New Brunswick, N.J.: Transaction Publishers.

Chisholm, Donald. 1989. *Coordination without hierarchy: Informal structures in multiorganizational systems.* Berkeley and Los Angeles: University of California Press.

CIDA (Canadian International Development Agency). 1997. Mainstreaming participatory development: Experiences and lessons of the Inter-Agency Group on Participation. Ottawa: CIDA (June).

Clague, Christopher, ed. 1997. *Institutions and economic development: Growth and governance in less-developed and post-socialist countries.* Baltimore, Md.: Johns Hopkins University Press.

———. 1994. The new institutional economics and economic development. Washington, D.C.: U.S. Agency for International Development and University of Maryland. Paper presented at the Conference on Economic and Political Institutions for Sustainable Development: Implications for Assistance (October 24–25).

Clark, John D. 1995. The state, popular participation, and the voluntary sector. *World Development* 23(4): 593–601.

————. 1991. *Democratizing development: The role of voluntary organizations*. West Hartford, Conn.: Kumarian Press.

Clarke, John D., and Winona Dorschel. 1998. Civil society participation in World bank country assistance strategies—Lessons from experience, FY 97–98. Washington, D.C.: World Bank, SDVNG. (April).

Cohen, Allan R., and David L. Bradford. 1990. *Influence without authority*. New York: John Wiley and Sons.

Cohen, John M., Merilee S. Grindle, and S. Tjip Walker. 1985. Foreign aid and conditions precedent: Political and bureaucratic dimensions. *World Development* 13(12): 1211–30.

Colburn, Forrest D. 1989. *Everyday forms of peasant resistance*. Armonk, N.Y.: M. E. Sharpe, Inc.

Collier, David. 1996. Trajectory of a concept: "Corporatism" in the study of Latin American politics. In *Latin America in comparative perspective: New approaches to methods and analysis*, edited by Peter Smith. Boulder, Colo.: Westview Press.

Connor, Katherine. 2000. *Contracting non-governmental organizations for HIV/AIDS: Brazil case study*. Washington, D.C.: U.S. Agency for International Development, Partnerships for Health Reform Project. Special Initiatives Report No. 30 (March).

Cooke, Bill. 1998. Participation, "process," and management: Lessons for development in the history of organization development. *Journal of International Development* 10(1): 35–54.

Coston, Jennifer M. 1999. Grassroots organizations and influencing public policy processes: Lessons from around the world. *International Journal of Organization Theory and Behavior* 2(1 and 2): 1–26.

————. 1998a. A model and typology of government-NGO relationships. *Nonprofit and Voluntary Sector Quarterly* 27(3): 359–83.

————. 1998b. Administrative avenues to democratic governance: The balance of supply and demand. *Public Administration and Development* 18(5): 479–93.

————. 1998c. The contribution of civil society organizations to democratization. *International Journal of Technical Cooperation* 4(2): 246–59.

Coston, Jennifer M., and Jennifer L. Butz. 1999. Mastering information: The birth of citizen-initiated voter education in Mongolia. *International Journal of Organization Theory and Behavior* 2(1&2): 107–41.

Crook, Richard C., and James Manor. 1998. *Democracy and decentralization in South Asia and West Africa: Participation, accountability, and performance*. Cambridge, U.K.: Cambridge University Press.

Crosby, Benjamin, and Carlos Gonzalez. 1992. *Financial sector reform in Honduras: A stakeholder analysis*. Tegucigalpa: U.S. Agency for International Development, Implementing Policy Change Project.

Dahl, Robert. 1971. *Polyarchy: Participation and opposition*. New Haven, Conn.: Yale University Press.

————. 1961. *Who governs?*. New Haven, Conn.: Yale University Press.

Dart, Jessica. 1999. A story approach for monitoring change in an agricultural extension project. Melbourne, Australia: Association for Qualitative Research. Paper presented at the Annual Conference (July).

Das Gupta, Monica, Helene Grandvoinnet, and Mattia Romani. 2000. State-community synergies in development: Laying the basis for collective action. Washington, D.C.: World Bank, Development Research Group. Draft.

DeJanvry, Alain, Elisabeth Sadoulet Dominguez, and Erik Thorbeke. 1993. Introduction. *World Development* 21(4): 565–75.

Diamond, Larry. 1994. Rethinking civil society: Toward democratic consolidation. *Journal of Democracy* 5(3): 4–17.

Diamond, Larry, and Marc F. Plattner, eds. 1996. *The global resurgence of democracy*. 2d ed. Baltimore, Md.: Johns Hopkins University Press.

Diamond, Larry, and Marc F. Plattner, eds. 1995. *Economic reform and democracy*. Baltimore, Md.: Johns Hopkins University Press.

Dominguez, Jorge I., ed. 1997. *Technopols: Freeing politics and markets in Latin America in the 1990s*. University Park, Pa.: Pennsylvania State University Press.

Dominguez, Jorge I., and Jeanne Kinney Giraldo. 1996. Conclusion: Parties, institutions, and market reforms in constructing democracies. In *Constructing democratic governance: Latin America and the Caribbean in the 1990s—themes and issues*, edited by Jorge I. Domínguez and Abraham F. Lowenthal, 3–41. Baltimore, Md.: Johns Hopkins University Press.

Druckman, Daniel. 1993. The situational levers of negotiating flexibility. *Journal of Conflict Resolution* 37: 236–76.

Dyer, William G. 1987. *Team building: Issues and alternatives*. 2d ed. Reading, Mass.: Addison-Wesley Publishing Co.

Echeverri-Gent, John. 1992. Politics of development and the development of politics: An inquiry into the political means of equitable development. *Contemporary South Asia* 1(3): 325–49.

Eckert, Robert J., and Merlyn H. Kettering. 1984. Development project start-up: A reference handbook on project implementation for technical assistance teams. Washington, D.C., and College Park, Md.: U.S. Department of Agriculture, Development Program Management Center, and University of Maryland, International Development Management Center (September).

EDI (Economic Development Institute). 1998. *Training program on social policy in transition economies (SPRITE): Status report*. Washington, D.C.: World Bank, EDI Evaluation Studies, No. ES98–2.

———. 1989. *A handbook for conducting a TeamUP workshop*. Washington, D.C.: World Bank, EDI Agricultural Management Training for Africa Project (June).

Edwards, Daniel B., and John Pettit. 1987. *Facilitator guide for conducting a project start-up workshop*. Washington, D.C.: U.S. Agency for International Development, Water and Sanitation for Health Project, WASH Technical Report No. 41 (June).

Edwards, Michael, and David Hulme, eds. 1992. *Making a difference: NGOs and development in a changing world*. London: Earthscan Publications Ltd.

Ensminger, Jan. 1992. *Making a market: The institutional transformation of an African society*. Cambridge, U.K.: Cambridge University Press.

Eurodad (European Network on Debt and Development). 2000. Poverty reduction strategies: What have we learned so far? Brussels: Eurodad (September).

Evans, Gareth. 1993. *Cooperating for peace*. St. Leonards, Australia: Allen and Unwin, Ltd.

Evans, Peter. 1996. Government action, social capital and development: Reviewing the evidence on synergy. *World Development* 24(6): 1119–32.

Farrington, John, Anthony Bebbington, Kate Wellard, and David J. Lewis. 1993. *Reluctant partners? Non-governmental organizations, the state and sustainable agricultural development*. London: Routledge.

Faure, Guy Olivier, ed. 1998. *Negotiation stories in developing countries*. Laxenburg, Austria: Processes of International Negotiation Project, International Institute for Applied Systems Analysis.

Ferlie, Ewan, Lynn Ashburner, Louise Fitzgerald, and Andrew Pettigrew. 1996. *The new public management in action*. Oxford: Oxford University Press.

Fernando, Jude L., and Alan W. Heston, eds. 1997. The role of NGOs: Charity and empowerment. *The Annals* 554 (November, Special Issue).

Ferris, James M., and Shui-Yan Tang. 1993. The new institutionalism and public administration: An overview. *Journal of Public Administration Research and Theory* 3(1): 4–11.

Fisher, Julie. 1998. *Non governments: NGOs and the political development of the third world*. West Hartford, Conn.: Kumarian Press.

Fiszbein, Ariel, and Pamela Lowden. 1998. *Working together for a change: Government, business and civic partnerships for poverty reduction in LAC*. Washington, D.C.: World Bank, Economic Development Institute.

Florini, Ann M., ed. 2000. *The third force: The rise of transnational civil society*. Washington, D.C.: Carnegie Endowment for International Peace.

Foley, Michael W., and B. Edwards. 1996. The paradox of civil society. *Journal of Democracy* 7(3): 38–53.

Foster, Phillips, Marcus D. Ingle, and Barton Clarke. 1990. Assessing the impact of farming systems research and development efforts: An action-training methodology. In *Methods for diagnosing research system constraints and assessing the impact of agricultural research*, vol. 2, edited by R. G. Echeverria, 161–73. The Hague: International Service for National Agricultural Research.

Fowler, Alan. 1997. *Striking a balance: A guide to enhancing the effectiveness of non-governmental organisations in international development*. London: Earthscan Publications Ltd.

———. 1991. The role of NGOs in changing state-society relations: Perspectives from Eastern and Southern Africa. *Development Policy Review* 9: 53–84.

Freeman, R. Edward. 1984. *Strategic management: A stakeholder approach*. Boston: Pitman Publishers.

Frischtak, Leila L. 1994. *Governance capacity and economic reform in developing countries*. Technical Paper No. 254. Washington, D.C.: World Bank.

Frischtak, Leila L., and Izak Atiyas, eds. 1996. *Governance, leadership, and communication: Building constituencies for economic reform*. Washington, D.C.: World Bank.

Gage, Robert W., and Myrna P. Mandell, eds. 1990. *Strategies for managing intergovernmental policies and networks*. New York: Praeger Publishers.

Garnett, Harry, Julie Koenen-Grant, and Catherine Rielly. 1997. Managing policy formulation and implementation in Zambia's democratic transition. *Public Administration and Development* 17(1): 77–91.

Garrity, Michele, and Louis A. Picard. 1991. Organized interests, the state, and the public policy process: An assessment of Jamaican business associations. *Journal of Developing Areas* 25 (April): 369–94.

Gasper, Des. 2000. Evaluating the "Logical Framework Approach"—towards learning-oriented development evaluation. *Public Administration and Development* 20(1): 17–29.

Geddes, Barbara. 1994. Challenging the conventional wisdom. *Journal of Democracy* 5(4): 104–18.

Ghai, Dharam, and Jessica M. Vivian, eds. 1992. *Grassroots environmental action: People's participation in sustainable development*. New York: Routledge.

Gillespie, Piers, Mona Girgis, and Peter Mayer. 1996. "This great evil:" Anticipating political obstacles to development. *Public Administration and Development* 16(5): 431–53.

Gilson, Lucy, Jane Doherty, Di McIntyre, Stephen Thomas, Vishal Briljal, and Chris Bowa. 1999. *The dynamics of policy change: Health care financing in South Africa, 1994–1999*. Washington, D.C.: U.S. Agency for International Development, Partnerships for Health Reform Project. Major Applied Research Paper 1, Technical Paper No. 1 (November).

Gittinger, J. Price. 1982. *Economic analysis of agricultural projects*. 2d ed. Baltimore, Md.: Johns Hopkins University Press.

Goldsmith, Arthur A. 1997. Private sector experience with strategic management: Cautionary tales for public administration. *International Review of Administrative Sciences* 23(1): 25–40.

Good, Kenneth. 1996. Towards popular participation in Botswana. *Journal of Modern African Studies* 34(1): 53–77.

Gran, Guy. 1983. *Development by people: Citizen construction of a just world*. New York: Praeger Publishers.

Gray, Barbara. 1989. *Collaborating: Finding common ground for multiparty problems*. San Francisco: Jossey-Bass Publishers.

Grindle, Merilee S. 1999. *In quest of the political: The political economy of development policy making*. Cambridge, Mass.: Harvard University, Center for International Development, CID Working Paper No. 17 (June).

———. 1996. *Challenging the state: Crisis and innovation in Latin America and Africa*. Cambridge, U.K.: Cambridge University Press.

———. 1991. The new political economy: Positive economics and negative politics. In *Politics and Policy Making in Developing Countries: Perspectives on the New Political Economy*, edited by Gerald M. Meier, 41–69. San Francisco: Institute for Contemporary Studies Press.

Grindle, Merilee S., ed. 1997. *Getting good government: Capacity building in the public sectors of developing countries*. Cambridge, Mass.: Harvard Institute for International Development.

———. 1980. *Politics and policy implementation in the third world*. Princeton, N.J.: Princeton University Press.

Grindle, Merilee S., and John W. Thomas. 1991. *Public choices and policy change: The political economy of reform in developing countries*. Baltimore, Md.: Johns Hopkins University Press.

Gulhati, Ravi. 1990. Who makes economic policy in Africa and how? *World Development* 18(8): 1147–61.

Haggard, Stephan, and Robert R. Kaufman. 1994. The challenges of consolidation. *Journal of Democracy* 5(6): 5–17.

Haggard, Stephan, and Robert R. Kaufman, eds. 1992. *The politics of economic adjustment*. Princeton, N.J.: Princeton University Press.

Haggard, Stephan, and Steven W. Webb, eds. 1994. *Voting for reform: Democracy, political liberalization, and economic adjustment*. New York: Oxford University Press.

Hansen, Gary. 1996. *Constituencies for reform: Strategic approaches for donor-supported civic advocacy programs*. Washington, D.C.: U.S. Agency for International Development, Center for Development Information and Evaluation, USAID Program and Operations Assessment Report No. 12 (February).

Harbeson, John W., Donald Rothchild, and Naomi Chazan, eds. 1994. *Civil society and the state in Africa*. Boulder, Colo.: Lynne Rienner Publishers.

Harriss, John, Jane Hunter, and Colin M. Lewis, eds. 1995. *The new institutional economics and third world development*. New York: Routledge.

Heap, Simon. 1998. *NGOs and the private sector: Potential for partnerships?*. Oxford, U.K.: International NGO Training and Research Center, Occasional Paper No. 27 (December).

Heclo, Hugh. 1977. *A government of strangers: Executive politics in Washington*. Washington, D.C.: Brookings Institution.

Heeks, Richard B., ed. 2001a. *Reinventing government in the information age*. London: Routledge.

———. 2001b. *Understanding e-governance for development*. Manchester, U.K.: University of Manchester, Institute for Development Policy and Management, I-Government Working Paper No. 11.

Hellstern, Gerd-Michael. 1986. Assessing evaluation research. In *Guidance, control, and evaluation in the public sector*, edited by Franz-Xaver Kaufmann, Giandomenico Majone, and Vincent Ostrom, 279–313. Berlin and New York: Walter de Gruyter and Company.

Hensher, Martin. 1999. The political and administrative environment in Central Asia: Implications for health sector reform. In *Implementing health sector reform in Central Asia: Papers from an EDI health policy seminar held in Ashgabat, Turkmenistan, June 1996*, edited by Zuzana Feachem, Martin Hensher, and Laura Rose, 95–106. Washington, D.C.: World Bank, Economic Development Institute.

Hirschman, Albert O. 1984. *Getting ahead collectively: Grassroots experiences in Latin America*. New York: Pergamon Press.

———. 1970. *Exit, voice, and loyalty: Responses to decline in firms, organizations, and states*. Cambridge, Mass.: Harvard University Press.

Hjern, Benny, and David O. Porter. 1981. Implementation structures: A new unit of administrative analysis. *Organization Studies* 2(3): 211–27.

Honadle, George, and Lauren Cooper. 1989. Beyond coordination and control: An interorganizational approach to structural adjustment, service delivery, and natural resource management. *World Development* 17(10): 1531–41.

Honadle, George, and Jerry VanSant. 1985. *Implementation for sustainability: Lessons from integrated rural development*. West Hartford, Conn.: Kumarian Press.

Horowitz, Donald L. 1989. Is there a third world policy process? *Policy Sciences* 22(2): 197–212.

Hulme, David, and Michael Edwards, eds. 1997. *NGOs, states and donors: Too close for comfort?*. New York: St. Martin's Press.

Hyden, Goren. 1992. Governance and the study of politics. In *Governance and politics in Africa*, edited by Goren Hyden and Michael Bratton, 1–27. Boulder, Colo.: Lynne Rienner Publishers.

———. 1990. Creating an enabling environment. In *The long-term perspective study of sub-Saharan Africa. Volume 3. Institutional and sociopolitical issues*, 73–81. Washington, D.C.: World Bank.

Idachaba, Francis S. 1998. *Instability of national agricultural research systems in sub-Saharan Africa*. The Hague: International Service for Agricultural Research, Research Report No. 13.

ICNL (International Center for Not-for-Profit Law). 1997. *Handbook on good practices for laws relating to non-governmental organizations*. Washington, D.C.: World Bank, Environmentally Sustainable Development Department. Draft (May).

IPC (Implementing Policy Change Project). 1996. *Decentralization as a means of building democracy: A seminar to study experience and prospects*. Washington, D.C.: U.S. Agency for International Development, Center for Democracy and Governance, Implementing Policy Change Project, Phase II (September).

Jelin, Elizabeth, and Eric Hershberg, eds. 1996. *Constructing democracy: Human rights, citizenship, and society in Latin America*. Boulder, Colo.: Westview Press.

Jones, Andrea L. 1990. Laying the groundwork for sustainability: Using action-planning to improve project design and implementation in Ghana and Guatemala. In *Institutional sustainability in agriculture and rural development: A global perspective*, edited by Derick W. Brinkerhoff and Arthur A. Goldsmith, 101–15. New York: Praeger Publishers.

Kardam, Nuket, and Yakin Erturk. 1999. Expanding gender accountability? Women's organizations and the state in Turkey. *International Journal of Organization Theory and Behavior* 2(1 and 2): 167–99.

Kerrigan, John E., and Jeff S. Luke. 1987. *Management training strategies for developing countries*. Boulder, Colo.: Lynne Rienner Publishers.

Kiggundu, Moses N. 1996. Integrating strategic management tasks into implementing agencies: From firefighting to prevention. *World Development* 24(9): 1417–31.

———. 1989. *Managing organizations in developing countries: An operational and strategic approach*. West Hartford, Conn.: Kumarian Press.

King, Cheryl S., Kathryn M. Feltey, and Bridget O. Susel. 1998. The question of participation: Toward authentic public participation in public administration. *Public Administration Review* 58(4): 317–27.

Kingdon, John W. 1995. *Agendas, alternatives and public policies*. 2d ed. Reading, Mass.: Addison-Wesley Publishing.

Klare, Michael T. 2001. *Resource wars: The new landscape of global conflict*. New York: Henry Holt and Company.

Klitgaard, Robert. 1991. *Adjusting to reality: Beyond "state versus market" in economic development*. San Francisco: Institute for Contemporary Studies Press.

Knack, Stephen, and Philip Keefer. 1995. Institutions and economic performance: Cross-country tests using alternative institutional measures. *Economics and Politics* 7(3): 207–27.

Kooiman, Jan, ed. 1993. *Modern governance: New government-society interactions*. London: Sage Publications.

Korten, David C. 1990. *Getting to the twenty-first century: Voluntary action and the global agenda*. West Hartford, Conn.: Kumarian Press.

Korten, David C., and Rudi Klauss, eds. 1984. *People centered development: Contributions toward theory and planning frameworks*. West Hartford, Conn.: Kumarian Press.

Koteen, Jack. 1989. *Strategic management in public and nonprofit organizations*. New York: Praeger Publishers.

Krueger, Anne O. 1993. *Political economy of policy reform in developing countries*. Cambridge, Mass.: Massachusetts Institute of Technology Press.

Kulibaba, Nicolas. 1996. *Good governance in sheep's clothing: Implementing the action plan for regional integration of the livestock trade in West Africa's central corridor*. Washington, D.C.: U.S. Agency for International Development, Center for Democracy and Governance, Implementing Policy Change Project, Case Study No. 3.

Kumar, Krishna, ed. 1997. *Rebuilding societies after civil war: Critical roles for international assistance*. Boulder, Colo.: Lynne Rienner Publishers.

Laking, Rob. 1999. Don't try this at home? A New Zealand approach to public management reform in Mongolia. *International Public Management Journal* 2(2): 217–36.

Lamb, Geoffrey. 1987. *Managing economic policy change: Institutional dimensions*. Washington, D.C.: World Bank, Discussion Paper No. 14.

Lamb, Geoffrey, and Rachel Weaving, eds. 1992. *Managing policy reform in the real world: Asian experiences*. Washington, D.C.: World Bank, Economic Development Institute.

Landau, Martin. 1991. On multiorganizational systems in public administration. *Journal of Public Administration Research and Theory* 1(1): 5–18.

Laothamatas, Anek. 1988. Business and politics in Thailand: New patterns of influence. *Asian Survey* 28(4): 451–70.

Lasswell, Harold. 1958. *Politics: Who gets what, when, how*. Cleveland, Ohio: Meridian Books.

Leonard, David K. 1991. *African successes: Four public managers of Kenyan rural development*. Berkeley and Los Angeles: University of California Press.

Leurs, Robert. 1998. Current challenges facing participatory rural appraisal. In *Who changes? Institutionalizing participation in development*, edited by James Blackburn with Jeremy Holland, 124–34. London: Intermediate Technology Publications.

Lewis, David, and Tina Wallace, eds. 2000. *New roles and relevance: Development NGOs and the challenge of change*. Bloomfield, Conn.: Kumarian Press.

Lewis, John P. 1989. Government and national economic development. *Daedalus* 118(1): 69–83.

Liebler, Claudia. 1994. *Making interdisciplinary teams work: A guide for team leaders and technical assistance managers*. Washington, D.C.: U.S. Agency for International Development, Water and Sanitation for Health Project, WASH Technical Report No. 92 (February).

Lindblom, Charles E. 1968. *The policy-making process*. Englewood Cliffs, N.J.: Prentice-Hall.

Lindblom, Charles E., and David K. Cohen. 1979. *Usable knowledge: Social science and social problem solving*. New Haven, Conn.: Yale University Press.

Lindenberg, Marc, and Benjamin Crosby. 1981. *Managing development: The political dimension*. Hartford, Conn.: Kumarian Press.

Lipsky, Michael. 1980. *Street-level bureaucracy: Dilemmas of the individual in public services*. New York: Russell Sage Foundation.

Lister, Sarah. 2000. Power in partnerships? An analysis of an NGO's relationships with its partners. *Journal of International Development* 12(2): 227–39.

Little, Ian M. D., and James A. Mirlees. 1991. Project appraisal and planning twenty years on. In *Proceedings of the World Bank annual conference on development economics 1990*, 351–82. Washington, D.C.: World Bank.

Lo, Amy. 1991. A balance of interests. *Free China Review* 41: 4–11.

Lowi, Theodore J. 1979. *The end of liberalism: The second republic of the United States*. 2d ed. New York: W. W. Norton and Company.

————. 1972. Four systems of policy, politics, and choice. *Public Administration Review* 32(4): 298–310.

Lowndes, Vivien, and Chris Skelcher. 1998. The dynamics of multi-organizational partnerships: An analysis of changing modes of governance. *Public Adminstration* 76(2): 313–35.

Malan, Jannie. 1997. *Conflict resolution wisdom from Africa*. Durban, South Africa: African Centre for the Constructive Resolution of Disputes (ACCORD).

Manor, James. 1999. *The political economy of democratic decentralization*. Washington, D.C.: World Bank.

Mark, Melvin, Gary T. Henry, and George Jules. 2000. *Evaluation: An integrated framework for understanding, guiding and improving policies and programs*. San Francisco: Jossey-Bass Publishers.

Martin, Gillian, and Winfried Hamacher, eds. 1997. *Lessons learned in environmental mediation: Practical experiences in north and south*. Geneva and Bonn: International Academy of the Environment and Deutsche Gesellschaft für Technische Zusammenarbeit (GTZ).

Mazmanian, Daniel A., and Paul A. Sabatier. 1989. *Implementation and public policy*. Lanham, Md.: University Press of America.

McCarthy, Kathleen D., Virginia A. Hodgkinson, Russy D. Sumariwalla, and Associates. 1992. *The nonprofit sector in the global community: Voices from many nations*. San Francisco: Jossey-Bass Publishers.

McGee, Rosemary, with Andy Norton. 2000. *Participation in poverty reduction strategies: A synthesis of experience with participatory approaches to policy design, implementation and monitoring*. Brighton, U.K.: University of Sussex, Institute of Development Studies, IDS Working Paper No. 109.

McNutt, John G., and Kathleen M. Boland. 1999. Electronic advocacy by nonprofit organizations in social welfare policy. *Nonprofit and Voluntary Sector Quarterly* 28(4): 432–52.

Meier, Gerald M., ed. 1991. *Politics and policy making in developing countries: Perspectives on the new political economy*. San Francisco: Institute for Contemporary Studies Press.

Migdal, Joel S. 1988. *Strong societies and weak states: State-society relations and state capabilities in the third world*. Princeton, N.J.: Princeton University Press.

Miles, Matthew B. 1981. *Learning to work in groups: A practical guide for members and trainers*. 2d ed. New York: Columbia University, Teachers College Press.

Miles, Matthew B., and A. Michael Huberman. 1994. *Qualitative data analysis: An expanded sourcebook*. 2d ed. Thousand Oaks, Calif.: Sage Publications.

Miller, John, and James Billings. 1995. *Protocol development project: Final report*. Washington D.C.: U.S. Agency for International Development, Center for Democracy and Governance, Implementing Policy Change Project.

Mitchell, Ronald, Bradley R. Agle, and Donna J. Wood. 1997. Toward a theory of stakeholder identification and salience: Defining the principle of who and what really counts. *Academy of Management Review* 22(4): 853–87.

Mitroff, Ian. 1983. *Stakeholders of the organizational mind*. San Francisco: Jossey-Bass Publishers.

Monke, Eric A., and Scott R. Pearson. 1989. *The policy analysis matrix for agricultural development*. Ithaca, N.Y.: Cornell University Press.

Montgomery, John D. 1988. *Bureaucrats and people: Grassroots participation in third world development*. Baltimore, Md.: Johns Hopkins University Press.

Morton, Alice L. 1997. Climbing the objective tree: Policy analysis and reform in the Philippines. In *Policy analysis concepts and methods: An institutional and implementation focus*, edited by Derick W. Brinkerhoff, 331–49. Greenwich, Conn.: JAI Press, Policy Studies in Developing Nations Series, Vol. 5.

Moser, Caroline O. N. 1995. Evaluating gender impacts. In *Evaluating country development policies and programs: New approaches for a new agenda*, edited by Robert Picciotto and Ray C. Rist, 105–19. San Francisco: Jossey-Bass Publishers, New Directions for Evaluation Series, No. 67.

Mosse, Roberto, and Leigh Ellen Sontheimer. 1996. *Performance monitoring indicators handbook*. Washington, D.C.: World Bank, Technical Paper No. 334.

Mugambe, Kenneth, and Caroline Robb. 2000. *Linking macro policy choices to poverty outcomes. Case example from Uganda*. Washington, D.C.: World Bank, Participatory Processes in Poverty Reduction Strategy Papers, Note No. 1.

Nabli, M., and Jeffrey Nugent. 1989. The new institutional economics and economic development. *World Development* 17(9): 1333–47.

Ndegwa, Stephen N. 1993. *NGOs as pluralizing agents in civil society in Kenya*. Nairobi: University of Nairobi, Institute for Development Studies, Working Paper No. 491.

Nelson, Joan M. 1999. *Reforming health and education: The World Bank, the IDB, and complex institutional change*. Washington, D.C.: Overseas Development Council, Policy Essay No. 26.

———. 1994a. Linkages between politics and economics. *Journal of Democracy* 5(4): 49–63.

Nelson, Joan M., ed. 1994b. *A precarious balance: An overview of democracy and economic reforms in Eastern Europe and Latin America*. San Francisco and Washington, D.C.: International Center for Economic Growth and Overseas Development Council.

———. 1989. *Fragile coalitions: The politics of economic adjustment*. Washington, D.C.: Overseas Development Council.

North, Douglass C. 1990. *Institutions, institutional change and economic performance*. Cambridge, U.K.: Cambridge University Press.

NPR (National Performance Review). 1996. *Reaching public goals: Managing government for results. Resource guide.* Washington, D.C.: NPR (October).

OED (Operations Evaluation Department). 1998. *Assessing development effectiveness: Evaluation in the World Bank and the International Finance Corporation.* Washington, D.C.: World Bank.

Olson, Mancur. 1965. *The logic of collective action: Public goods and the theory of groups.* Cambridge, Mass.: Harvard University Press.

Osborne, David, and Ted Gaebler. 1992. *Reinventing government: How the entrepreneurial spirit is transforming the public sector.* Reading, Mass.: Addison-Wesley Publishing Company.

Ostrom, Elinor. 1990. *Governing the commons: The evolution of institutions for collective action.* New York: Cambridge University Press.

Ostrom, Elinor, Larry Schroeder, and Susan Wynne. 1993. *Institutional incentives and sustainable development: Infrastructure policies in perspective.* Boulder, Colo.: Westview Press.

O'Toole, Laurence J. 2000. Research on policy implementation: Assessment and prospects. *Journal of Public Administration Research and Theory* 10(2): 263–89.

Ottaway, Marina, and Thomas Carothers, eds. 2000. *Funding virtue: Civil society aid and democracy promotion.* Washington, D.C.: Carnegie Endowment for International Peace.

Otto, Dianne. 1996. Non-governmental organizations in the United Nations system: The emerging role of international civil society. *Human Rights Quarterly* 18: 107–41.

Palumbo, Dennis J., and Donald J. Calista, eds. 1990. *Implementation and the policy process: Opening up the black box.* New York: Greenwood Press.

Pateman, Carole. 1970. *Participation and democratic theory.* New York: Cambridge University Press.

Patton, Michael Q. 1980. *Qualitative evaluation.* Beverly Hills, Calif.: Sage Publications.

———. 1978. *Utilization-focused evaluation.* Beverly Hills, Calif.: Sage Publications.

Paul, Samuel. 1992. Accountability in public services: Exit, voice, and control. *World Development* 20(7): 1047–60.

———. 1983. *Strategic management for development programmes: Guidelines for action.* Geneva: International Labor Organization, Management Development Series No. 19.

Paul, Samuel, and Sita Sekhar. 2000. *Benchmarking urban services: The second report card on Bangalore.* Bangalore, India: Public Affairs Centre (June).

Pearce, Jenny. 1997. Between co-option and irrelevance? Latin American NGOs in the 1990s. In *NGOs, states and donors: Too close for comfort?*, edited by David Hulme and Michael Edwards, 257–75. New York: St. Martin's Press.

Perez-Aleman, Paola. 2000. Learning, adjustment and economic development: Transforming firms, the state and associations in Chile. *World Development* 28(1): 41–55.

Peters, B. Guy. 1998. Managing horizontal government: The politics of co-ordination. *Public Administration* 76(2): 295–313.

Picciotto, Robert. 1995. *Putting institutional economics to work: From participation to governance*. Washington, D.C.: World Bank, Discussion Paper No. 304.

Picciotto, Robert, and Ray C. Rist, eds. 1995. *Evaluating country development policies and programs: New approaches for a new agenda*. San Francisco: Jossey-Bass Publishers, New Directions for Evaluation Series, No. 67.

Picciotto, Robert, and Eduardo Weisner, eds. 1998. *Evaluation and development: The institutional dimension*. New Brunswick, N.J.: Transaction Publishers.

Polidano, Charles. 1999. The new public management in developing countries. Manchester, U.K.: University of Manchester, Institute for Development Policy and Management, Public Policy and Management Working Paper No. 13 (November).

Powell, Walter W., and Paul J. DiMaggio, eds. 1991. *The new institutionalism in organizational analysis*. Chicago: University of Chicago Press.

Pressman, Jeffrey L., and Aaron B. Wildavsky. 1973. *Implementation*. Berkeley and Los Angeles: University of California Press.

Pretty, Jules, and Hugh Ward. 2001. Social capital and the environment. *World Development* 29(2): 209–27.

Putnam, Robert. 1993. *Making democracy work: Civic traditions in modern Italy*. Princeton, N.J.: Princeton University Press.

Putney, Pamela. 2000. *Best practices case study: The Nepal safe motherhood network*. Washington, D.C.: U.S. Agency for International Development, Partnerships for Health Reform Project.

Rausser, Gordon C. 1990. A new paradigm for policy reform and economic development. *American Journal of Agricultural Economics* 72: 821–30.

Reisinger, William, Arthur Miller, and Vicki Hesli. 1995. Public behavior and political change in post Soviet states. *Journal of Politics* (November): 941–70.

Ribot, Jesse C. 1995. From exclusion to participation: Turning Senegal's forestry policy around? *World Development* 23(9): 1587–99.

Rielly, Catherine. 1994. *Cabinet profiles*. Washington, D.C.: U.S. Agency for International Development, Center for Democracy and Governance, Implementing Policy Change Project (February).

Rietbergen-McCracken, Jennifer, ed. 1996. *Participation in practice: The experience of the World Bank and other stakeholders*. Washington, D.C.: World Bank, Discussion Paper No. 333.

Rivlin, Alice M. 1971. *Systematic thinking for social action*. Washington, D.C.: Brookings Institution.

Robb, Caroline M. 1999. *Can the poor influence policy? Participatory poverty assessments in the developing world*. Washington, D.C.: World Bank, Directions in Development Series.

Rodrik, Dani. 1993. The positive economics of policy reform. *American Economic Association Papers and Proceedings* 83(2): 356–61.

Roe, Emery M. 1991. Development narratives, or making the best of blueprint development. *World Development* 19(4): 287–300.

Rondinelli, Dennis A. 1999. Market-supporting governance in an era of economic globalization: Challenges for governments in developing countries. *Politics, Administration and Change* 31 (January-June): 1–27.

———. 1998. Privatization, governance, and public management: The challenges ahead. *Business and the Contemporary World* 10(2): 149–70.

———. 1983. *Development projects as policy experiments: An adaptive approach to development administration*. New York: Methuen.

Rossi, Peter H., Howard E. Freeman, and Mark W. Lipsey. 1999. *Evaluation: A systematic approach*. 6th ed. Thousand Oaks, Calif.: Sage Publications.

Rothchild, Donald. 1994. Structuring state-society relations in Africa: Toward an enabling political environment. In *Economic change and political liberalization in sub-Saharan Africa*, edited by Jennifer A. Widner, 201–29. Baltimore, Md.: Johns Hopkins University Press.

Rowe, Nicholas. 1989. *Rules and institutions*. Ann Arbor, Mich.: University of Michigan Press.

Sabatier, Paul A., ed. 1999. *Theories of the policy process*. Boulder, Colo.: Westview Press.

Sabatier, Paul A., and Hank C. Jenkins-Smith, eds. 1993. *Policy change and learning: An advocacy coalition approach*. Boulder, Colo.: Westview Press.

Sachikonye, Lloyd. 1995. *Democracy, civil society, and the state: Social movements in Southern Africa*. Harare, Zimbabwe: Southern African Political Economy Series Trust.

Salamon, Lester M. 1987. Of market failure, voluntary failure, and third-party government: Toward a theory of government-nonprofit relations in the modern welfare state. *Journal of Voluntary Action Research* 16(1 and 2): 29–49.

Salamon, Lester M., and Helmut K. Anheier, eds. 1997. *Defining the nonprofit sector: A cross-national analysis*. Manchester and New York: Manchester University Press.

Sarris, Alexander H. 1990. *A macro-micro framework for analysis of the impact of structural adjustment on the poor in sub-Saharan Africa*. Ithaca, N.Y.: Cornell University, Food and Nutrition Policy Program, Monograph No. 5 (September).

Schamis, Hector E. 1999. Distributional coalitions and the politics of economic reform in Latin America. *World Politics* 51(2): 236–68.

Schedler, Andreas, Larry Diamond, and Marc F. Plattner, eds. 1999. *The self-restraining state: Power and accountability in new democracies*. Boulder, Colo.: Lynne Rienner Publishers.

Schmeer, Kammi. 1998. *Interest mapping for health system institutional reform in Ecuador*. Washington, D.C.: U.S. Agency for International Development, Partnerships for Health Reform Project. In Briefs, No. 26 (November).

Schmidt, Gregory D. 1991. Linking action training to bureaucratic reorientation and institutional reform. *Public Administration and Development* 11: 39–55.

Schneider, Anne L., and Helen Ingram. 1997. *Policy design for democracy*. Lawrence, Kans.: University of Kansas Press.

Schon, Donald A., and Martin Rein. 1995. *Frame reflection: Toward the resolution of intractable policy controversies*. New York: Basic Books.

Schubeler, Peter. 1996. *Participation and Partnership in Urban Infrastructure Management*. Washington, D.C.: World Bank, Urban Management Program Policy Paper No. 19 (June).

Scribner, Susan, with Benjamin L. Crosby. 1997. *Increasing the influence of the private sector in policy reforms in Africa*. Washington, D.C.: U.S. Agency for International Development, Center for Democracy and Governance, Implementing Policy Change Project, Monograph No. 3 (December).

Siegal, Daniel, and Jenny Yancey. 1992. *The rebirth of civil society: The development of the nonprofit sector in East Central Europe and the role of Western assistance*. New York: Rockefeller Brothers Fund.

Silverman, Jerry M. 1997. Analyzing the role of the public sector in Africa: Implications for civil service reform policy. In *Policy analysis concepts and methods: An institutional and implementation focus*, edited by Derick W. Brinkerhoff, 159–87. Greenwich, Conn.: JAI Press, Policy Studies and Developing Nations Series.

Silverman, Jerry M., Merlyn H. Kettering, and Terry D. Schmidt. 1986. *Action-planning workshops for development management*. Washington, D.C.: World Bank, Technical Paper No. 56.

Smillie, Ian, and Henny Helmich, eds. 1999. *Stakeholders: Government-NGO partnerships for international development*. London: Earthscan Publications Ltd.

Smith, Brian H. 1987. An agenda of future tasks for international and indigenous NGOs: Views from the north. *World Development* 15(Supplement): 87–93.

Smith, Peter. 2000. A comment on the limitations of the logical framework method, in reply to Gasper, and to Bell. *Public Administration and Development* 20(5): 437–42.

Smucker, Bob. 1991. *The non-profit lobbying guide*. San Francisco: Jossey-Bass and the Independent Sector.

Smulovitz, Catalina, and Enrique Peruzzotti. 2000. Societal accountability in Latin America. *Journal of Democracy* 11(4): 147–58.

Snyder, Monteze, Fran Berry, and Paul Mavima. 1996. Gender policy in development assistance: Improving implementation results. *World Development* 24(9): 1481–96.

Spector, Bertram. 1994. *Strengthening institutions for conflict prevention*. Potomac, Md.: Center for Negotiation Analysis. Working Paper (July).

Stone, Deborah. 1996. *Policy paradox: The art of political decision making*. New York: W. W. Norton and Company.

Stover, John, and Alan Johnston. 1999. *The art of policy formulation: Experiences from Africa in developing national HIV/AIDS policies*. Washington, D.C.: U.S. Agency for International Development, Global Bureau, Office of Population, Health, and Nutrition, The POLICY Project, Occasional Paper No. 3 (August).

Taylor, Lance, ed. 1990. *Socially relevant policy analysis: Structuralist computable general equilibrium models for the developing world*. Cambridge, Mass.: Massachusetts Institute of Technology Press.

Tendler, Judith. 1997. *Good government in the tropics*. Baltimore, Md.: Johns Hopkins University Press.

Teune, Henry, ed. 1995. Local governance around the world. *The Annals* 540 (July, Special Issue).

Thomas, John. 1995. *Public participation*. San Francisco: Jossey-Bass Publishers.

Thomas, Vinod, Ajay Chhibber, Mansoor Dailami, and Jaime de Melo, eds. 1991. *Restructuring economies in distress: Policy reform and the World Bank*. New York: Oxford University Press.

Thompson, Graheme, Jennifer Frances, Rosalind Levacic, and Jeremy Mitchell, eds. 1991. *Markets, hierarchies and networks: The coordination of social life*. Newbury Park, Calif.: Sage Publications.

Thompson, John. 1995. Participatory approaches in government bureaucracies: Facilitating the process of institutional change. *World Development* 23(9): 1521–54.

Turner, Mark, and David Hulme. 1997. *Governance, administration, and development: Making the state work*. West Hartford, Conn.: Kumarian Press.

UNDP (United Nations Development Programme). 1994. *Process consultation for systemic improvement of public sector management*. New York: UNDP.

United Nations. 1992. *An agenda for peace: Preventive diplomacy, peacemaking and peacekeeping*. New York: United Nations.

Uphoff, Norman. 1998. Understanding social capital: Learning from the analysis and experience of participation. In *Social capital*, edited by Ismael Serageldin and Partha Dasgupta, 215–46. New York: Oxford University Press.

———. 1993. Grassroots organizations and NGOs in rural development: Opportunities with diminishing states and expanding markets. *World Development* 21(4): 607–22.

Uruena, Mary-lis. 1996. Service delivery surveys and performance measurement. Washington D.C.: World Bank, Economic Development Institute. Summary Proceedings of a Workshop for El Salvador, Guatemala, and Nicaragua, April 22–26.

Ury, William, Jeanne Brett, and Stephen Goldberg. 1991. Designing an effective dispute resolution system. In *Negotiation theory and practice*, edited by J. William Breslin and Jeffrey Z. Rubin, 295–314. Cambridge, Mass.: Program on Negotiation Books.

USAID (U.S. Agency for International Development). 2000. Monitoring the policy reform process. Washington, D.C.: USAID, Center for Development Information and Evaluation. *Recent Practices in Monitoring and Evaluation: Tips*, No. 14.

———. 1999. *Accelerating the implementation of HIV/AIDS prevention and mitigation programs in Africa*. Washington, D.C.: USAID, Bureau for Africa, Office of Sustainable Development, and Global Bureau, Center for Population, Health, and Nutrition, Working Paper, Draft (September).

———. 1996. Preparing a performance monitoring plan. Washington, D.C.: USAID, Center for Development Information and Evaluation. *Recent Practices in Monitoring and Evaluation: Tips*, No. 7.

Wallis, Joe, and Brian Dollery. 2001. Government failure, social capital and the appropriateness of the New Zealand model for public sector reform in developing countries. *World Development* 29(2): 245–63.

Waterbury, John. 1989. The political management of economic adjustment and reform. In *Fragile coalitions: The politics of economic adjustment*, edited by Joan M. Nelson, 39–57. Washington, D.C.: Overseas Development Council.

Weiss, Carol H. 1989. Congressional committees as users of analysis. *Journal of Policy Analysis and Management* 8(3): 411–31.

———. 1972. *Evaluation research: Methods of assessing program effectiveness*. Englewood Cliffs, N.J.: Prentice-Hall.

Weiss, Carol H., ed. 1977. *Using social research in public policy making*. Lexington, Mass.: Lexington Books.

Western, David, and R. Michael Wright, eds. 1994. *Natural connections: Perspectives in community-based conservation*. Washington, D.C.: Island Press.

White, Louise G. 1997. Interactive policy analysis: Process methods for policy reform. In *Policy analysis concepts and methods: An institutional and implementation focus*, edited by Derick W. Brinkerhoff, 287–309. Greenwich, Conn.: JAI Press, Policy Studies in Developing Nations Series, Vol. 5.

———. 1990. *Implementing policy reforms in LDCs: A strategy for designing and effecting change*. Boulder, Colo.: Lynne Rienner Publishers.

Whitely, Paul F. 1995. Rational choice and political participation: Evaluating the debate. *Political Research Quarterly* 48(1): 211–33.

WHO (World Health Organization). 2000. *The world health report 2000. Health systems: Improving performance*. Geneva: WHO.

Wholey, Joseph S. 1979. *Evaluation: Promise and performance*. Washington, D.C.: Urban Institute.

Wildavsky, Aaron. 1974. *The politics of the budgetary process*. 2d ed. Boston: Little, Brown and Company.

Williamson, Oliver. 1979. Transaction-cost economics: The governance of contractual relations. *American Journal of Sociology* 87: 548–77.

Winter, Soren. 1990. Integrating implementation research. In *Implementation and the policy process: Opening up the black box*, edited by Dennis J. Palumbo and Donald J. Calista, 19–39. New York: Greenwood Press.

Woolcock, Michael. 1998. Social capital and economic development: Towards a theoretical synthesis and policy framework. *Theory and Society* 27: 151–208.

World Bank. 1997. *World development report 1997: The state in a changing world*. Washington, D.C.: World Bank.

———. 1996. *The World Bank participation sourcebook*. Washington, D.C.: World Bank, Environmentally Sustainable Development Department.

Zakaria, Fareed. 1997. The rise of illiberal democracy. *Foreign Affairs* (November/December): 22–43.

Zapata, Francisco. 1998. Trade unions and the corporatist system in Mexico. In *What kind of democracy? What kind of market? Latin America in the age of neoliberalism*, edited by Philip D. Oxhorn and Graciela Ducatenzeiler, 151–67. University Park, Pa.: Pennsylvania State University Press.

Zartman, I. William, ed. 1998. *Traditional African conflict resolution approaches*. Washington, D.C.: Johns Hopkins University, Paul H. Nitze School of Advanced International Studies.

Zuckerman, Elaine. 1991. The social costs of adjustment. In *Restructuring economies in distress: Policy reform and the World Bank*, edited by Vinod Thomas, Ajay Chhibber, Mansoor Dailami, Jaime de Melo, 247–75. New York: Oxford University Press.

About the Authors

Derick W. Brinkerhoff is a principal social scientist with Abt Associates Inc. For ten years he was the research director for USAID's IPC Project. Dr. Brinkerhoff has worked with public agencies, NGOs, and the private sector across a broad range of development sectors in many developing and transitioning countries, with an emphasis on Africa. Prior to joining Abt in 1993, he spent ten years at the University of Maryland's International Development Management Center, including six years as the center's associate director for research and four years as resident advisor to Haiti's planning ministry; two years in USAID as a public sector management specialist; and several years free-lance consulting. He was a Peace Corps volunteer in Chad for three years. Dr. Brinkerhoff has published extensively, including five books, numerous articles, and book chapters. He holds a doctorate in public policy and administration from Harvard University. He is also an adjunct faculty member at Johns Hopkins University's School of Advanced International Studies.

Benjamin L. Crosby is a director of Management Systems International (MSI) and for ten years served as the technical assistance director for IPC. Dr. Crosby has over thirty years of experience with public sector, private sector, and NGO management problems in over thirty countries in Latin America, Asia, Africa, Eastern Europe, and the Middle East. He has also worked extensively with private sector firms in Latin America on problems of strategy development and the management of political risk. Prior to joining MSI in 1990, Dr. Crosby was a MacArthur Scholar in Residence at the Overseas Development Council for a year. He spent fifteen years on the faculty of the Central American Institute of Management (INCAE) in Nicaragua and Ecuador, where he was professor of public management and business policy. He is the author of numerous articles, conference papers, book chapters, and editorials. He is co-author with Marc Lindenberg of *Managing Development: The Political Dimension*. Dr. Crosby holds the Ph.D. in political science from Washington University.

# Also from Kumarian Press...

International Development

Advocacy for Social Justice: A Global Action and Reflection Guide
David Cohen, Rosa de la Vega, and Gabrielle Watson

Patronage or Partnership: Local Capacity Building in Humanitarian Crises
Edited by Ian Smillie for the Humanitarianism and War Project

Sustainable Livelihoods: Building on the Wealth of the Poor
Kristin Helmore and Naresh Singh

Transcending Neoliberalism:
Community-Based Development in Latin America
Edited by Henry Veltmeyer and Anthony O'Malley

War's Offensive on Women:
The Humanitarian Challenge in Bosnia, Kosovo and Afghanistan
Julie A. Mertus for the Humanitarianism and War Project

Conflict Resolution, Environment, Gender Studies, Global Issues, Globalization, Microfinance, Political Economy

Bound: Living in the Globalized World
Scott Sernau

Capitalism and Justice: Envisioning Social and Economic Fairness
John Isbister

Exploring the Gaps: Vital Links Between Trade, Environment and Culture
James R. Lee

The Hidden Assembly Line:
Gender Dynamics of Subcontracted Work in a Global Economy
Edited by Radhika Balakrishnan

Inequity in the Global Village: Recycled Rhetoric and Disposable People
Jan Knippers Black

Mainstreaming Microfinance:
How Lending to the Poor Began, Grew, and Came of Age in Bolivia
Elisabeth Rhyne

Reconcilable Differences: Turning Points in Ethnopolitical Conflict
Edited by Sean Byrne and Cynthia L. Irvin

Where Corruption Lives
Gerald Caiden, O.P. Dwivedi, and Joseph Jabbra

Visit Kumarian Press at **www.kpbooks.com** or
call **toll-free 800.289.2664** for a complete catalog.

Kumarian Press, located in Bloomfield, Connecticut, is dedicated to publishing and distributing books and other media that will have a positive social and economic impact on the lives of peoples living in "Third World" conditions no matter where they live.